DAVE MATTHEWS BAND
UNDER THE MICROSCOPE
By Toby Wine

Cherry Lane Music Company
Educational Director/Project Supervisor: Susan Poliniak
Director of Publications: Mark Phillips
Publications Coordinator: Rebecca Skidmore

ISBN 978-1-60378-004-9

Visit our website at www.cherrylaneprint.com

TABLE OF CONTENTS

Introduction 3

About the Book 4

About the Author 4

Acknowledgments 4

The Best of What's Around 5

What Would You Say 19

Satellite 30

Warehouse 46

So Much to Say 58

Crash Into Me 70

Too Much 80

Rapunzel 96

Don't Drink the Water 113

Stay (Wasting Time) 134

The Space Between 144

Grey Street 151

American Baby 157

Louisiana Bayou 165

INTRODUCTION

The term "grass roots" gets thrown around a lot, but in the case of Dave Matthews Band the term is fitting enough to warrant its application. Due to the band's beginnings on the Virginia club scene, the combination of their charismatic leader's strong songs and vocals, and the instrumental prowess of his bandmates, the group quickly attracted a heavy local following that grew exponentially during increasingly wide-reaching tours. Of course, the sort of lasting commercial and artistic success enjoyed by Dave Matthews Band is never as quick or easy as is often portrayed from the outside—it takes talent, all manner of specific musical skills, and a tremendous work ethic to make something like this happen.

While working as a bartender back in 1991 in Charlottesville, Virginia, South African–born Matthews was introduced to two local pros—drummer Carter Beauford and saxophonist LeRoi Moore—who soon recruited teenage bass prodigy Stefan Lessard to round out their rhythm section. Fellow bartender Peter Griesar (keyboards) and violin pro Boyd Tinsley also became fixtures, although Griesar would eventually leave the band in 1993. With a three-song demo in hand, the band was able to secure bookings for the Charlottesville Earth Day Festival and a private rooftop party that was their first official gig under the Dave Matthews Band moniker. Weekly hits at the nightclubs Eastern Standard and Trax helped spread the word, and burgeoning audiences soon followed. Live recordings of gigs at the Muse Music Club on Nantucket Island, Massachusetts, and the Flood Zone in Richmond, Virginia, would become the band's first album, the independently-released 1993 effort *Remember Two Things*. It quickly became a gold-seller, in large part due to their popularity on the college music scene. This had the major labels perking up their ears, and before long the band had a deal with RCA and a big-league debut with 1994's *Under the Table and Dreaming*. "What Would You Say" became a hit single and a heavily rotated video on MTV. Much of the next year was spent on the road.

Crash, the band's second RCA album, hit the stores in the spring of 1996 while the boys kept their noses to the grindstone, selling out bigger and bigger arenas with each passing day. Songs like the Grammy-winning "So Much to Say," as well as "Crash Into Me" and "Too Much" (all three included in this book) became big hits and fan favorites. Two live recordings followed, including the five-song EP *Recently* (originally released on the band's Bama Rags label in 1994 and reissued by RCA in 1997), and *Live at Red Rocks 8.15.95*. Their third studio album, the Steve Lilywhite–produced *Before These Crowded Streets*, was released in April 1998, debuting in the top spot on the *Billboard* charts. The album features a variety of guests including Alanis Morissette, the Kronos Quartet, banjo-player Bela Fleck, and guitarist Tim Reynolds, a frequent contributor to the band's recordings and live performances. Also joining the mix was keyboardist Butch Taylor, now a steady (albeit unofficial) member of the ensemble.

The long gap between *Before These Crowded Streets* and the 2002 release of the band's fourth studio album, *Busted Stuff* was filled by three more live recordings, including *Live at Luther College*, which found Dave in a duo setting with Tim Reynolds, *Listener Supported*, recorded at the Continental Airlines Arena in New Jersey, and *Live in Chicago 12.19.98*, featuring, among others, saxophonist Maceo Parker of the James Brown Band. *Busted Stuff* included reworkings of a number of songs that had been leaked over the internet during the previous year, as well as new numbers such as the Grammy-nominated hit single "Where Are You Going" (used in the Adam Sandler movie *Mr. Deeds*). Less than four months later, fans were rewarded with another live album, *Live at Folsom Field, Boulder Colorado*, which was also made available as a DVD.

This has never been a band that rested on their laurels. Their incredible worldwide popularity was the result of a lot of hard work—and, of course, great playing and material—and post-*Folsom Field* was not the time to sit around collecting accolades. Matthews went off on another duo tour with Tim Reynolds, released a solo album (*Some Devil*), and then went back on the road with Reynolds and Phish guitarist Trey Anastasio. Meanwhile, other band members pursued their own projects, including violinist Boyd Tinsley's solo debut, *True Reflections*. They reconvened for a massive free concert in New York City's Central Park on September 24, 2003 (a benefit for local public schools), later released on both CD and DVD. A steady stream of live recordings followed, including *The Gorge* and the first two entries in the *Live Trax* series.

Stand Up, the band's fifth studio album, was released on May 10, 2005, followed by a summer tour that ended with a concert at Red Rocks Amphitheatre in Colorado to benefit the victims of Hurricane Katrina. A "best of" album (*The Best of What's Around Vol. 1*) was issued in November of the following year, while the band returned to the studio with producer Mark Batson at the onset of 2007 to begin work on their latest, forthcoming studio recording. Through it all, they've maintained a hectic, globetrotting pace of live appearances, the best of which have made their way into stores as the latest releases in the *Live Trax* series. The trademark eclecticism present in the band's earliest work remains in place as they've stubbornly resisted the formulaic and the predictable. Their vast repertoire draws inspiration from rock, folk, funk, jazz, and world music, filtering each through their collective musical identities to emerge as something that sounds fresh, new, and very much Dave Matthews Band. Rather than concern themselves with what "kind" of band they are, they simply create music they love and share it. We're eager to hear what they'll share with us next.

ABOUT THE BOOK

Dave Matthews Band Under the Microscope presents a cross-section of songs from the band's lengthy career and subjects them to rigorous analysis. They are presented in chronological order and each is prefaced by a variety of preparatory exercises designed to set the guitarist on the right path to playing this often very demanding music. The theoretical analysis breaks down each tune into four distinct categories—harmony, rhythm, scales, and composition—and each is discussed in technical but no-nonsense language. In the end, it is our sincere hope that you will learn to play and enjoy the music of Dave Matthews Band, gain a deeper understanding of its structure and organization, and increase your own instrumental proficiency and musicianship in general.

ABOUT THE AUTHOR

Toby Wine is a native New Yorker and a freelance guitarist, composer, arranger, and educator. He is a graduate of the Manhattan School of Music, where he studied composition with Manny Albam and Edward Green. Toby has performed with Philip Harper (formerly of the Jazz Messengers), Bob Mover, Ari Ambrose, Joe Shepley, Michael and Carolyn Leonhart (both of Steely Dan), Peter Hartmann, Ian Hendrickson Smith, and the New York–based R&B/salsa collective Melee, among others. His arrangements and compositions can be heard on recordings by Phillip Harper (*Soulful Sin, The Thirteenth Moon*, Muse Records), Ari Ambrose (*Early Song*, Steeplechase), and Ian Hendrickson Smith (*Up in Smoke*, Sharp Nine). Toby leads his own trio and septet, does studio sessions, and works as a sideman with a variety of tri-state–area bandleaders. He spent four years as the music librarian for the Carnegie Hall Jazz Band and has performed orchestration and score preparation duties for jazz legend Ornette Coleman. He is the author of numerous Cherry Lane publications, including *1001 Blues Licks, The Art of Texas Blues, 150 Cool Jazz Licks in Tab, Steely Dan Legendary Licks*, and *Metallica Under the Microscope*.

ACKNOWLEDGMENTS

Many thanks are due to Cherry Lane's head honcho, John Stix, and to my friend and editor, Susan Poliniak, for her insight, guidance, and absurdly patient good nature. Additional thanks to the extended Cherry Lane family for all that they do so well. Thanks as well to my parents, Rosemary and Jerry, and to Lissette, Bibi, Bob, Jack, Noah, Enid, Mover, Humph (R.I.P.), and all of the great teachers I've ever had.

THE BEST OF WHAT'S AROUND
From *Under the Table and Dreaming* (1994)

Let's kick things off with the opening track from Dave Matthews Band's major-label debut, *Under the Table and Dreaming*. "The Best of What's Around," with its intriguing blend of funk, folk, and pop flavors, introduced the best-kept secret in indie rock to mainstream audiences around the world for the first time.

THEORY

Harmony

Dave Matthews' diverse songwriting style makes good use of traditional pop harmonies, with melodies supported by underlying guitar and keyboard chords, instrumental riffs, and static, single-chord funk vamps. One of the most common ways of understanding what's happening harmonically in a given piece of music is with *Roman numeral analysis*, in which each chord is assigned a Roman numeral indicating its place and function within the key. Since we'll be doing a lot of this type of analysis throughout the book, let's take a moment to review some of the basic principles of harmony and how it is generated. To begin with, most of the music of the Western world is based upon the major diatonic scale, the modes related to it, and the alterations to these. Here are the major scales in the keys of C and E, respectively.

These should be familiar enough. Note that the major scale is constructed with the following interval sequence: whole step–whole step–half step–whole step–whole step–whole step–half step. By following that sequence exactly you can construct major scales beginning on any note.

Next, for each step of the scale, a proper corresponding *triad* (three-note chord) of specific quality—here, major, minor, or diminished—can be created by stacking a couple of notes above it in intervals of a major or minor 3rd as dictated by the key. Just think of this as skipping every other scale note and then stacking things up.

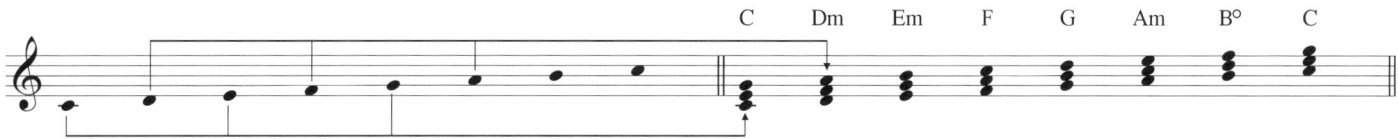

The resulting triads are, in sequence, major, minor, minor, major, major, minor, and diminished. If a fourth note is added to the equation, *7th chords* are created.

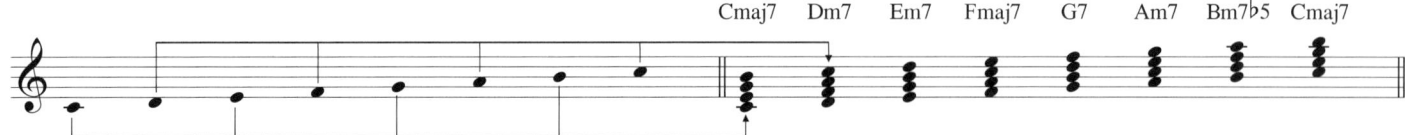

Notice that the chord built on the scale's 5th degree becomes a *dominant 7th chord*, and the chord built on the 7th degree becomes a *minor 7th flat 5 chord* (also referred to as a *half diminished*). As long as we remain *diatonic*—that is, within one key and without using *borrowed tones* (pitches that are not members of that particular key)—the qualities of these chords remain consistent and can be referred to by Roman numerals representing the steps of the major scale. In a major key, I is always major, iii is minor (note the lower case letters for minor and diminished chords), IV is major, etc. Entire songs and progressions can be analyzed with these numerals and can be easily transposed to other keys using this approach. For example, I–IV–V in C would be C–F–G. In E it would be E–A–B major, and in D♭ it would be D♭–G♭–A♭. So far, so good. We should now have a clear picture of how chords are formed and what their qualities are in any given key. Now, let's return to the music at hand.

"The Best of What's Around" is interesting in that it toggles back and forth between the keys of C and A major. Because the vi chord in the key of C is A minor, the effect is basically that of repeated shifts between A major and A minor tonalities. When the song begins, we're in the key of C, with a four-measure progression that's played twice. A Roman numeral analysis of this section would look like this.

Notice the second chord in measure 3; C5/B is essentially a tonic (I) power chord played above the 7th scale degree (B), a passing bass note that connects I to vi. These are often referred to as *slash chords*—the functional aspect of the chord is shown to the left of the slash, while the note in the bass is shown to the right. Slash chords may be *inversions*, in which a chord tone other than the root is played in the bass, or *passing chords*, as seen here, that merely connect one more "common" chord to another. Occasionally, they may function as stand-alone harmonies in their own right, as we'll see during the course of this book. Suffice it to say, C5/B takes on an entirely different sound and meaning if the band stays on it for four measures, instead of for the short time found here.

Another oddity worth mentioning in this section is the final chord, Dadd4, which is shown here as the II chord (with capital letters) because of the presence of the F♯, the major 3rd of the chord. Here's our first taste of Dave Matthews' unique approach to harmony. It's a typical Dave Matthews Band voicing as well, combining fretted notes with the open G string a mere half step above the F♯ on the D string, causing an intriguing minor 2nd rub.

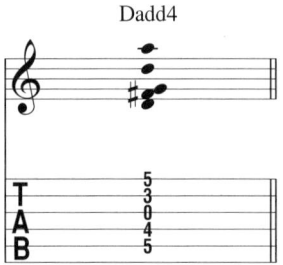

As the chorus is introduced for the first time, the action shifts abruptly to the key of A, with the following four-measure sequence, which is also played twice. Note the change of key signature to three sharps, which removes any mystery about what key we're now in.

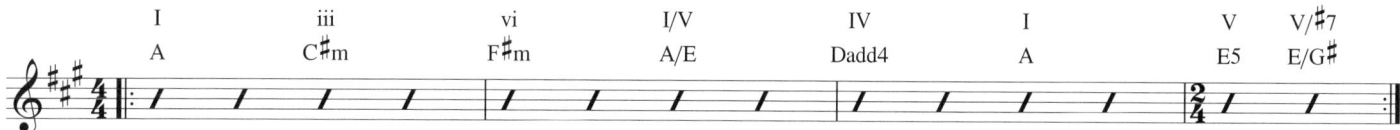

The slash chords above represent inversions, in that the bass notes in each are normally found within the chord (unlike the B played below C5 in the earlier verse section). A/E is the tonic triad (A major) with its 5th in the bass, while E/G♯ is the V chord with its 3rd in the bass. The Dadd4 chord returns in this section, but it is functioning as the IV chord instead of the II as it did in the key of C. It's still a bit of an oddity, though, because the open G string ringing in the middle of the chord is from outside the key of A. By temporarily lowering the A scale's 7th degree from G♯ to G, Matthews very briefly introduces an A Mixolydian mode (A–B–C♯–D–E–F♯–G) flavor to the chorus (more on modes later). Even though it's extremely short-lived, the Mixolydian sonority returns in the bridge. The section is prefaced by a syncopated two-measure riff beginning with an Am chord followed by the descending bass notes G, F♯, and F. Think of this section as a short return to the key of C and its relative minor chord (Am, the vi chord in that key). Here's the bridge that follows.

Things start off simply enough, mimicking the chorus as we move from I to iii. Bm represents the ii chord and G the ♭VII. However, we could also potentially look at this section from a Mixolydian (the mode built on the D major scale's 5th degree) standpoint, and consider A the V chord, C♯ the vii, Bm the vi, and G the IV in the key of D! Things are rarely as simple as they seem at first, a point further illustrated by the returning two-measure riff at the end of the phrase, which marks a move back to the key of C and its vi chord, Am. While this type of analysis may seem daunting at first, the logic governing music's harmonic laws is well worth the time taken to understand and utilize it.

Rhythm

Rhythm—whether it's in the funky guitar parts, clockwork ensemble playing, or vocal gymnastics—is the force that drives the Dave Matthews Band engine. All of their diverse world-beat influences, exotic timbres, and eclectic drum patterns wouldn't be worth much if they didn't get the people out of their seats and dancing. The group repeatedly demonstrates their awareness of this fact by making precise grooves and rock-solid time the backbone of all of their songs. In order to ensure an equally unshakeable rhythmic performance from yourself, it is highly recommended that you practice each new part with a metronome at a reduced tempo, and then ratchet things up to speed only when they're as unassailably sturdy as can be. The ultimate goal should be to play the complete song along with the recording, as the demands of matching the band's real-time performance will leave little doubt as to whether you can really play it or not.

"The Best of What's Around" is less complex than most of the group's compositions in terms of rhythmic demands, but there are still a few moments that bear closer examination. First, while the song is played in a comfortable, medium-tempo 4/4 groove, there is the occasional 2/4 measure that pops up in the chorus and fade-out coda section. This one shouldn't throw you for much of a loop, but it's still recommended that you slow the section down and count out the beats in each measure so that you're exactly sure where each note you play is falling in the individual measures. Next, it's imperative that you have a strong grasp of 16th note and broken 16th note figures, as the guitar parts here and in many other Dave Matthews Band songs are often dominated by 16th note funk strumming rhythms. Many musicians use a sequence of syllables to verbalize 16th notes for their own understanding of a passage or as a way of describing it to other players in a rehearsal or on a recording. These syllables are shown in the example below, above the corresponding 16th notes on the staff.

Here's a measure of broken 16th notes and the syllables that would be used to verbalize them.

Musicians might say, "that lick begins on the 3–and" or "that riff starts on 2–e," meaning the third 16th note of beat 3 in the former and the second 16th note of beat 2 in the latter. To further complicate matters, dots and ties can be introduced to the equation, allowing for rhythms that cross both beats and barlines. In case you've forgotten, a dot after a note instructs you to add an additional half of that note's rhythmic value to its duration, so that a dotted half note would last three beats rather than two, while a dotted quarter would last one and a half beats instead of one. Ties simply tell you to add up the durations of the connected notes (and notice that the tied notes after the first are not re-attacked).

Try your hand at the extended exercise that follows, in which the syllables above the staff have been removed. Sing the figures on any single pitch you like, or drum them out on a tabletop while tapping your foot to a steady quarter note pulse. Proceed slowly and repeat these figures until you're comfortable—you'll be seeing many of them in "The Best of What's Around."

If you made it through that one flawlessly the first time, give yourself a pat on the back and get yourself some studio work. However, if you're like the vast, vast majority of the guitar playing population, there were, at best, a few glitches. Simply go back, try repeating each measure three or four times until it's perfect, and then go on to the next. Even if you understand what's happening intellectually, the eyes and brain must still be trained to recognize these figures and translate them into the sound they represent. If you saw measure after measure of quarters and half notes, you'd likely need little more than a glance to grasp them, and would probably be able to read a measure or two ahead at minimum. That kind of fluency can be attained with more complex figures like those in the exercise above, but you'll need the same level of dedication and daily practice you might have mustered shedding your pentatonic scales and favored blues licks. It might not be as much fun, but it may prove to be more valuable in the long run.

Scales

The guitar parts in "The Best of What's Around" are almost exclusively strumming chord figures, so there isn't any single-line scale playing to speak of, per se. However, a discussion of the scales and modes employed both in the song-writing process and in the melodic lines of the vocals should prove illuminating. We've also learned that every chord and progression has a scale as its basis, so we'd be remiss in skimming over the topic here. The C major scale provides the genesis for the chords and melodic figures in the opening verse, before the music shifts to the key of A and the A major scale (A–B–C♯–D–E–F♯–G♯). Both are shown below with a typical two-octave fingering.

Before we go any further, let's brush up for a moment on the subject of modes. These Latin-named modes are derived from the major scale and begin on the following scale degrees.

1. Ionian (major scale)
2. Dorian
3. Phrygian
4. Lydian
5. Mixolydian
6. Aeolian (natural minor scale)
7. Locrian

If we use the C major scale (C–D–E–F–G–A–B) as an example, the Dorian mode begins on D (D–E–F–G–A–B–C), the Mixolydian mode begins on G (G–A–B–C–D–E–F) and the Aeolian mode begins on A (A–B–C–D–E–F–G). Each has a unique sound and application. Guitarists frequently use the Dorian and Aeolian modes to solo over minor 7th chords, while the Mixolydian mode works well over a dominant 7th chord. A progression that moves back and forth between, say, F minor and E♭7, might be approached with the F Dorian and E♭ Mixolydian modes, respectively. It's always a good idea to know what the "parent" major scale is in relation to any mode you might be playing. For instance, in the rhetorical solo progression above, the F Dorian mode is derived from an E♭ major scale (beginning on its 2nd degree), while the E♭ Mixolydian mode is taken from the A♭ major Scale (and begins on its 5th degree).

In our earlier harmonic discussion of "The Best of What's Around," we saw that the song bounces back and forth between the keys of C and A major, but since the C major sections begin with an Am chord, we can think of this more in terms of a shift from A Aeolian (A–B–C–D–E–F–G) to A Ionian (major scale). If you're following along, it should be obvious by now that the C major scale and A Aeolian modes contain identical pitches and simply begin on different notes. However, the key *sound* in the song is that of the shift between A minor and A major, so it's useful to think of the minor sections as A Aeolian rather than C major. Without belaboring the point (wait . . . too late), you may also recall that the bridge section of the song contains a G chord, which belongs in the key of D major (as the IV) rather than in A. The passage never quite sounds or feels like a key change, though, and it would be a stretch to say that it was in D (D–E–F♯–G–A–B–C♯) or A Mixolydian (A–B–C♯–D–E–F♯–G), the mode built on the D major scale's 5th degree. Think of the G chord as a temporary move outside the key of A, or as an early return to the A natural minor sound in the little two-measure riff that immediately follows.

Composition

"The Best of What's Around" gives us the merest taste of what would soon become a distinct and richly varied compositional style. We've already discussed some of Matthews' quirky little devices, such as the Dadd4 voicing with the minor 2nd rub between F♯ and G in the middle, and the shifting between C major, A major, and A Mixolydian sounds. Let's take a moment to look at three other principles he employs here.

First, like any good songwriter, Matthews knows when to re-use his earlier material. Strong motifs are never merely introduced, heard once, and then never heard from again. Instead, they return to bring a satisfying sense of unity to the song. Even at this early stage in his compositional development, Matthews has the good sense to let us savor his best ideas rather than bombarding us with a million new sections and themes. Even if a songwriter has ten great ideas, we don't need to hear them all in one tune. There will be more songs to write down the road, and a chance for them all to be heard eventually. Next, in the closing "Oh, oh, hey la" motif that repeats during the fade out, Matthews employs a technique that becomes a staple of his writing style: a repeated melodic figure above a base of shifting harmonies and bass notes. The melody takes on a different emotional aspect with each new harmony heard below, and Matthews knows how to use this approach to wring every drop of emotion out of his songs. Finally, check out the way this section—and the earlier choruses built on the same chord progression—seems to dovetail around on itself. The 2/4 measure deceives the listener into thinking that the A chord that follows is resolving the progression on beats 3 and 4, rather than restarting it at the top of a fresh measure of 4/4. It's a clever, inventive bit of songwriting that's fresh and unpredictable, and gives the fadeout a sense of the infinite. What sounds at first like the end of a phrase reveals itself over and over again to be, paradoxically, the beginning.

TECHNIQUE

The technical demands of "The Best of What's Around" can be broken down into two categories: the mastering of the individual chord voicings in the song, and the rhythmic right-hand strumming patterns applied to them. To that end, the following exercise contains a sequence of all of the chords from the song's chorus and outro, and should be played slowly and repeatedly until the transitions from voicing to voicing are smooth and comfortable.

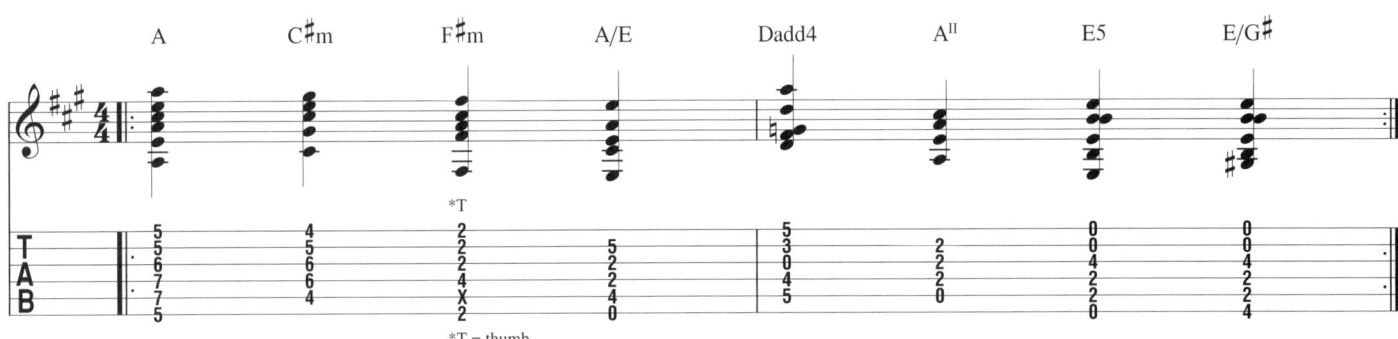

Hopefully, you were familiar enough with the common barre chords above, but the inversions (A/E, E/G♯) and "Matthews-isms" (the thumbed F♯ root and Dadd4 voicing) may be new to you. You might want to create your own variation of this exercise and only include those chords that you find difficult or unfamiliar. Stay calm, take a deep breath, and then move *slowly* and steadily back and forth between them for twenty minutes or so. Chord playing on the guitar is frequently a matter of *muscle memory* (training the mind and fingers to immediately recall the shape of a D major, G♭ suspended, or B13 voicing, for example), but few players are patient enough to slog through the hundreds or thousands of careful repetitions needed to acquire it. Many will spend a decade or more struggling with one technical hole or another rather than sit down for that focused, grueling hour that may solve the problem once and for all!

You're back so soon? Just kidding. Hopefully, the chords above are under your fingers and ready to be recalled at a moment's notice. There's more work to be done, though, if you want to recreate the song exactly, as you'll see in the complete transcription that follows this discussion. Multiple acoustic guitars are layered throughout and each contains a number of intricate variations in which bits and pieces of chords are played rather than full five- or six-string voicings. The example below, containing a segment of the two-guitar accompaniment to the opening verse, demonstrates some of the band's trademark arranging for the instrument. Proper fingering is essential so you can put yourself in position to execute each new "grip." For instance, use your ring finger for the opening A on the D string, and your pinky for the slide up to D on the low E string in the second measure (in both parts). Work through the excerpt below, and then examine the way each guitar part evolves during the course of the full song.

Finally, let's talk briefly about our right-hand strumming technique. Much of what the guitar does in a typical Dave Matthews Band song is strum precise rhythmic parts that both provide the harmony and serve as a percussive addition to the drums and bass, rather than playing a lot of single-note lines and solos, which are often taken by the saxophone and violin. Many players find a strumming style that's personal and works well for them, and it's likely that you have by now as well. However, two things you might want to consider are whether you'll be pivoting primarily at your wrist or your elbow, and how you'll be taking care of the many muted tones (each marked by an "X" in the notation) you'll encounter in this music and most other instances in which you need to play a strummed chord part. One problem you may run into if you're primarily an elbow-pivoting–type strummer is fatigue; if you have to keep it going for more than a few minutes at a time, your arm may stiffen or experience painful cramps. The wrist isn't immune to these symptoms by any means but, in general, it seems to resist the issues the larger joint seems particularly susceptible to. Many of the best rhythm guitarists leave their upper arm fairly stationary and allow their wrists, relaxed to the point of limpness, to take care of all the work. Watch some of your favorite players if you have a chance and take note of their technique. Matthews himself is primarily a "wrist" strummer, and does it brilliantly.

Which brings us to the other consideration: muted or muffled tones. While some players use the side of their pick hand to mute the strings as needed, most (Dave included) simply release the pressure applied by their fret hand without actually lifting off from the strings. This allows for a quick on-and-off technique and a nearly infinite number of rhythmic possibilities at any given moment (the one instance where this technique doesn't quite work is when playing a chord with a number of open strings—logic dictates that you can't release fret-hand pressure from strings that aren't fretted). Try the exercise below with a loose-wristed strummed style and fret-hand muted tones, and then move on to the whole song and put the technique into practice.

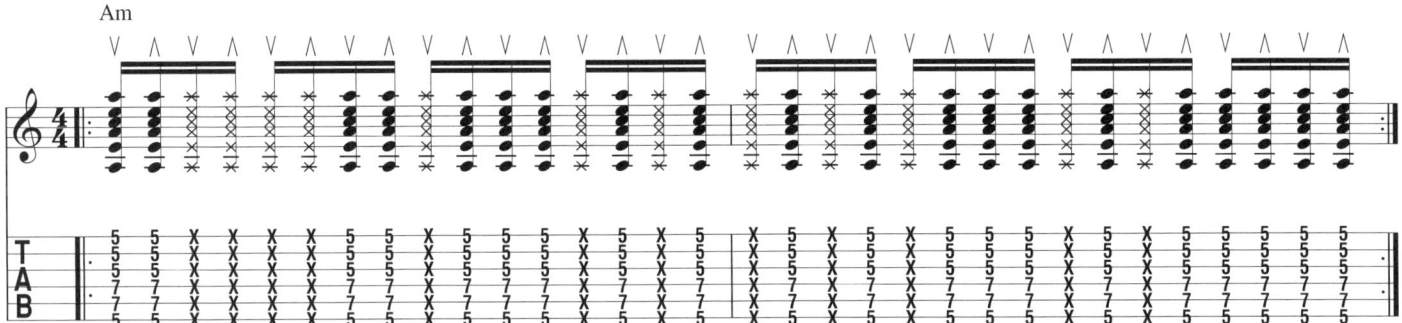

THE BEST OF WHAT'S AROUND

Written by
David J. Matthews

A
C♯m
F♯m
A/E
Dadd4
A[II]
E5
E/G♯
5fr.
4fr.
2fr.
3fr.
134211
13421
T 3111
*T=thumb
3114
32 14
111
114
3114

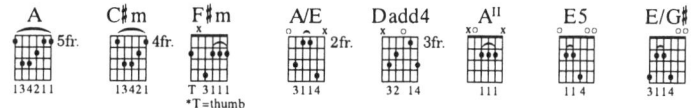

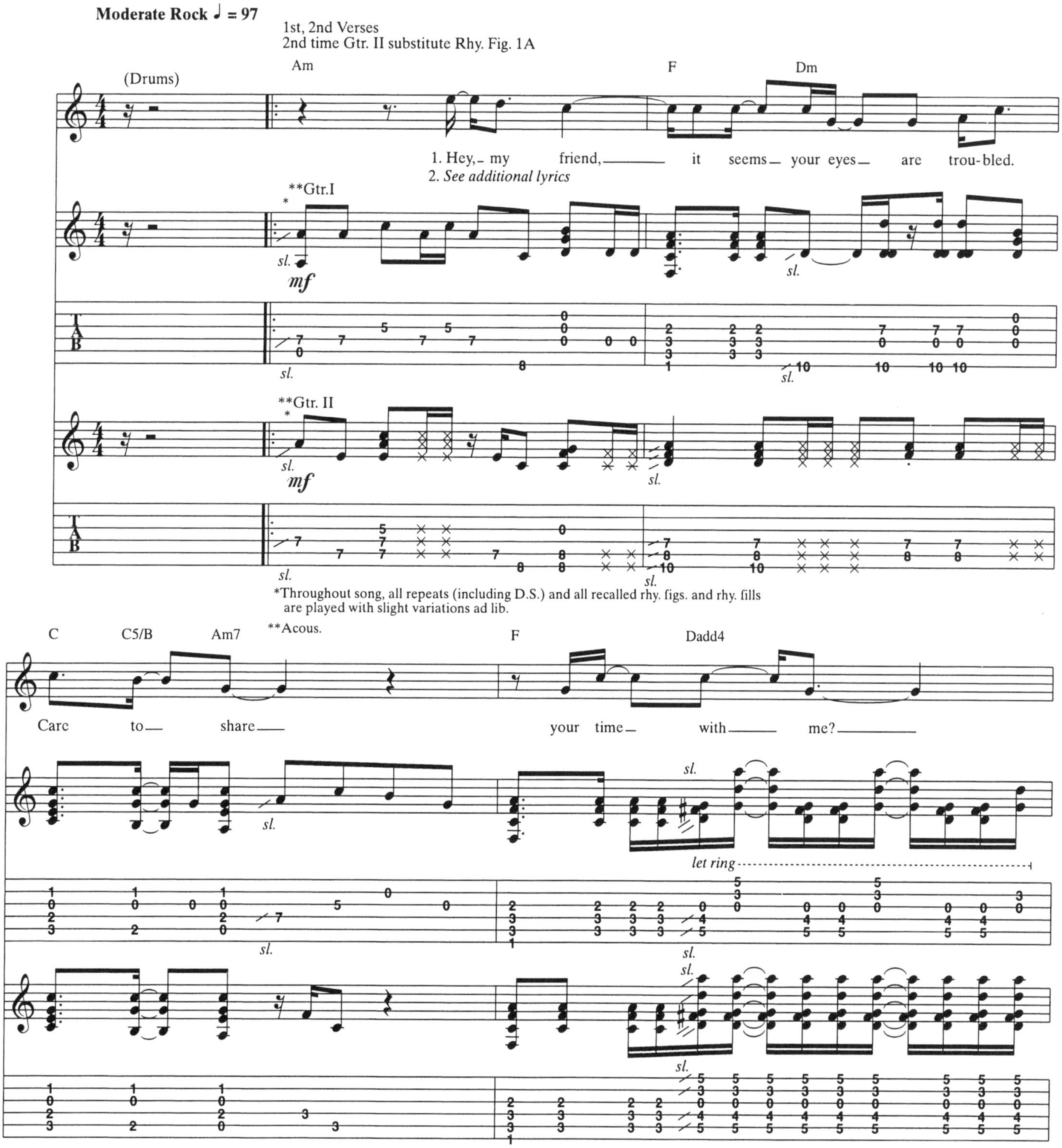

Moderate Rock ♩ = 97
1st, 2nd Verses
2nd time Gtr. II substitute Rhy. Fig. 1A
(Drums)
Am
F
Dm
1. Hey, my friend, it seems your eyes are trou-bled.
2. See additional lyrics
**Gtr. I
mf
sl.
let ring
**Gtr. II
*Throughout song, all repeats (including D.S.) and all recalled rhy. figs. and rhy. fills are played with slight variations ad lib.
C
C5/B
Am7
**Acous.
Dadd4
Care to share your time with me?

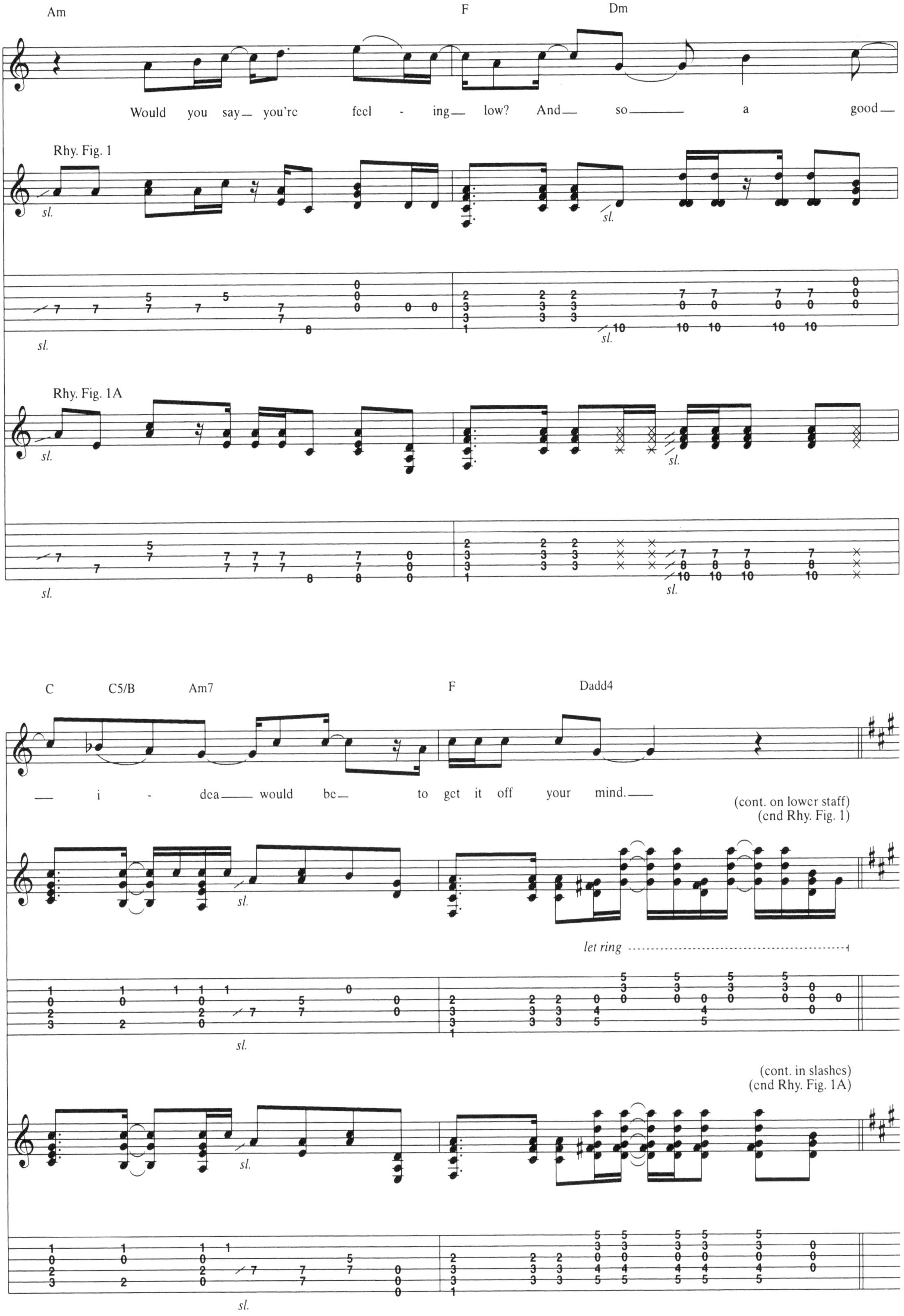
Am
F
Dm
Would you say you're feel - ing low? And so a good
Rhy. Fig. 1
sl.
Rhy. Fig. 1A
C
C5/B
Am7
Dadd4
i - dea would be to get it off your mind.
(cont. on lower staff)
(end Rhy. Fig. 1)
let ring
(cont. in slashes)
(end Rhy. Fig. 1A)

1.3. See,— you and me— have a— bet-ter time— than— most can dream. Have—
2. *See additional lyrics*

it bet-ter than— the best, so— can a-pull on through—

Additional Lyrics

2. And if you hold on tight to what you think is your thing,
   You may find you're missing all the rest.
   Well, she run up into the light surprised.
   Her arms are open. Her minds's eye is...

2nd Chorus:
Seeing things from a better side than most can dream.
On a clearer road I feel, oh, you could say she's safe.
Whatever tears at her, whatever holds her down.
And if nothing can be done, she'll make the best of what's around. *(To Bridge)*

WHAT WOULD YOU SAY
From *Under the Table and Dreaming* (1994)

One of the band's earliest hit singles, "What Would You Say" has a freewheeling, funky vibe that easily communicates the fun the band has playing together and for their listeners. It reappears on the *Live at Folsom Field* concert CD and DVD, in which the looks on the bandmembers' faces show plainly that they're having a blast. Let's take a closer look.

THEORY

Harmony

"What Would You Say" is a fairly straightforward tune; the band often opens this one up for extended jamming during live performances. It is divided into three distinct sections delineated by their differing harmonic foundations. The first section opens the song and continues under both the verses and the chorus with slight variations throughout.

Matthew's funky two-measure acoustic part moves back and forth between an A9 chord and an A triad with a G in the bass—essentially an A7 chord in 3rd inversion. This chord is sometimes played without its full compliment of notes, transforming it into either a G6 or Gadd2 chord, which makes for a subtle difference but has no bearing on its harmonic function. If you recall our earlier discussion of the harmonized major scale, the 5th degree will always become a dominant chord if the 7th is included. By working down the scale backwards from A, we find ourselves in the key of D, making both the A9 chord and the A/G different ways of playing the V. However, this doesn't quite jibe with either the key signature (three sharps) or the sound of the tune, both of which are clearly in A. So what's going on? Essentially, "What Would You Say" is a modal tune, and these sections are based on the A Mixolydian mode (A–B–C♯–D–E–F♯–G). If we look at the song from this perspective, we can consider A9 to be the I chord, A/G the I chord in 3rd inversion (with its ♭7th in the bass), and the G6 and Gadd2 chords the ♭VII in A. Two of the defining characteristics of modal music are the absence of a dominant chord on the 5th degree and, consequently, the absence of a *leading tone*. This important note—the 7th scale degree in a major scale and the major 3rd of the V chord—is responsible for the tension built by the dominant chord and resolved upon arriving at the tonic. Play though the example in A below and pay particular attention to the action of the leading tone, G♯, as it repeatedly resolves upwards to A by gravitational force.

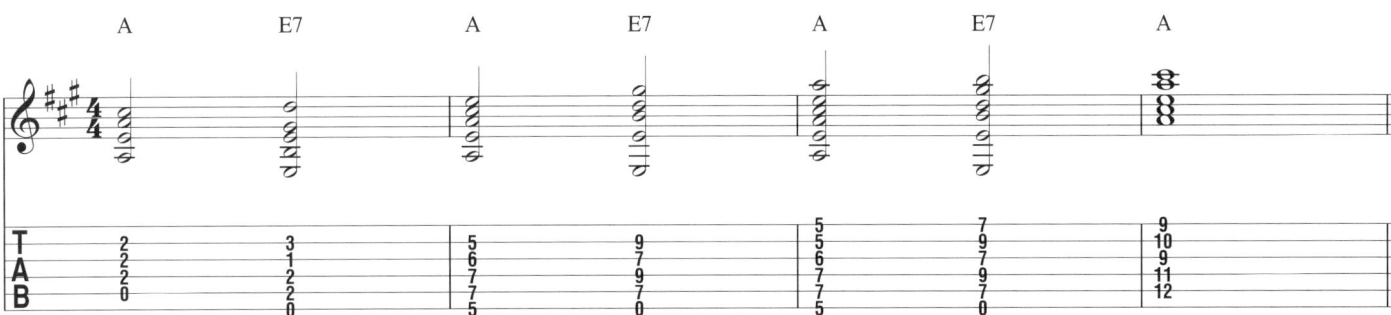

In the Mixolydian-based sections of "What Would You Say," there is no leading tone, as the G♯ that would serve that function is lowered to a G♮, and the modal nature of these parts has a distinctively different sound than a major scale–based composition. When the tune shifts temporarily to 3/4 during its pre-chorus section, the mode shifts as well to A Aeolian. Again, if you recall our earlier discussion on the topic, the Aeolian mode is built on the major scale's 6th degree, so the parent scale here is C major. Analyzed from the point of view of A Aeolian, Am is the i chord, G is the ♭VII, F is the ♭VI, and Esus4 is the V chord (again, no leading tone here).

Finally, a third progression emerges that serves as a backdrop to LeRoi Moore's saxophone solo. The first three chords—A7sus4, A7, and A5—represent the I chord in the original A Mixolydian tonality. The C7 chord that follows is, functionally, the V chord in the key of F major, but it serves instead here as a kind of non-harmonic passing chord leading us down to E7sus4, the final chord in the progression (and the V chord in the key of A). This chord lacks the G♯ that would change things from an A Mixolydian tonality into A major, allowing Moore to take a predominantly modal approach to his solo. Also, check out the nifty voice leading employed by Matthews to get from C7 to E7sus4—not the most common transition.

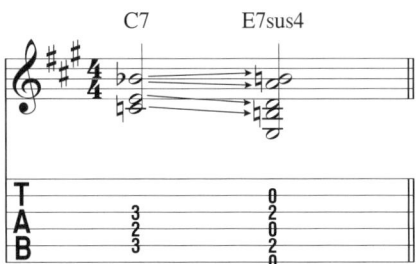

Voice leading is the art of moving through harmonies with smooth steps from each chord tone to the next, particularly as concerns the inner voices. Take a look at the example below, which includes the same progression but with much less artfully voiced chords.

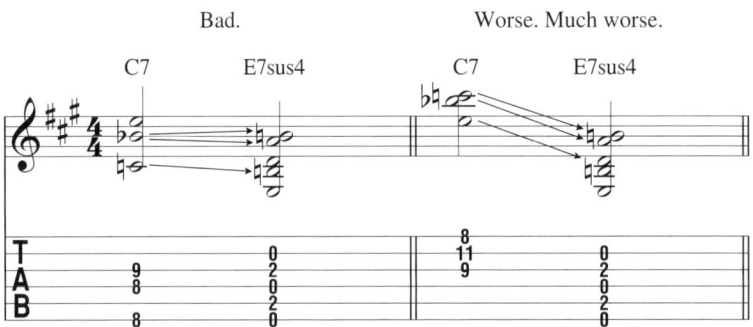

The second example is pretty exaggerated, as most guitarists would likely have a bit more common sense than to jump around so jarringly. Nevertheless, voice leading is an important consideration in both composition and chord playing, and it would behoove you to give it a closer look if you're not doing so already.

Rhythm

Once again, rhythm plays a central role in a Dave Matthews Band song, and the main two-measure riff at the heart of the song has enough rhythmic thrust to propel things along nicely. Matthews, like all great songwriters, has an almost instinctive grasp of the three central elements of music (harmony, melody, and rhythm) and the delicate balancing act each must perform within the course of a piece.

"What Would You Say" has a pretty bare-bones harmonic base, which allows both melody, and especially rhythm, to come to the fore. If the song had a million chords and jumped from key to key constantly, the busy, syncopated guitar riff would serve more as a distraction than anything else. Likewise, a complex melody would suffer and the listener would likely be overwhelmed by everything that was going on at once. Give a listen to some of your favorite music by other artists, be they rock, country, jazz, or classical stylists, and see where and how this important principle is applied in their music.

Okay, back to the song at hand. While the opening riff repeats during much of the bulk of the tune, it's subjected to subtle rhythmic variations that combine eighth notes and 16th notes with a variety of rests, dots, and ties. Listening carefully to the recording is always a great way to grasp the rhythms employed in a song (as well as all of the other elements), but it isn't enough. The recording should never be used as a crutch to help you past either your inability to read music or your unwillingness to spend the time in doing so. You need to examine the notated music and learn exactly where in a given measure each note falls; there shouldn't be any guesswork involved. For example, here's the measure immediately preceding Matthews' vocal entrance. Guitar 1, playing an octave figure, is shown in the notation, while Guitar 2, playing the A/G chord, is shown above the staff in rhythm slashes.

Remember when we talked about the "e–and–a" syllables used to verbalize 16th note figures? Let's use them now. The dotted eighth note that opens the measure lasts for 3/4 of the first beat, so that the first 16th note falls on the "a" of beat 1. We rest for an eighth note (first half of beat 2), and then hit that low G again on the "and" of beat 2. Notice that Guitar 2 splits away here into its own rhythmic figure, resting on the "a" of beat 2 and the downbeat of beat 3. Guitar 1 plays on beat 3, rests for a 16th note ("e"), and then plays two 16ths on the "and" and "a" of beat 3. Guitar 2 punches an A/G chord into the space where Guitar 1 rests, then plays all four 16th notes on beat 4 while sliding the chord voicing down a fret and back up again. Meanwhile, Guitar 1 completes the measure by resting on the downbeat of beat 4, playing two 16th notes on the "e" and "and," and then resting for the final 16th of the measure. Whew! And that's only one measure. Before you close this book in disgust and go back to jamming along with the album, realize that this type of rhythmic analysis goes by more quickly with each new attempt. If you stick with it, you'll be taking in entire measures at a glance and moving on to even more complex figures and phrases before you know it. So, take the time to break down any measure you don't immediately and completely understand, play or tap out the rhythms slowly, and then bring it all back up to speed once you're clear on where each and every note should be falling.

Before we move on, take note of the time signature change that occurs in the pre-chorus. The shift here from 4/4 to 3/4 is a relatively simple one in that all we're doing is dropping a beat off the end of each measure, with a quarter note chord part that makes counting along an easy matter. In the fifth measure of this section, we jump back to 4/4 with a dotted quarter figure, so keep up that counting to avoid any confusion over where "1" is.

Scales

We've already said that the chords and melody of "What Would You Say" are derived primarily from the Mixolydian and Aeolian modes. Now, let's look at a few different ways of playing them on the instrument.

A Aeolian Mode (Fingering 1) A Aeolian Mode (Fingering 2)

The two modes above are each shown in an *open-position* fingering (utilizing, as the name employs, a number of open strings) and in a more common fingering beginning with the 2nd finger on the low E string's 5th fret. Get them under your fingers and try soloing over the recording of the song, using A Mixolydian over each section except the pre-chorus where you should shift to A Aeolian. You'll likely find yourself hitting many of the same notes sung by Matthews and the back-up vocalists.

While there's no guitar solo here to speak of, there are some tasty solo spots from LeRoi Moore on saxophone and Blues Traveler frontman John Popper sitting in for a guest spot on harmonica. Both combine Mixolydian ideas with licks from the A major pentatonic scale and the A blues scale. Popper in particular leans heavier in the direction of the Mixolydian mode while Moore plays from more of a blues scale base. Here are the most common fingerings for the major pentatonic and blues scales, although I strongly suspect that you already know the latter if you're anything like 99.9% of the world's guitar-playing population.

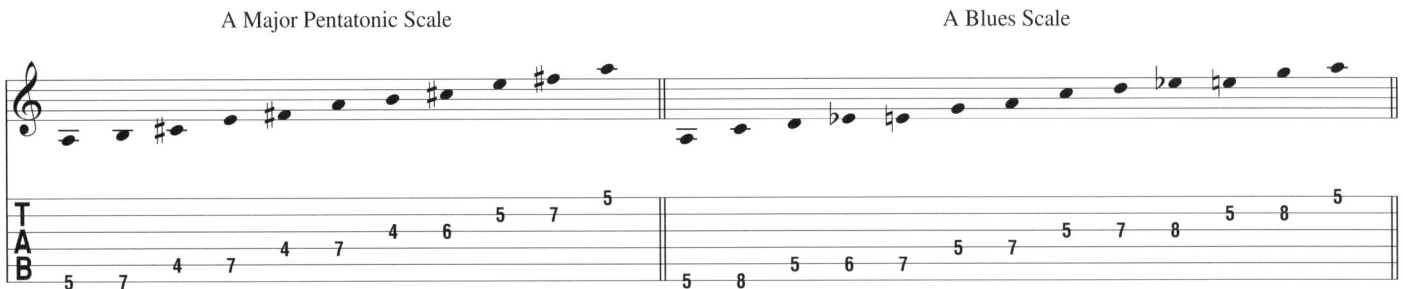

A Major Pentatonic Scale A Blues Scale

Try improvising over the solo section of the tune by using only one scale or mode at first. When each is comfortably under your fingers and their distinctively different sounds are in your ears, trying mixing and matching tones from all three (A Mixolydian mode, A major pentatonic scale, and A blues scale).

Composition

"What Would You Say" doesn't reinvent the wheel compositionally, with its relatively simple structure and repeated returns to the central riff that begins the song—and that's exactly the point. When you have something good, it's not necessary to keep adding more and more to it. Restraint is just as important—perhaps more so—than many of the sophisticated writing techniques one could apply. In fact, restraint *is* a sophisticated writing technique, and one that requires a fair amount of maturity to develop. If all we heard was that two-measure phrase over and over again, we'd probably get a little bored, but Matthews breaks things up in several different ways.

First, there's that pre-chorus section that presents shifts in both time signature (from 4/4 to 3/4) and tonality from A Mixolydian to A Aeolian. Secondly, there are the recurring *stop-time* figures in which the entire band drops out, leaving the vocal to stand alone for a moment or two. The fact that these breaks don't always occur in exactly the same place helps to keep things interesting as well. Finally, the vocal melody of the song uses a type of *call-and-response* arrangement in which Dave's solo vocal is often answered by a harmonized group vocal that fills in the space while he's taking a breath. It's a compositional technique that goes back centuries before the first recorded music, but it's just as effective now as it ever was in the past.

TECHNIQUE

It's a relatively simple song, but "What Would You Say" presents a few technical challenges outside of those involved with the execution of the main riff. Here it is in its original song-opening guise, before any alterations have been made. Note, however, that we've collapsed the two-guitar line so it's playable by just one.

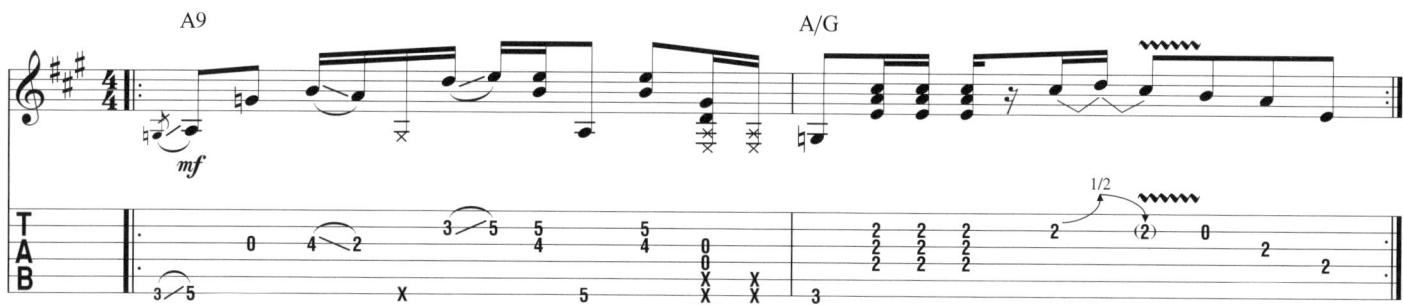

There are a few different ways to play this figure, but Dave does it like this. Begin with your middle finger hitting the A on the low E string, and then use your index finger for the slide down the G string that begins on beat 2. Use your ring finger for the slide up the B string that follows, with your middle finger back on the low E string and your pinky taking the G-string note. This should allow you to use your index finger to mute the unused open strings by lying gently above them on the 4th fret. In the second measure, the index finger is used to barre the 2nd fret of the D, G, and B strings while the middle finger remains on the low E. Dave performs a quick shift of position to bend and release the B string at the 2nd fret with his middle finger, using the index finger for a little assistance behind it. Strike the B string only once, push it up a half step to D, and then return to the original unbent pitch, C♯. The next time you pick should be on the open B-string eighth note that follows. Each of the slides in the phrase are picked only once, so use enough finger pressure as you slide up or down to ensure that the note you land on can be heard clearly.

WHAT WOULD YOU SAY

Written by
David J. Matthews

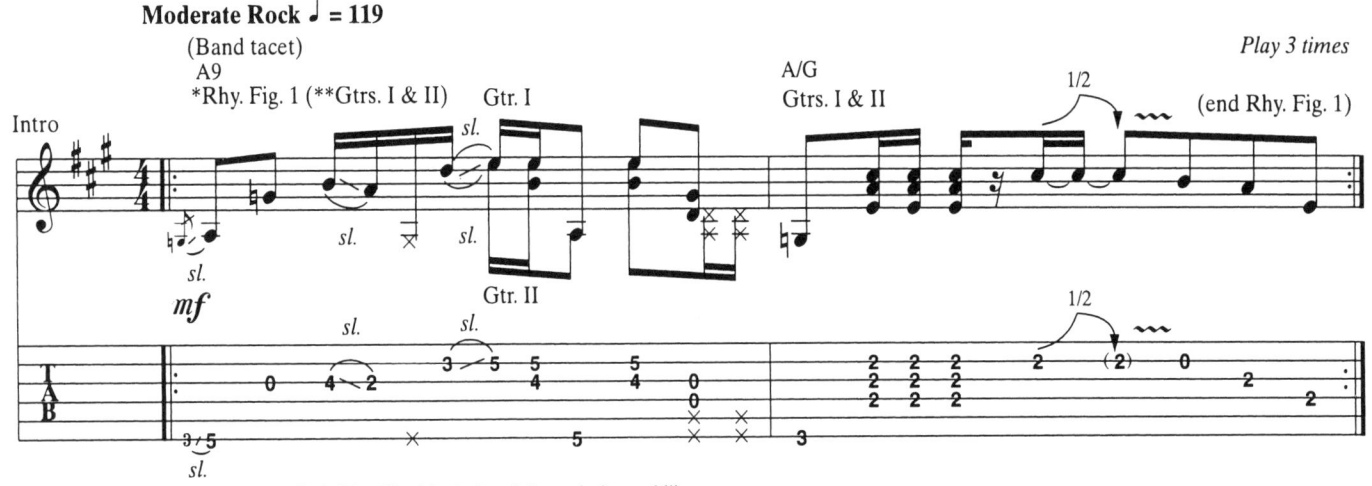

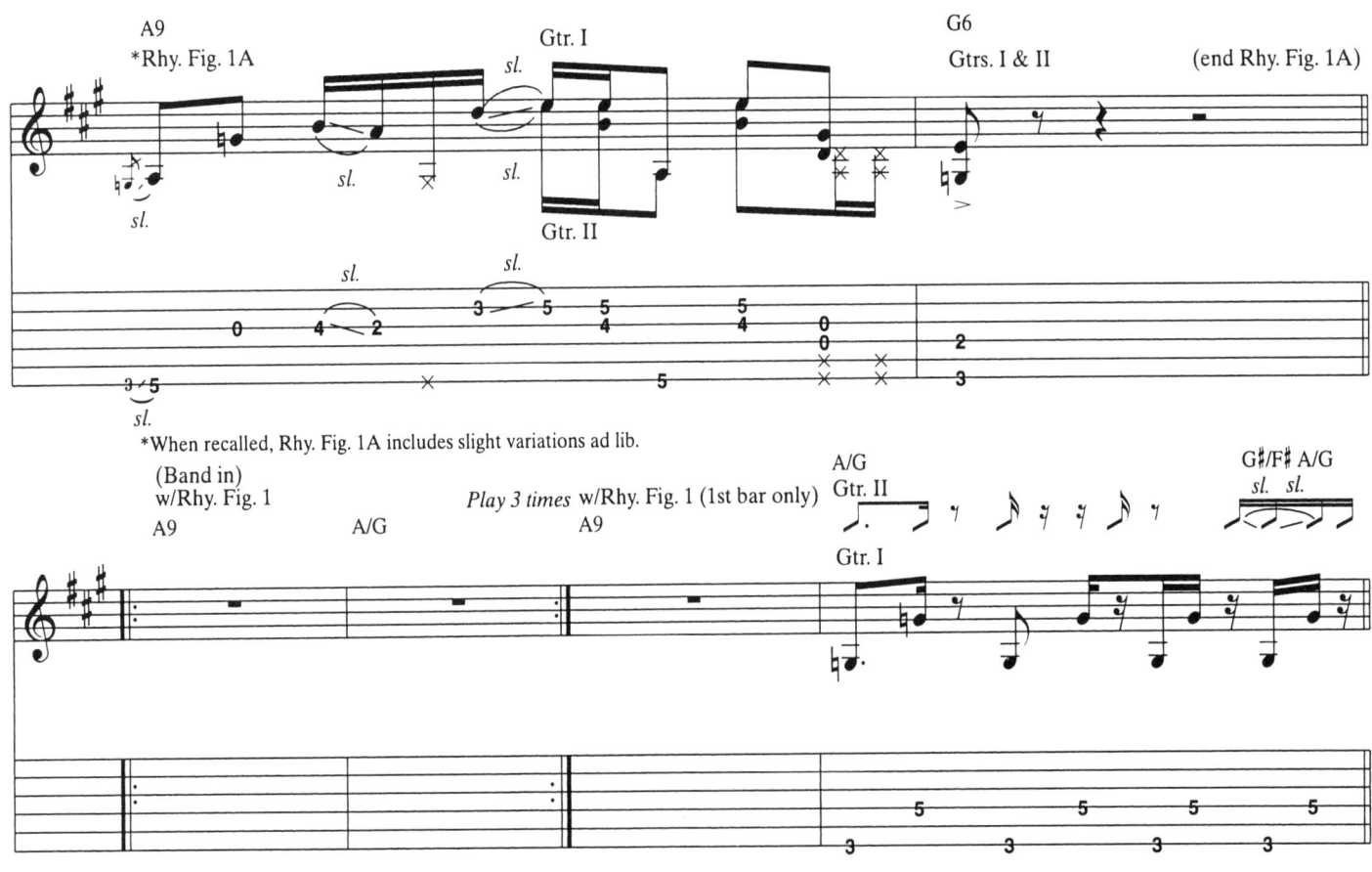

1st, 2nd, 3rd Verses
w/Rhy. Fig. 1 (3½ times)
3rd time w/Fill 1

A9   A/G   A9

1. Up and down the pup-pies' hair fleas and ticks jump ev-'ry-where ('cause of o-rig-
2.3. *See additional lyrics*

A/G   A9

i - nal   sin).   Down the hill fell Jack and Jill, and

2nd & 3rd times Gtrs. I & II substitute Rhy. Fig. 1A

A/G   A9

you came tum-bling af - ter ('cause of o - rig-

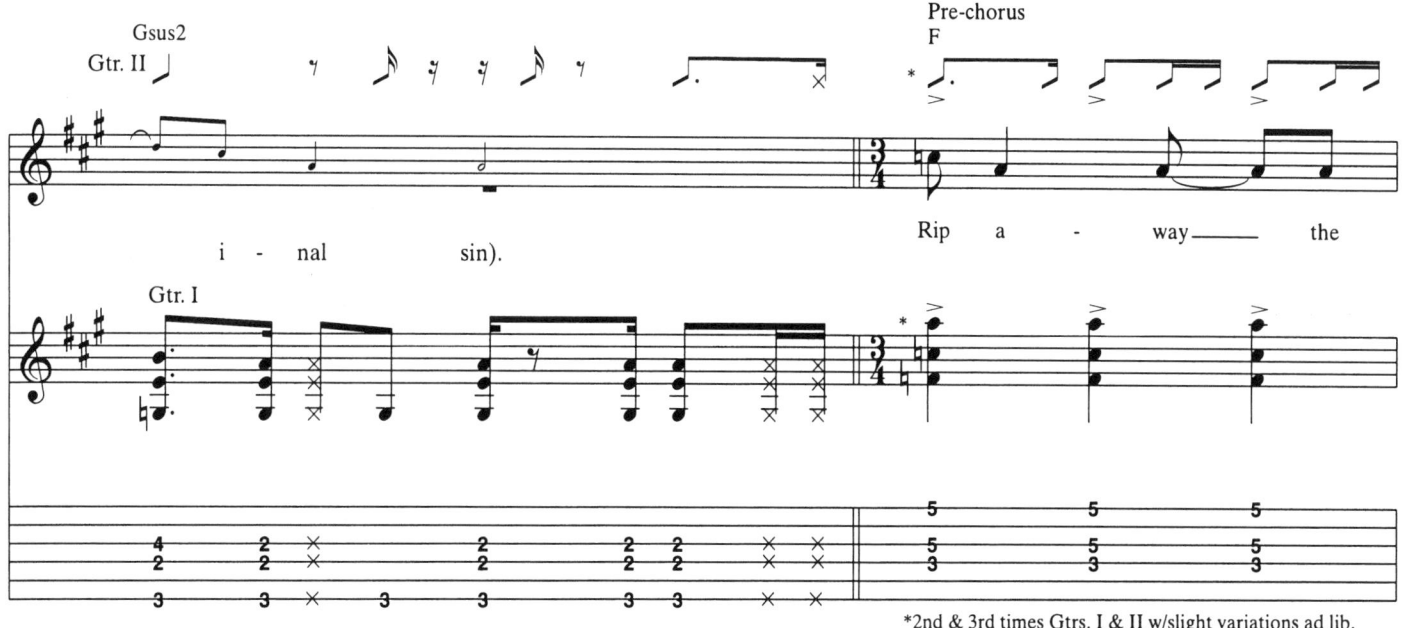

Gsus2
Gtr. II

Pre-chorus
F

i - nal   sin).   Rip a - way the

Gtr. I

*2nd & 3rd times Gtrs. I & II w/slight variations ad lib.

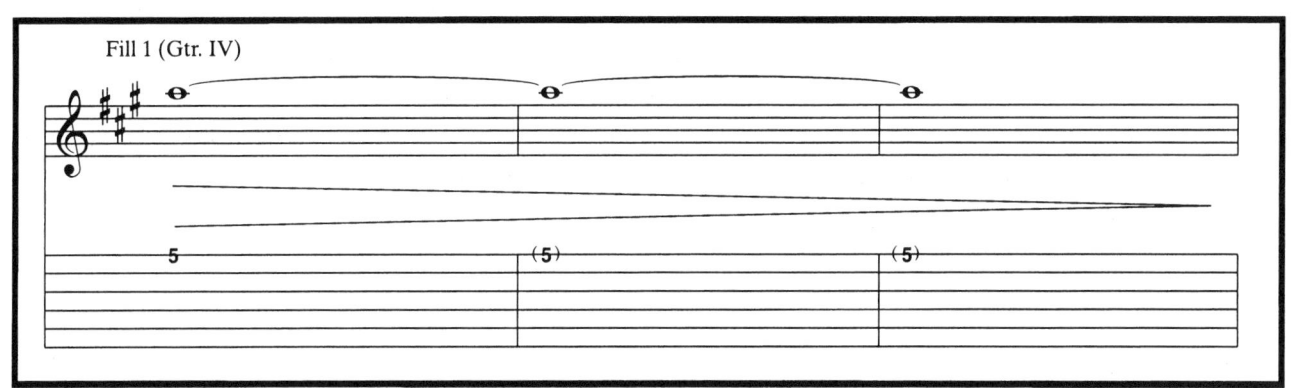

Fill 1 (Gtr. IV)

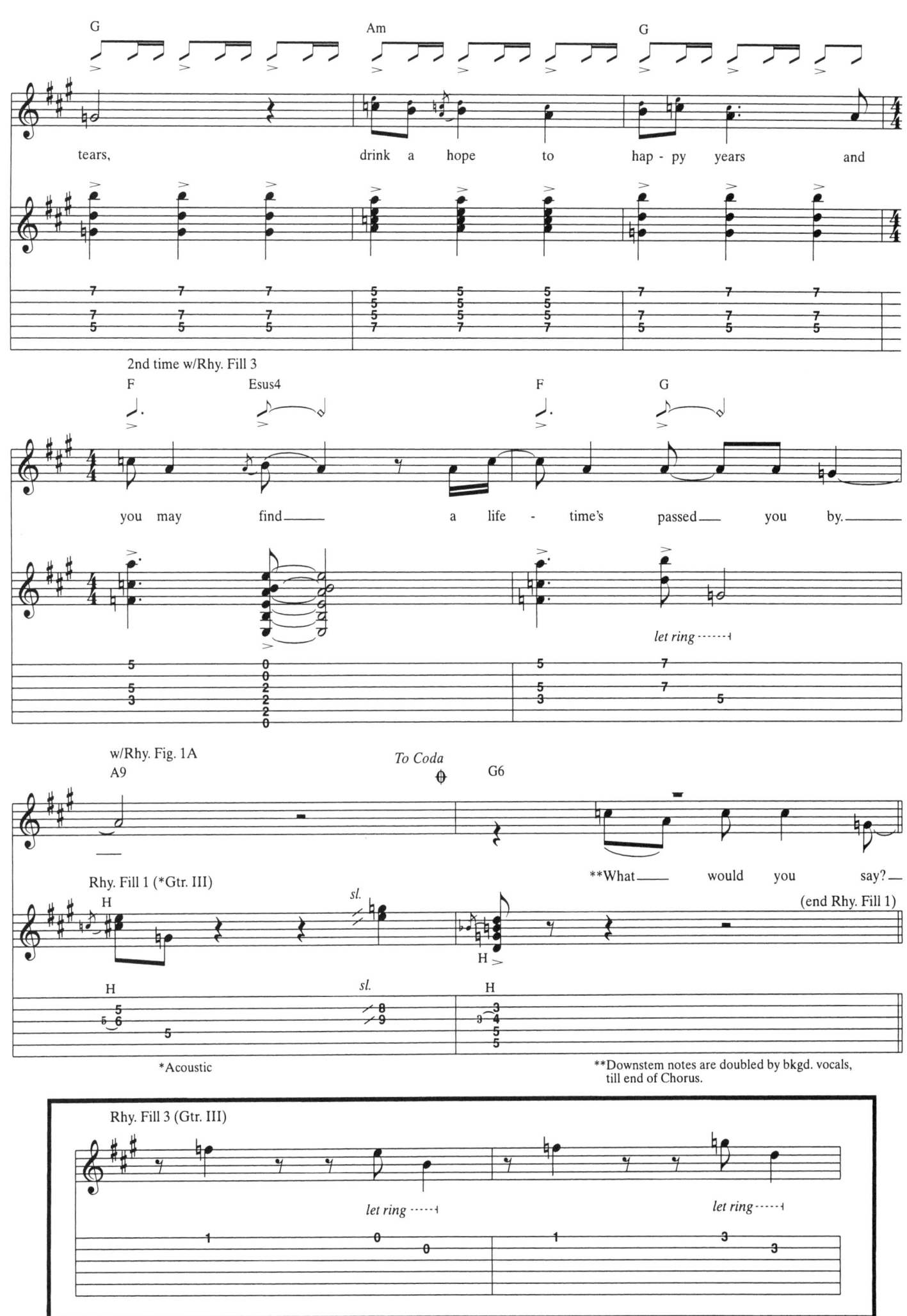

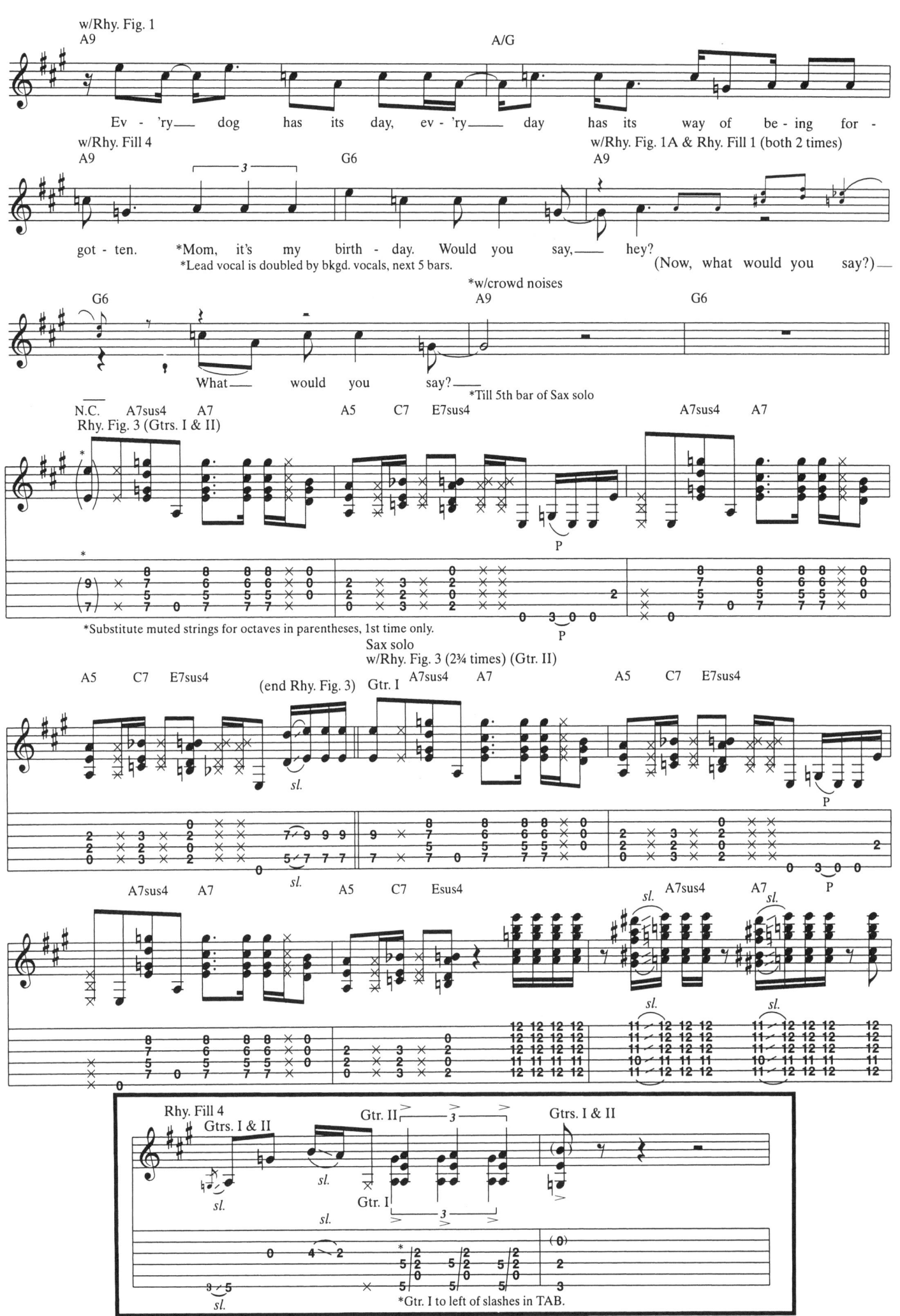

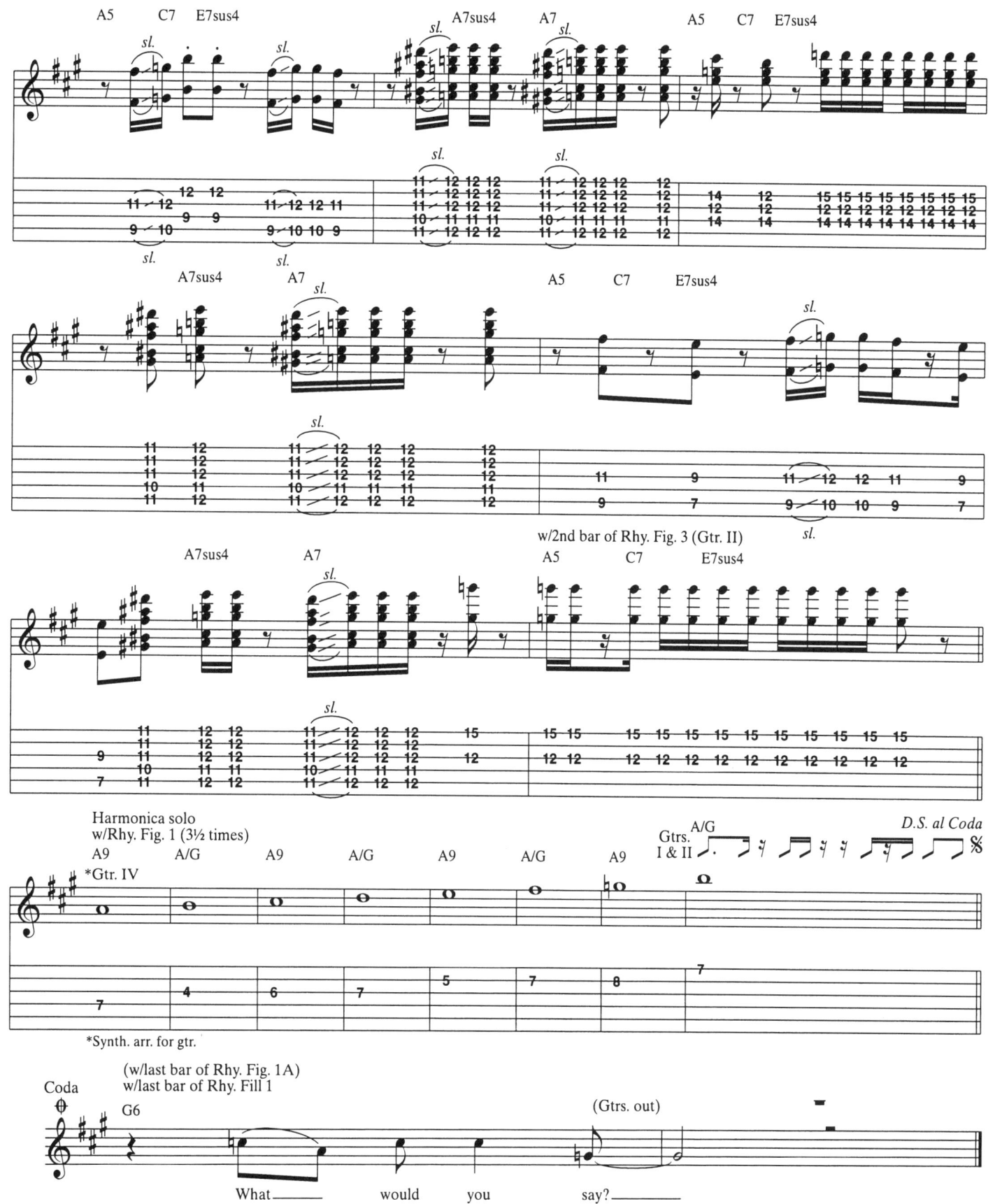

Additional Lyrics

2.3. I was there when the bear ate his head, thought it was a candy.
   (Everyone goes in the end.)
   Knock, knock on the door. Who's it for? There's nobody in here.
   (Look in the mirror, my friend.)

2nd, 3rd Pre-chorus:
I don't understand, at best, and cannot speak for all the rest.
The morning rise, a lifetime's passed me by.
 What would you say?

SATELLITE
From *Under the Table and Dreaming* (1994)

The gently undulating "Satellite" displays an entirely different sensibility than the funky jams heard on "What Would You Say" and "The Best of What's Around." Dave Matthews Band has always been known for their versatility and wide-ranging influences, and "Satellite" is a prime example of their eagerness to dip into a wide pool of sounds and grooves.

THEORY

Harmony

"Satellite" is a strictly diatonic song, in that it remains in the key of A♭ major from start to finish. This doesn't mean that the song is devoid of harmonic interest—only that Matthews has been particularly resourceful in creating that interest by employing some fairly unconventional devices. While the chorus and bridge sections of the song include standard chord progressions that are easily analyzed, the verses of the song are constructed over a pattern of intervals heard as a number of layered, single-note parts played by multiple acoustic guitars and Boyd Tinsley's violin. At first, it's hard to say exactly what's happening harmonically as there aren't any actual chords being played, but as the vocal begins, Stefan Lessard enters on bass and clears things up a bit. His simple part, which moves between A♭ and E♭ bass notes, creates the sensation of shifting from the tonic (I) to the dominant chord (V) in each alternating measure and also gives us a rhythmic handle to latch onto by playing mostly dotted half notes (one note per measure of 3/4). With the arrival of the chorus, we enter more common harmonic territory, as the sequence of A♭, D♭6/9, B♭m7, and E♭7add4 chords represents the I, IV, ii, and V chords in A♭, respectively. The addition of chord extensions (the 6 and 9 above the D♭ chord, and the added 4 on the E♭7 chord) to the basic tones underneath does not alter their functions in the key in any way—they merely provide some added color and complexity. The bridge of the song changes the chord sequence slightly, with the A♭, Cm, D♭add2, and B♭m chords representing the I, iii, IV, and ii chords in the key. It's a small difference but a significant one, as the introduction of the Cm chord gives us a sound we hadn't heard up to this point in the composition. In a piece constructed with a small, select group of harmonic materials, each new addition really makes an impact.

Rhythm

"Satellite" can accurately be described as a waltz. In a waltz, the rhythm section—be it a group of string basses in the old Viennese ballroom style, or the tandem of Stefan Lessard and Carter Beauford in Dave Matthews Band—plays what is essentially a "one" feel, with a single bass note in each measure. This might be a dotted half note, as mentioned above, or a short quarter note followed by two beats of rest. There may be the occasional fill or passing note but these do not obscure the highly emphasized downbeat of each measure, leading to a kind of loping rhythm to which dancers have always been drawn. When Lessard and Beauford enter, they immediately clear up any rhythmic confusion with their simple parts emphasizing the downbeat of each measure. Prior to that, the layered single-note lines of the intro often obscure "one" with their unpredictable groupings. Take a look at the opening guitar part.

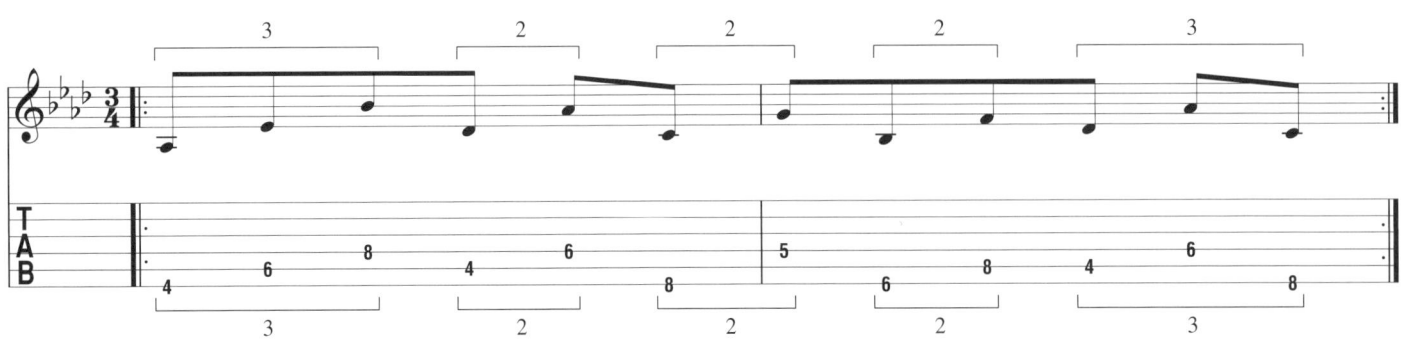

The two-measure phrase includes 12 eighth notes in total, broken into groups of three and two (these groups are indicated by the brackets above and below the staff). By dividing the notes in this fashion, the placement of the barline and beat 1 (the downbeat) of each measure is cleverly obscured. What looks at first glance like rhythmic sameness—a steady flow of eighth notes—is instead transformed into a complex and disorienting guitar part. In the song's ninth measure, a second part is added, as shown in the example below.

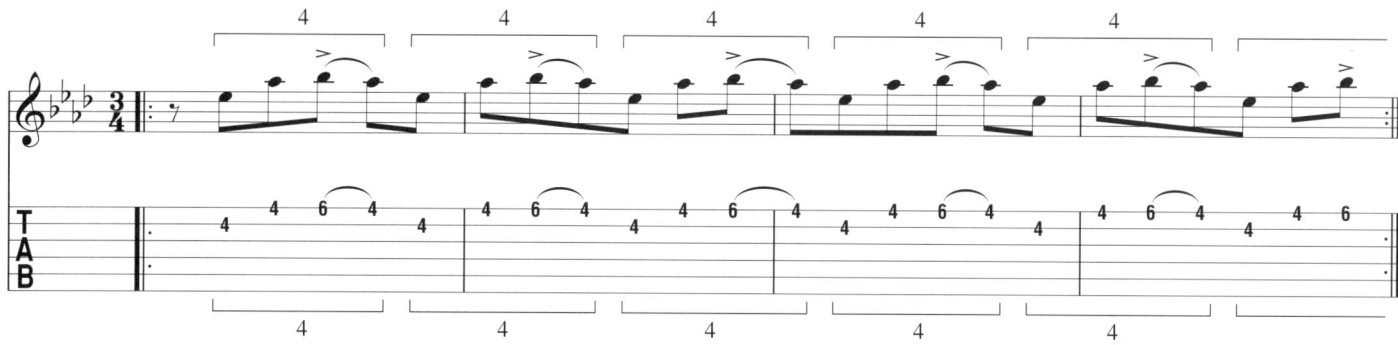

This one's even more unusual, it that it takes a four-note phrase and begins it in three different places before repeating from the beginning. The first time we hear it, it begins after an eighth note rest on the downbeat and falls on the "and" of beat 1, It begins again on the final eighth note of the first measure (the "and" of 3), and then falls on the "and" of 2 in the second measure before starting afresh in measure 3. This is a prime example of what musicians mean by *playing over the barline:* phrases that begin or end without regard for the artificial barriers set up by measures and time signatures. Advanced drummers (i.e., Carter Beauford) often play fills or solo phrases that work this way and intentionally avoid pounding the downbeat of a measure. These licks cross the barline and end in unpredictable places, demanding that all players involved count each beat so as not to lose their place. Before we move on, try tapping out the rhythms in the exercise below, a study in increasingly difficult over-the-barline phrasing that you may struggle with at first but should help you deal with these challenging moments when you encounter them down the line. Keep a steady quarter note pulse going with your foot and add an emphatic accent to the downbeat of each measure if you can. It's a bit like tapping your head and rubbing your stomach at the same time—but then again, so is playing music.

Scales

We've already said that "Satellite" is entirely diatonic and employs notes and chords derived exclusively from the A♭ major scale (A♭–B♭–C–D♭–E♭–F–G). The intro and verse sections of the song are based on a steady eighth note pattern of interesting intervallic leaps within the scale, while the chorus and bridge are sung over chords generated by the scale's harmonization. In the examples that follow, we'll examine a few different ways of playing this scale and take a peek at the tip of the iceberg in terms of the possible intervallic patterns within them. Let's begin with the two most common fingerings for the A♭ major scale, shown on the next page.

Fingering 1   Fingering 2

The first fingering is in 3rd position (i.e., the index finger plays all notes on the 3rd fret, the middle finger plays those on the 4th, etc.) while the second is in 4th position (use your index finger for the 4th-fret notes, your middle finger for the 6th-fret notes, and your pinky for those on the 8th fret). Both of these fingerings involve only three fingers and notes per string, but if you want a real finger-buster, try this one, which requires the use of all four fingers per string.

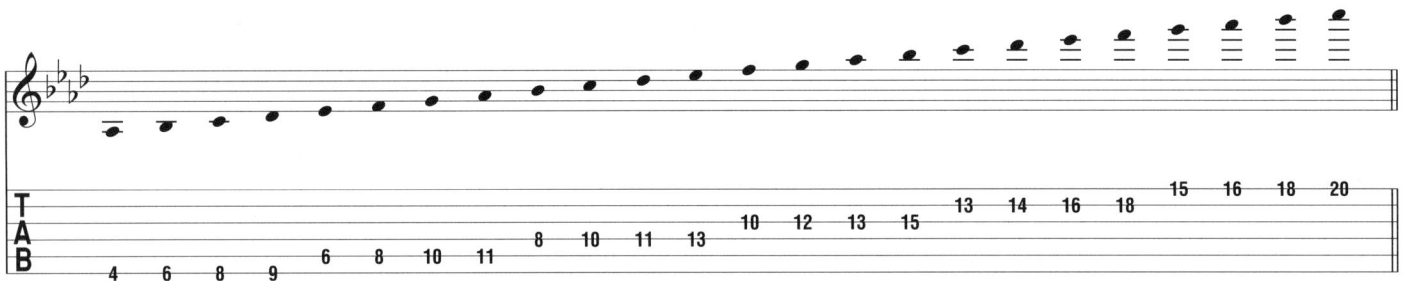

This fingering might seem unwieldy at first, but like all new things, it should be approached slowly and with a great deal of patience. A few weeks of diligent practice on the four-notes-per-string scale fingering can yield a greatly enhanced range on the fingerboard and increased functional stretching ability for both single lines and chords.

Next, let's look at a handful of interval studies using the Ab major scale and its 4th-position fingering. This first one goes up and down the scale in a series of diatonic 3rds. Work slowly and do your best to stay in position throughout.

Now, let's do the same with diatonic 4ths. This one uses a lot of "rolling" of one finger from string to string on the same fret.

This next exercise moves in diatonic 5ths; you'll recognize a lot of these moves when you play through the main guitar part in "Satellite."

So far, so good. We've gone through most of the various diatonic intervals in the patterns above, so why not finish things off with the last two: diatonic 6ths and 7ths. The 6ths, which we'll look at first, necessitate a fair amount of stretching and string-skipping. Take your time with these.

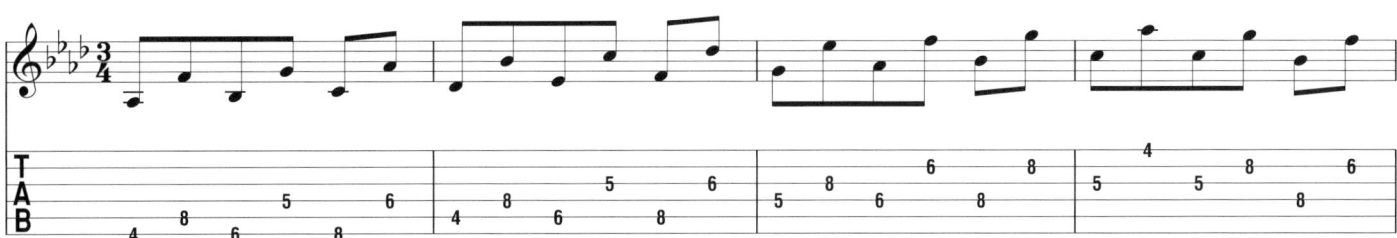

Finally, here's a sequence of diatonic 7ths that has you skipping strings all over the place. Work this one and the rest up to speed, and then make up some of your own drills by combining the various intervals, taking a multi-directional approach, or introducing rhythmic variants or odd note groupings to the equation. You're only limited by your imagination and willingness to work hard in the practice room.

Composition

"Satellite" is a prime example of Dave Matthews' economical songwriting approach, in which he draws from a relatively small number of raw materials but knows just how to use them for maximum impact. The song follows the familiar verse–chorus–bridge format of many pop tunes but its layered single-note lines and soaring, harmonized vocals leave us with something that's far from ordinary. There are a number of trademark Matthews devices in effect here, from the stop-time breaks in the intro to the subtle harmonic differences between the chorus and bridge sections. The latter is a fairly uncommon occurrence; in "The Best of What's Around," we observed a similar scheme, in which both chorus and bridge begin with the same chord rather than moving to another key entirely as is much more commonly seen. In both instances, Dave avoids any sense of monotony by virtue of melodic, rather than harmonic, variation, while the rhythm changes the underlying groove to help delineate each new section. Matthews also uses layered eighth note lines instead of full chords as accompaniment to the verse sections of the song, bringing in each layer individually during the intro that precedes it. He starts with overdubbed acoustic steel string guitars doubling the central part, brings in a third guitar for a higher register counter-line, and then has violinist Boyd Tinsley enter the mix with a series of bowed eighth notes that enriches the arrangement even further.

"Satellite" has a vaguely Celtic flavor, with its open harmonies, Irish waltz rhythms, and lyrical melody, and Tinsley's violin takes us closer to the Emerald Isle if only in spirit. The layered lines are scaled back upon Matthews' vocal entrance so as not to overwhelm or distract; in later verses, Tinsley's part returns in an unobtrusive way, and there's even a subtle slide guitar part buried discreetly beneath it all. Dave is a musician blessed with good taste, economical sensibilities, and a gift for melody.

TECHNIQUE

If you worked through the "Scales" portion of this song's lesson, you've already had a bit of a technical workout on the A♭ major scale and should be prepared to tackle the single-note lines on which the verses are built. However, the second layer in this section (shown in the notated music as "Gtr. 3") employs three common guitar techniques (pull-offs, slides, and vibrato) that deserve a closer look. Here's a four-measure excerpt that includes all three.

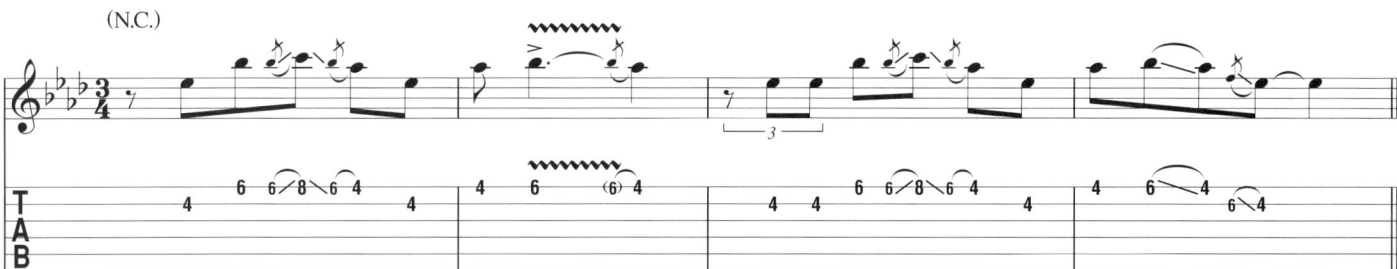

Play the example without any of the added articulations indicated so you get the basic rhythms and pitches of the phrase under your fingers. Now, let's add the details. Begin the first measure with your index finger on the B string, and then use your ring finger to play the B♭ on the high E string's 6th fret. Strike the B♭ again and slide up a whole step to the 8th fret immediately; that second B♭ should take up only a fraction of a second. Next, slide back down to B♭ quickly and pull-off to A♭ on the 4th fret in one movement. Remember that a *pull-off* is executed by lifting your finger away from a given (first) note while pulling down on the string slightly at the same time. This allows you to sound another lower pitched (second) note, provided that you pull off and down with sufficient force.

In the excerpt's second measure, play the Bb on the high E string with your ring finger, and then apply a bit of vibrato to the note by repeatedly shaking your fret hand up and down, slightly bending the string, while holding the note. The speed and distance a string is bent determines the depth and intensity of the vibrato. Generally, vibrato is used to give a note a slightly detuned, wobbly effect without changing the pitch more than a quarter tone (except in rare exaggerated cases where it can be used for comic effect) and to mimic a singer's approach to sustained pitches. When people say someone "really sings" on guitar, they usually mean that the player has an especially beautiful, controlled vibrato that brings to mind a great vocalist. They'll also probably have a strong handle on other aspects of articulation—those details that turn mere notes into actual music—such as the slides found in our excerpt. The key to clean, accurate sliding is firm finger pressure that allows the *target note* (the destination to which you're sliding) to be heard clearly. Note that the slides in this example are *slur slides*, in which the target note is not re-picked. This kind of slide is the one most commonly encountered, but there are instances of sliding (usually involving a longer distance up or down the fretboard) in which the target note *is* picked. The third measure of the example above echoes the first with a slight rhythmic variation, while the final measure includes both a slide from B♭ to A♭ (in which each pitch lasts an eighth note) and another *grace note* slide like those in the earlier measures, in which the tiny, upstemmed pitch lasts for but a split second.

Try your hand at the little etude below that includes the three techniques described above.

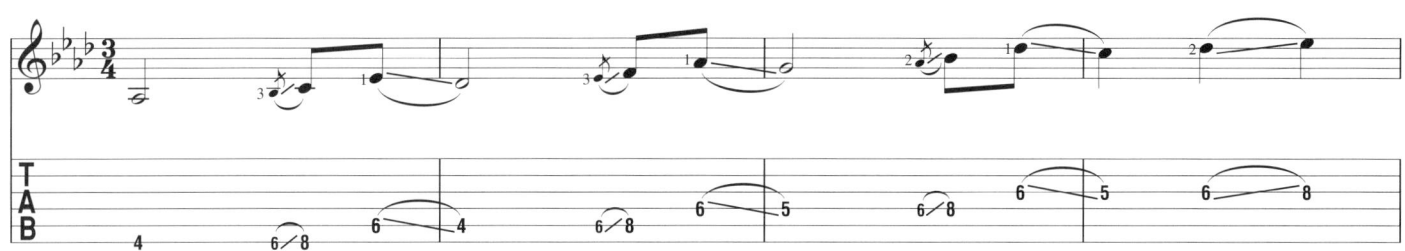

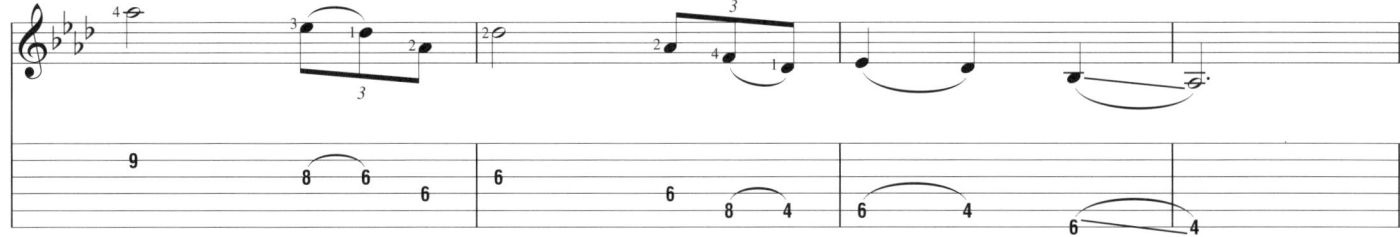

Moving on, there's the matter of the little slide guitar part barely heard under the song's second verse. Obviously, slide guitar technique is a topic big enough for its own book, but there are some pointers we can discuss here that should help you to play the part, shown below.

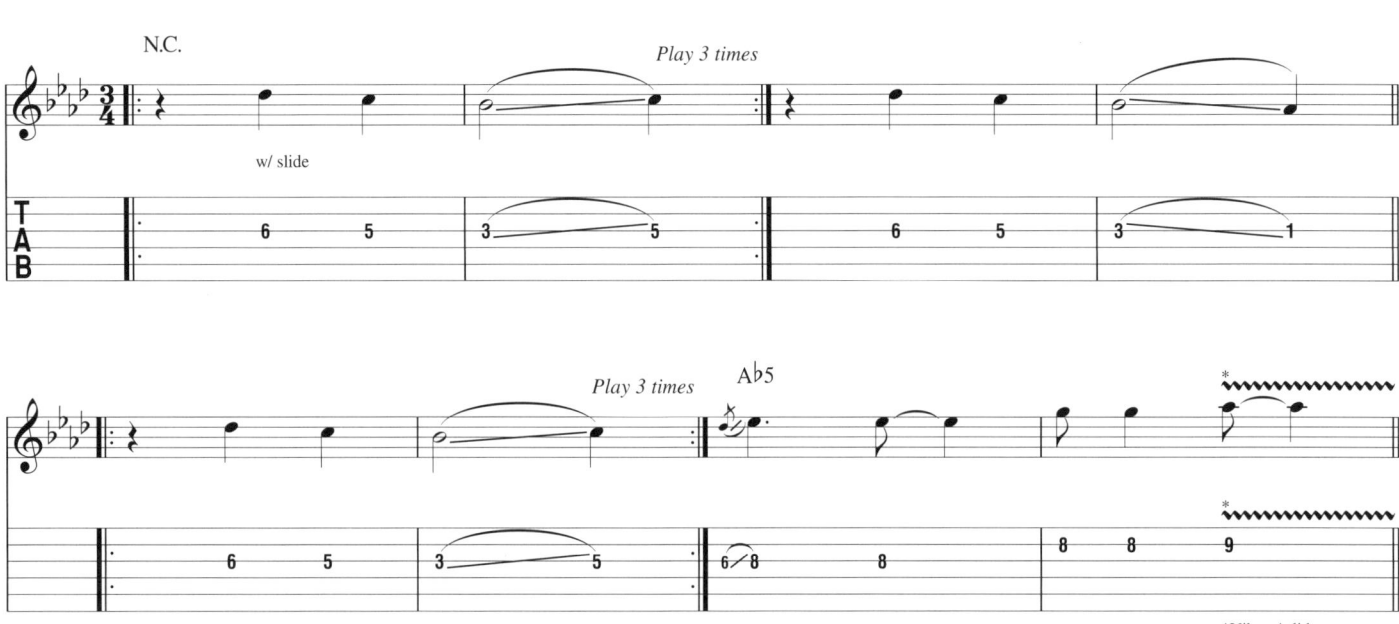

To begin with, slides themselves are usually made of either glass or brass, and each has a unique tone and weight. The choice of slide material is entirely yours; many guitarists who play slide frequently own and use both. Then, there is the matter of which finger to wear it on, with the most common choices being the ring finger or pinky. Whichever you choose, the fingers behind the slide should be flattened as much as possible and kept parallel with it to minimize string noise. The pick hand should perform a similar maneuver, with the fingers that are not gripping the pick (as well as the side of the hand) helping to mute the unused strings. The higher the string height or *action* on your instrument, the easier it should be to execute slide phrases. In addition, the slide should never be pressed down *into* the strings—rather, it should be laid gently *on* them, directly above the fret wire. Above all, you'll need to be patient if playing slide is new to you; pay particular attention to your intonation. It's a delicate art that can quickly erode into a whiny, detuned mess if it's not approached with appropriate care. The example taken from "Satellite" is actually a good place to start, as it's repetitious and rhythmically undemanding. Be sure to slide from note to note only where indicated, making the other notes discrete from each other and clearly defined. Add a little vibrato to the final note of the example by moving the slide a short distance from left to right, rather than up and down as would be the case if one where playing otherwise.

Before moving onto the complete song, let's look at a final technique you'll need. Both the chorus and bridge sections include fingerpicking passages in which the pick is put down or palmed, and the thumb is used to pluck low strings while the index, middle, and ring fingers pluck the higher strings above. Here's the basic pattern played during the chorus.

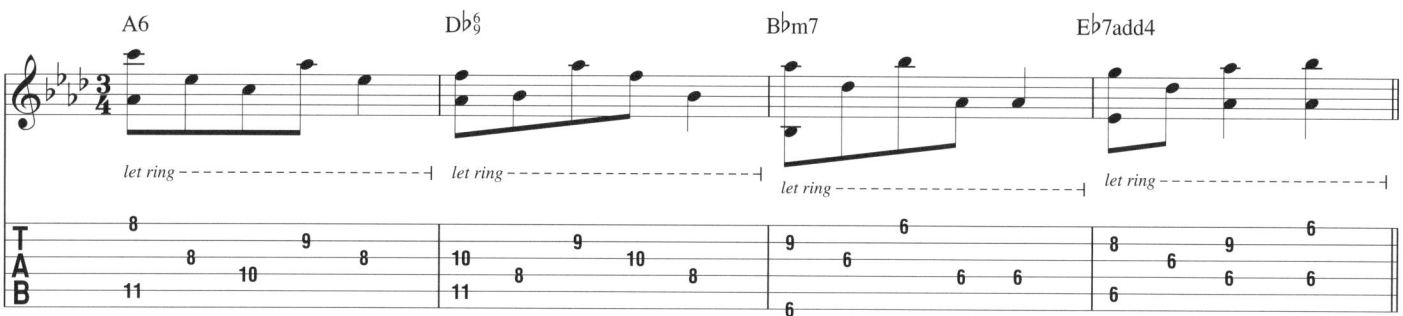

Each measure introduces a new chord voicing that is held and allowed to ring for three full beats. Begin each measure by grabbing the lower pitch with your thumb and the higher one with your ring finger, and then finish off with a combination of index, ring, and middle fingers. This kind of playing is often fairly instinctual: If you begin a phrase with the correct fingers, the others should just fall into line. As with any new technique, take your time and slow things down enough to execute them perfectly before bringing the tempo back up to its full speed.

The fingerpicked accompaniment to the bridge (below) is particularly quick. A number of fingerpicking schemes are possible here, but the most logical answer is probably the correct one. Use your thumb, index, middle, and ring fingers to play the notes on the D, G, B, and high E strings, respectively. The 16th notes fly by at this tempo (125 beats per minute), so work your way up to speed gradually. A passage like this has to be smooth, consistent, and without any rhythmic hiccups to be effective. Good luck!

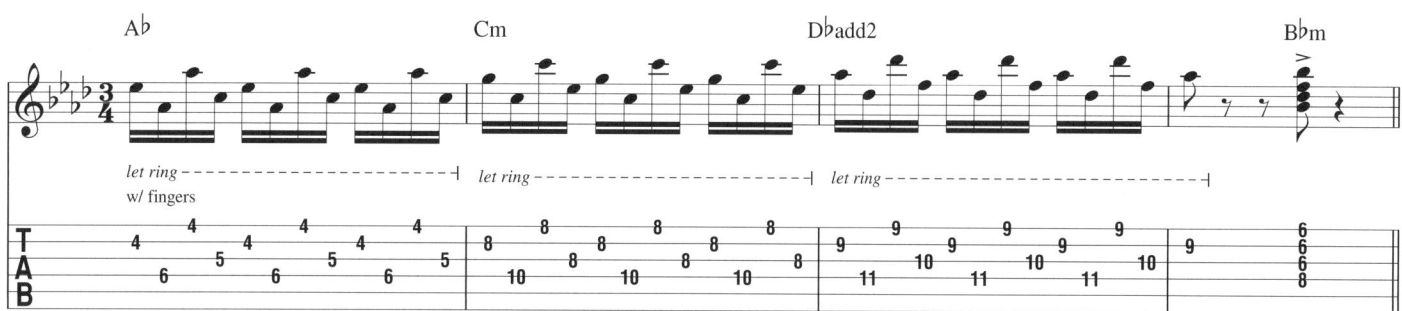

SATELLITE

Written by
David J. Matthews

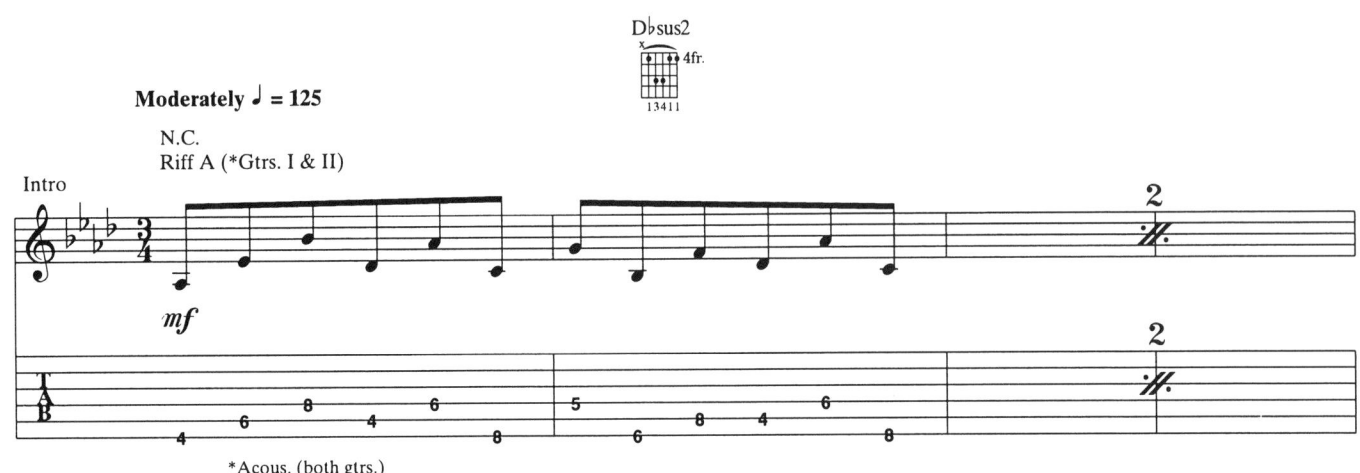

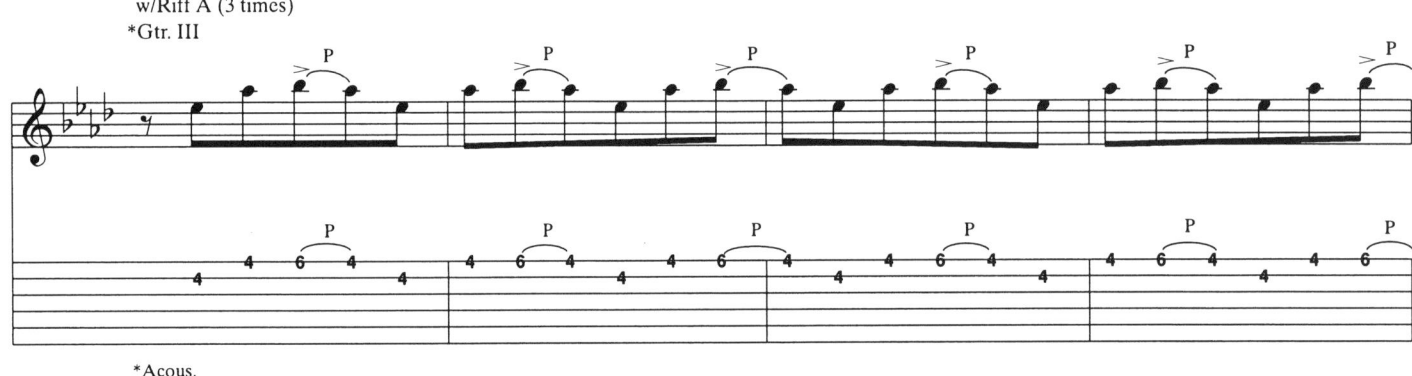

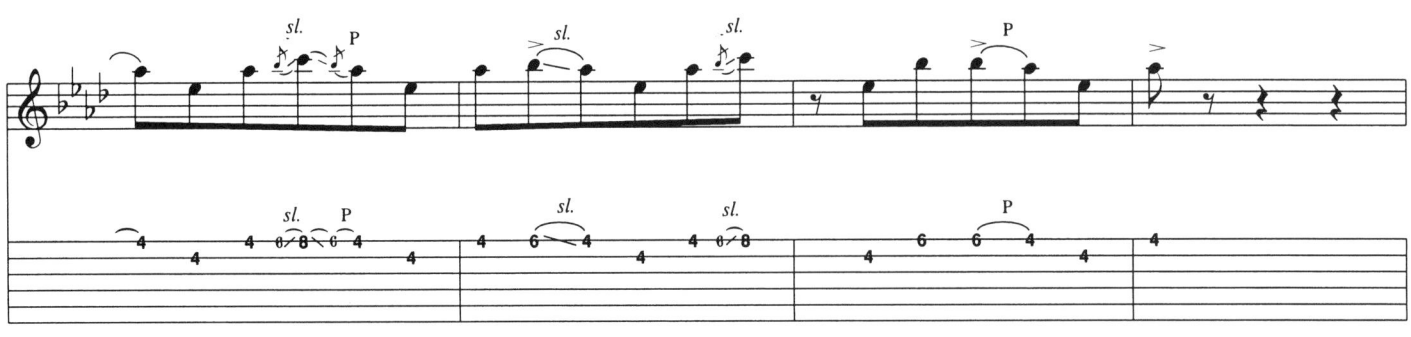

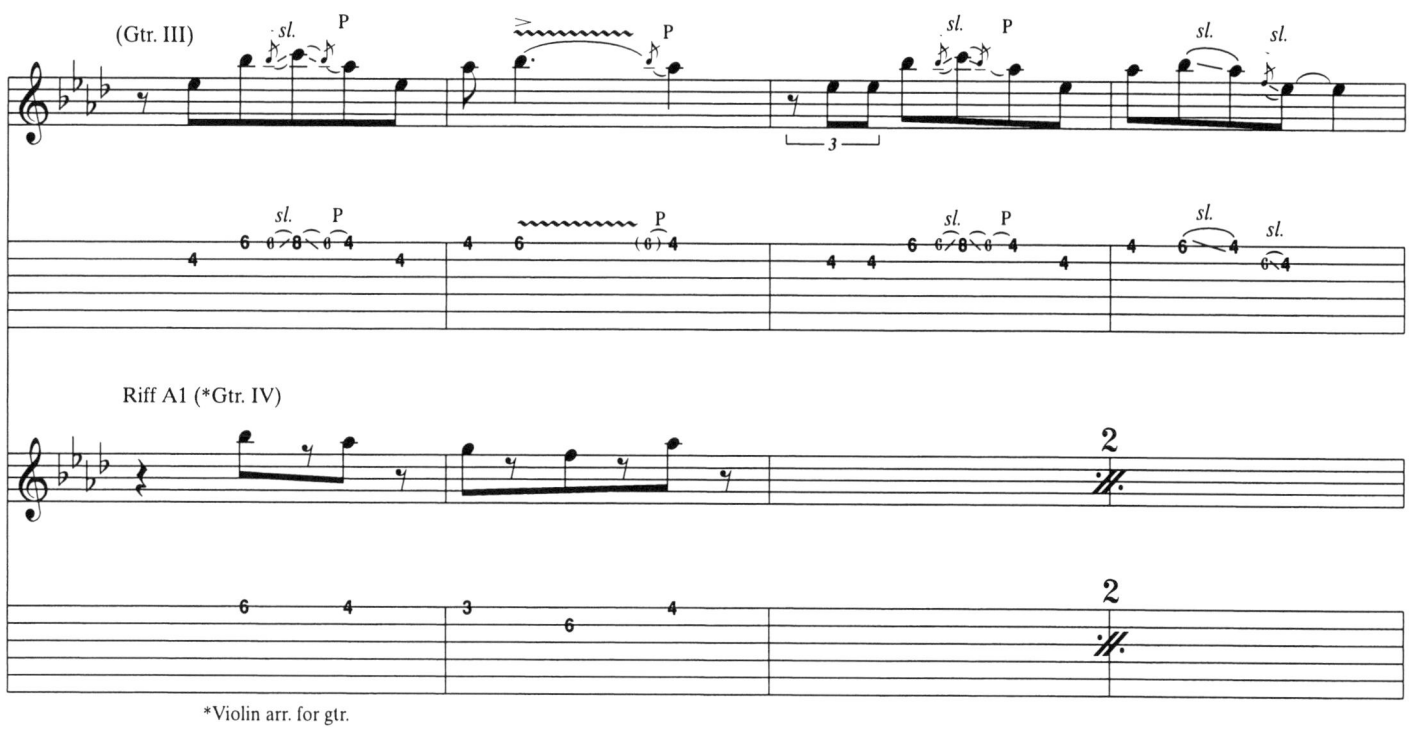

Riff A1 (*Gtr. IV)

*Violin arr. for gtr.

(end Riff A1)

w/Riff A1
(Gtr. III)

1. Sat - el -

(Gtr. III out)

1st, 2nd, 3rd Verses
w/Riff A (1¾ times)
2nd time w/Riff A1 (1¾ times) & Riff B
3rd time w/Riff A1 (1 time only)

N.C.

(1.3.) lite   in   my   eyes,   like   a   dia - mond   in   the   sky.
(2.) lite   head - lines   read.   Some - one's   se - crets   you've   seen,   eyes   and

*Harmony is sung 3rd time only.

How   I   won - der.   Sat - el - lite   strong   from   the   moon,
cars   have   been.   Sat - el - lite   dish   in   my   yard,

and   the   world   your   bal - loon.   Peep - ing   Tom   for   the
tell   me   more,   tell   me   more.   Who's   the   king   of   your

Riff B (*Gtr. V)   Play 3 times

w/slide

*Acous.

Play 3 times   (Gtr. V out)

*Vib. w/slide.

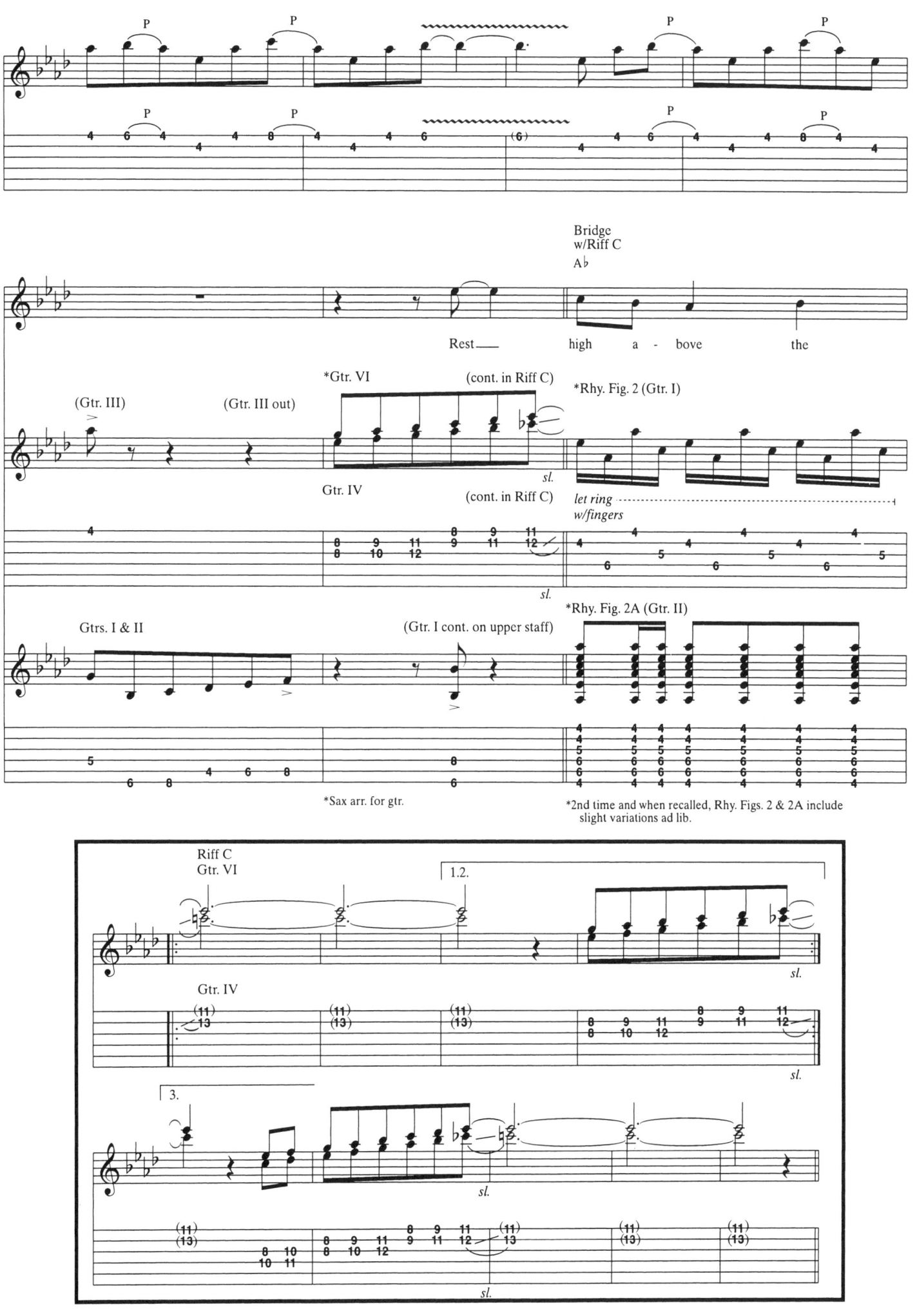

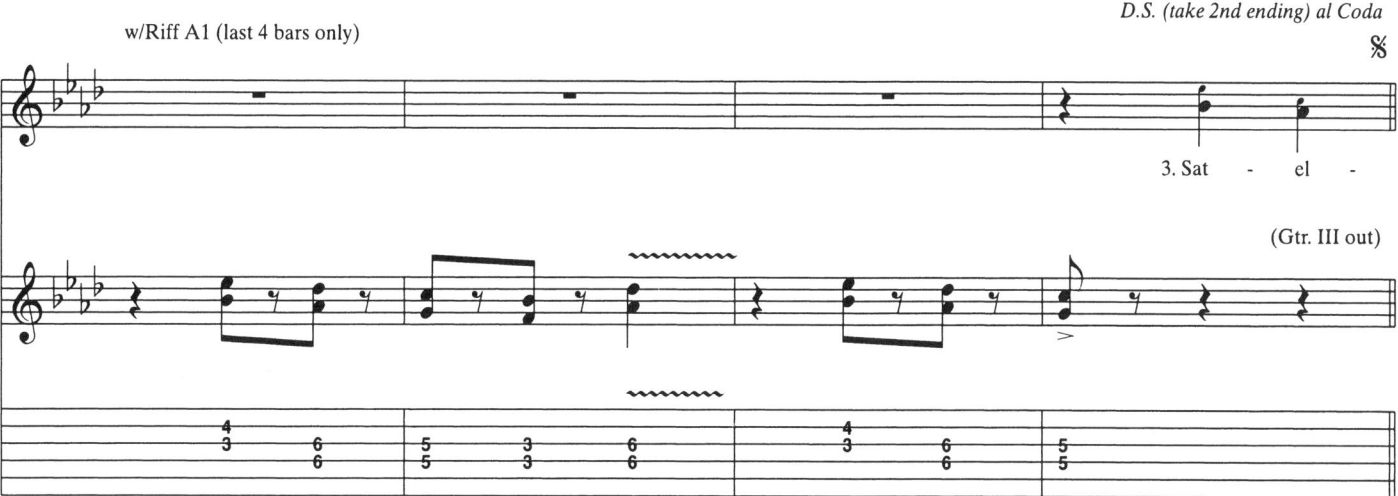

w/Riff A1 (last 4 bars only)

3. Sat - el -

(Gtr. III out)

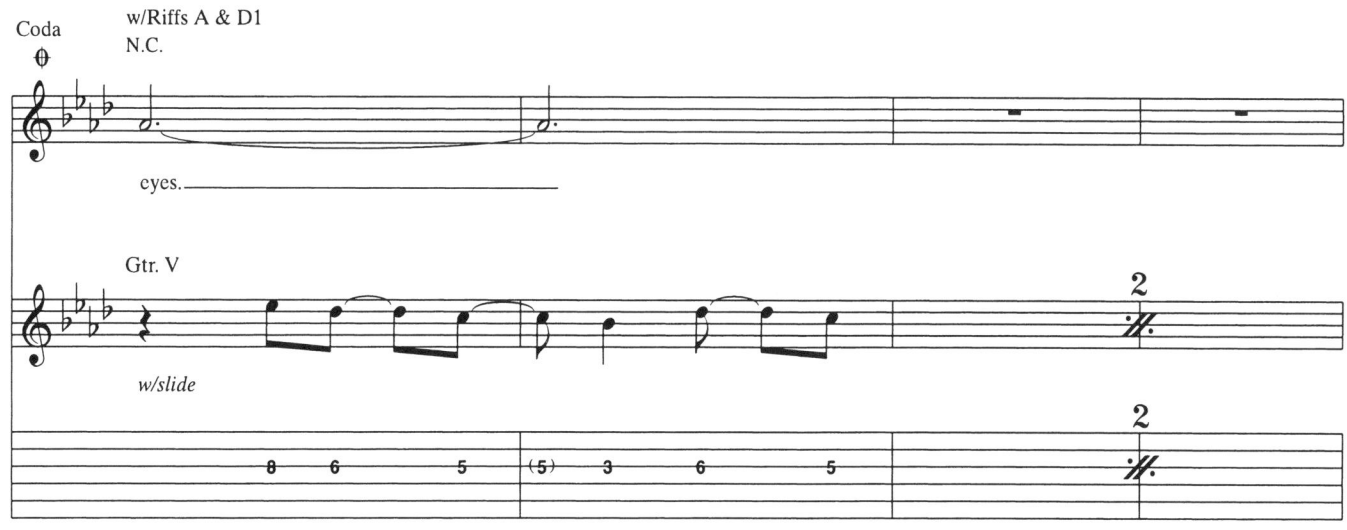

Coda

w/Riffs A & D1
N.C.

eyes.

Gtr. V

w/slide

w/Riff A1 (last 4 bars only)

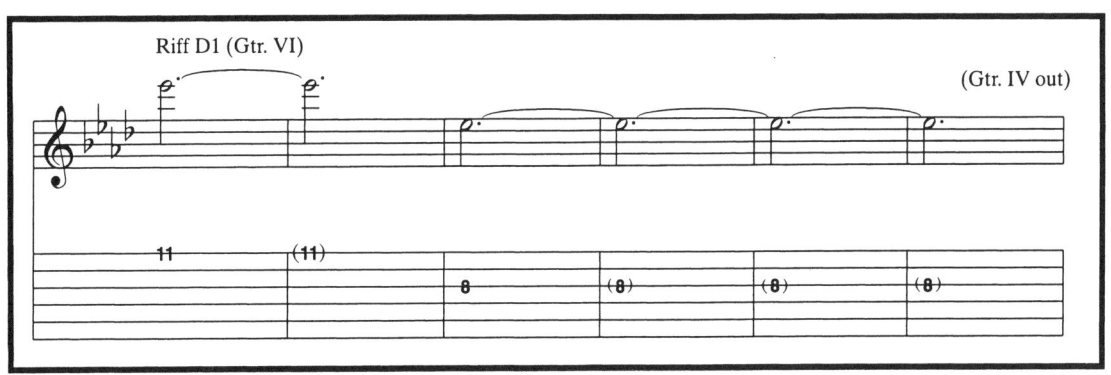

Riff D1 (Gtr. VI)

(Gtr. IV out)

WAREHOUSE
From *Under the Table and Dreaming* (1994)

The eclecticism of Dave Matthews Band is apparent not only from album to album and song to song, but even within the confines of a single composition. On "Warehouse," the band shifts from a dark and mysterious soundscape to an upbeat, major-keyed dance groove, and later to a relaxed, quasi-calypso feel. Let's dig in.

THEORY

Harmony

The central motif of "Warehouse" is a looping, single-note line based on the B Aeolian mode (B–C♯–D–E–F♯–G–A), the 6th mode of the D major scale. The minor chord and key center built on a major scale's 6th degree is called its *relative minor,* and the process can be reversed so that the major scale and chord built on the minor's 3rd degree is called its *relative major.* The relative minor of C is A minor, the relative major of Cm is E♭, and so forth.

In the early stages of "Warehouse," in which that serpentine line repeats so hypnotically, we're in full modal territory, staying strictly within B Aeolian. When the pre-chorus arrives, we shift to the relative major key of D. While the guitars continue to play single-note patterns, the bass begins to move around a bit, and the combined effect is that of shifting from A major to D major to a G major chord with an added 2nd. These harmonies represent the V, I, and IV chords in the key of D major, respectively. The song saves its biggest harmonic move for the chorus, which isn't heard until seconds before the song hits the three-minute mark. Here, the band moves to B major, with the familiar progression B–E–F♯–E, the I–IV–V–IV in the new key (don't miss the key signature change).

This represents the third time in the four songs we've examined so far that Matthews includes some sort of *modal interchange*—an instance in which the basic root remains the same (in this case, B) but the mode which is built on it changes. "Warehouse" moves from the B Aeolian mode to the B major scale—in "The Best of What's Around," it was a shift from A Aeolian to A major, and in "What Would You Say," we saw A Mixolydian become A Aeolian right before the big chorus break. Clearly, this is a device Dave relishes. He also has shown a knack for returning smoothly to the earlier modalities of these songs. In "Warehouse" he ends the chorus with a rising progression from G major to A major that leads neatly back to the opening motif in B Aeolian. These chords represent the ♭VI and VII chords in the mode, respectively.

Rhythm

"Warehouse" is full of diverse, propulsive rhythms, but it's a fairly straightforward piece in terms of the guitar playing involved. The rhythmic variety in the song is generated more by the work of bassist Stefan Lessard and drummer Carter Beauford than by anything else; observe what happens to the whole vibe of the tune when they make their entrances at the beginning of the second verse. Of course, that's not to say that guitars don't have a crucial rhythmic role in the song. The central riff, made up of a steady flow of 16th notes, glues the whole thing together and has a kind of perpetual, clockwork aspect to it. The open-string line played above the lower B Aeolian lick breaks up the 16-notes-per-measure in particularly interesting fashion.

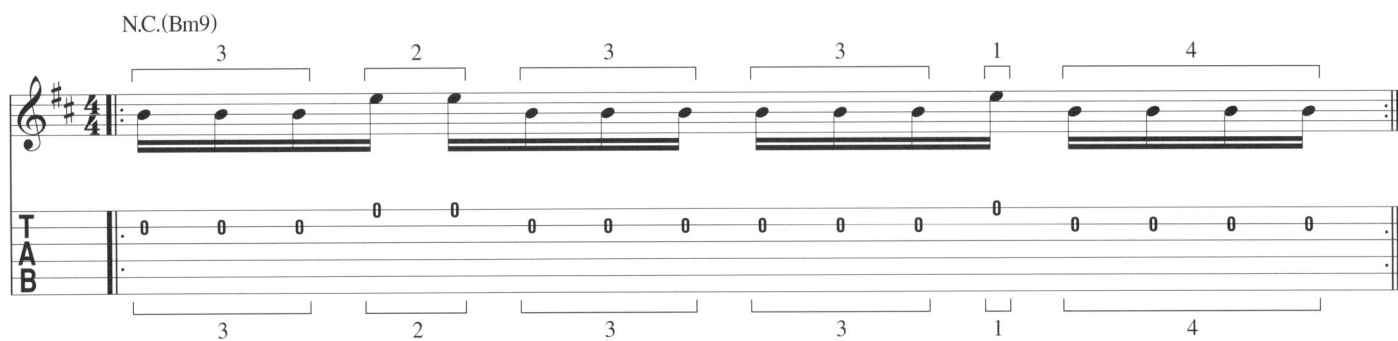

As seen in "Satellite," Matthews takes an instance of rhythmic sameness—continuous 16th notes—and transforms it into something interesting by employing interesting groupings. In the example above, the brackets represent groups of 3, 2, 3, 3, 1, and 4, an unpredictable scheme that contrasts nicely with the steadier line played by the other guitars (which basically breaks the measure down into eight groups of two). The next example shows the final two measures of the chorus, where G- and A-major barre chords are strummed in a 16th note rhythm.

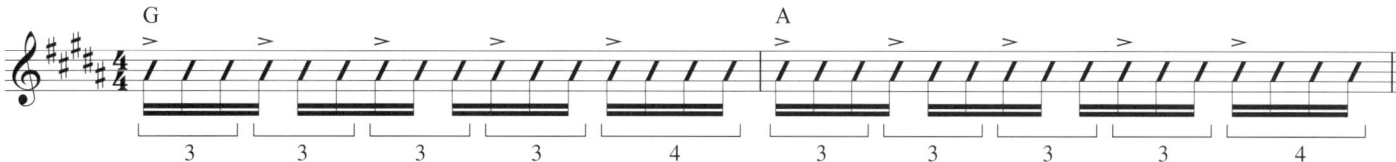

Here, Matthews uses accents (shown above the staff) to attack the chords with greater force and alleviate the sameness of the steady 16th note rhythm. Instead of using different pitches to break up the phrase as in the earlier example, the accents are employed here to subdivide the measure into groups of 3, 3, 3, 3 and 4. It's just another demonstration of Dave's inherently percussive approach to the guitar, which eschews flashy licks and solos in favor of driving parts that are as rhythmically important to the song as anything Lessard and Beauford play on bass and drums.

Before we move on, let's take a look at the chorus, where the band shifts suddenly from the key of D major to B major, and we find ourselves in sunnier territory where calypso and Latin influences meet "Louie, Louie." Check out the two guitar parts in this section, with the barre chords shown above the staff in rhythm slashes.

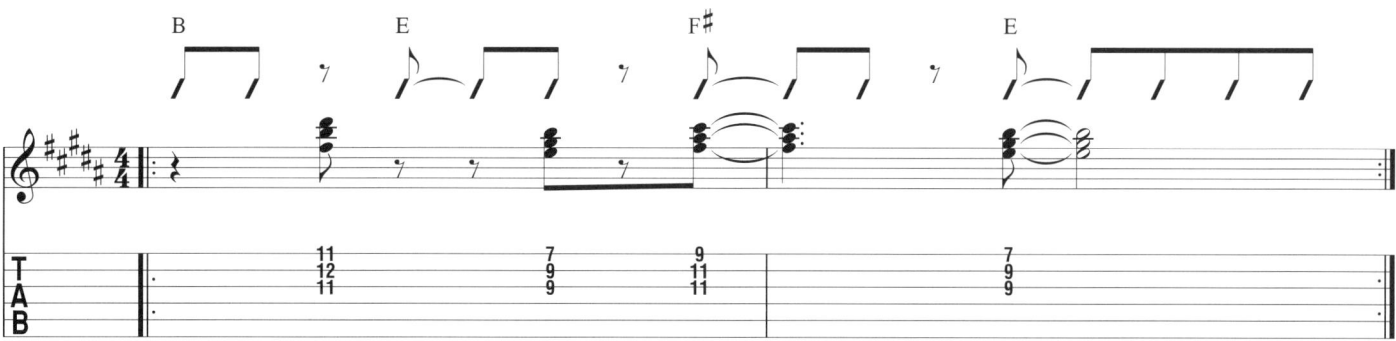

What's particularly interesting here is the way in which the two syncopated parts intertwine with each other, landing on the same beat in certain instances and filling the rhythmic gaps at others. Play through each part carefully, making absolutely sure that you know where everything falls within the measure. The ties, dots, and eighth note rests place many of the chords on the "ands" of the beat, leading to a somewhat off-kilter feeling. It's not enough to listen to the recording and mimic it from there, although that does have value. You need to know exactly where the first E chord falls in the upper part ("and" of 2) and when it's answered by the triad on the upper strings ("and" of 3). Take the guesswork out of your playing and you'll be able to tackle any situation with increased confidence and authority.

Scales

In the harmonic examination of "Warehouse," it was noticed that the bulk of the song is derived from the B Aeolian mode, with later sections built upon its relative major scale, D, and on the B major scale after the big key change in the chorus. Let's take a look at some common two-octave fingerings for these scales and modes, beginning with the B Aeolian mode in a three-notes-per-string fingering much like that employed in the song.

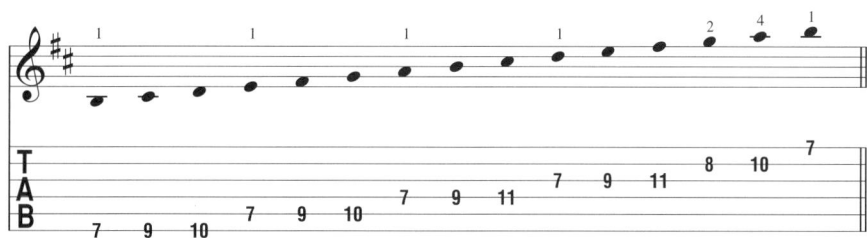

Next, let's take a look at two fingerings for the D major scale. The first uses the same three-notes-per-string scheme and begins on the low E string, while the second starts on the A string and follows a similar pattern with a few minor fingering alterations.

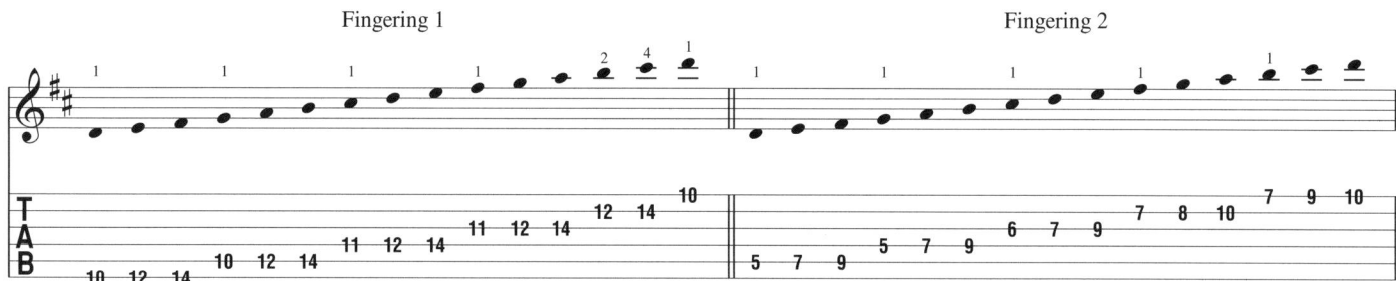

Finally, here's the B major scale beginning on both the low E and A strings, and employing the same fingering patterns used for the D major scale. All of the fingerings in this section are *moveable,* so all you need to do to play them in another key is to shift everything up or down the appropriate number of frets. Just be sure that everything moves in parallel fashion and you'll be golden.

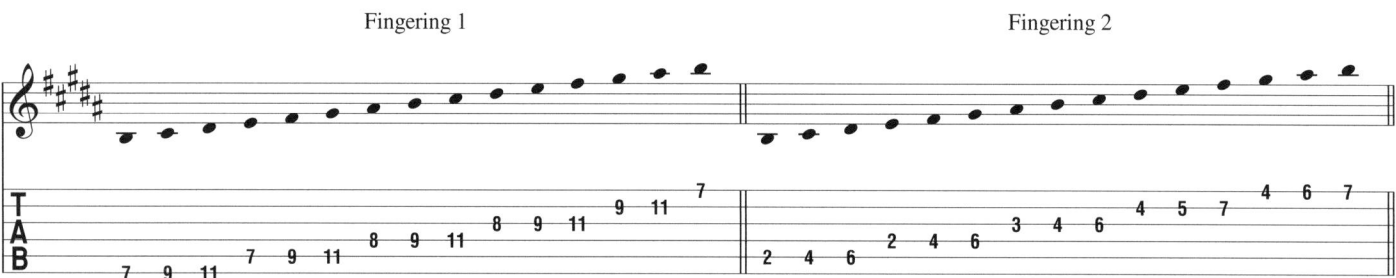

We'll get into some variations on the Aeolian mode in the "Technique" section of this chapter, but until then try playing all of the fingerings shown above in a variety of keys while putting them through whatever permutations you'd like. If you want a real challenge, try applying the intervallic studies we used on the A♭ major scale during our examination of "Satellite" to the B and D major scales here, and then put the B Aeolian mode to the same test. You'll be flying through them and all over the fingerboard before you know it if you do your homework in the shed!

Composition

"Warehouse" is a great example of Matthews' ability, even relatively early in his evolution as a songwriter, to create mood and atmosphere with just a few basic compositional techniques. The main guitar part, which essentially outlines a Bm chord with the 9th rubbing right up against the minor 3rd, has a particularly evocative sound, and he milks it for all it's worth. Remember our earlier discussion about re-using your strongest materials? Dave does it here, returning time and again to that mysterious sonority. The open string part layered above it further enriches the phrase by adding the 11th to the chord on the ringing high E string. That brings us to what has become one of Matthews' most favored compositional devices, the *upper pedal point.*

A pedal point is a note or series of notes that repeats while things around it (above or below) move and shift. Dave often employs these pedal points on the upper strings of the guitar while moving around on the lower strings or letting the band move from chord to chord while he remains in one place. We'll see a lot more of this before the end of this book, as these pedal points are a kind of unifying force within his music.

So, what else is going on here? Well, there are the stop-time interjections of the rhythm section in the first verse, a nice juxtaposition of the quieter, steady guitar parts and the louder blasts of the bass and drums. This use of *dynamics* (manipulation of volume) is another way in which Matthews and the band create interest without using a whole kitchen sink's worth of material. Music is often about contrast, and the band fully exploits the whole range of contrasts at their disposal. Contrasts between loud and soft, fast and slow (listen to the long, sustained notes Dave sings above the busy 16th note guitar parts in the opening verse), textures, grooves, and moods, are all vital parts of their approach. The band has a wide palette of timbres available and uses them to great effect, whether they're the trills played above the main riff by the saxophone and violin, the wood blocks and miscellaneous percussion added by Carter Beauford, or the overdubbed guitars playing in different registers throughout the song. Of course, there are also the great contrasts among the song's verse, pre-chorus, and chorus sections, which shift in mood from the opening sense of dread and anticipation to the more upbeat vibe in the D major section, and the breezy, relaxed feeling of the B major chorus. In "Warehouse," we also find Matthews breaking out of the restrictions of common four-, eight-, and 16-measure section lengths as he extends the first pre-chorus past its obvious ending and turns it into an 11-measure form with the repeated lyric "around, and around, around." It's the sign of a rapidly maturing songwriter, and one who has the confidence to let the melody guide him instead of forcing the music into predetermined phrase lengths and chord progressions.

TECHNIQUE

The big technical challenges of "Warehouse" are the double-picked notes of the song's main riff and the stretching aspects of its three-notes-per-string fingering. Forgive this author for repeating himself, but the *only* way to strengthen technique and master difficult passages is by slowing them way down and practicing them at a greatly reduced speed until all aspects of the music—pitches, rhythms, articulation, tone, etc—have been mastered. To that end, let's look at a few drills that may help to get you in shape to play this sometimes-challenging song. The first is merely a trip up and down the B Aeolian mode, using the three-notes-per-string fingering and double-picked notes found in the tune. Stay strictly with *alternate picking* (downstroke, upstroke, downstroke, upstroke) throughout the example; this should be your default right-hand approach, and should be altered only when the situation expressly calls for it.

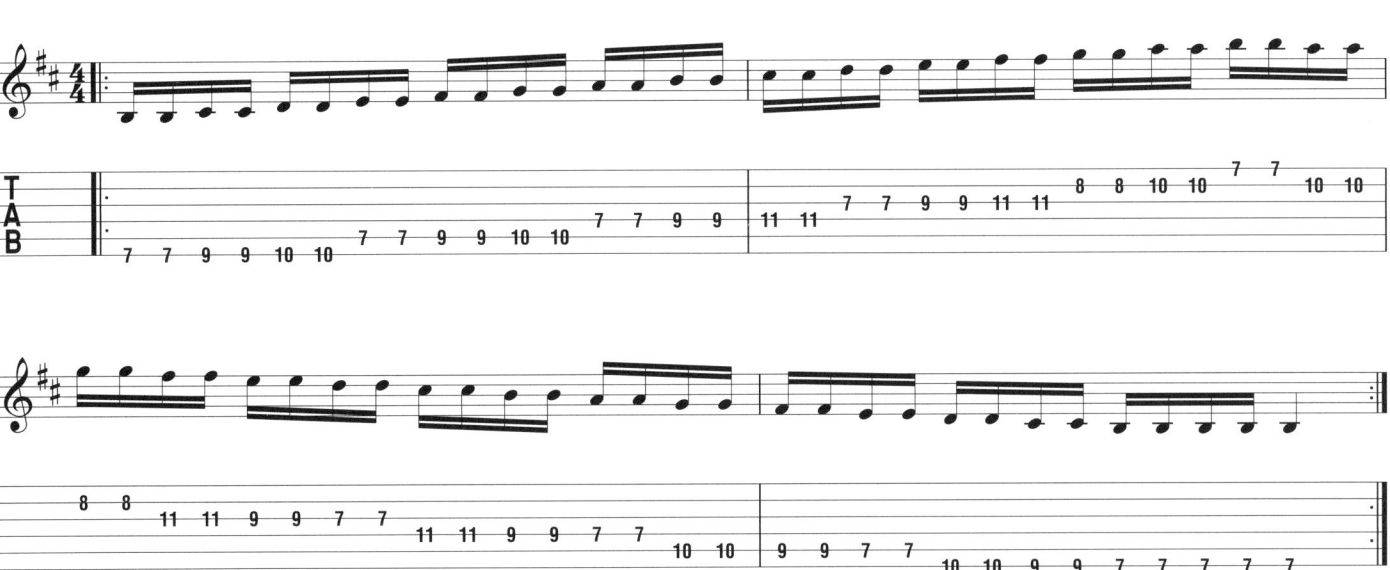

Let's move on to a tougher exercise that mimics the song's opening riff but puts it through a series of multi-directional permutations that move through the mode. If you look at the first four pitches in the Gtr. 1 part, you'll see that it begins on the root (B), moves up a 5th (F♯), moves up another 5th (C♯), and then moves up a minor 2nd to D. This exercise does exactly that, and then it goes up one more scale degree (to E) and reverses the process, all the while staying strictly within the parameters of B Aeolian and its 7th-position fingering. Because of this, some of the 5ths are perfect and others are flat, while some of the 2nds are minor and others are major. It's a completely diatonic exercise, so these alterations have been made to stay within the key.

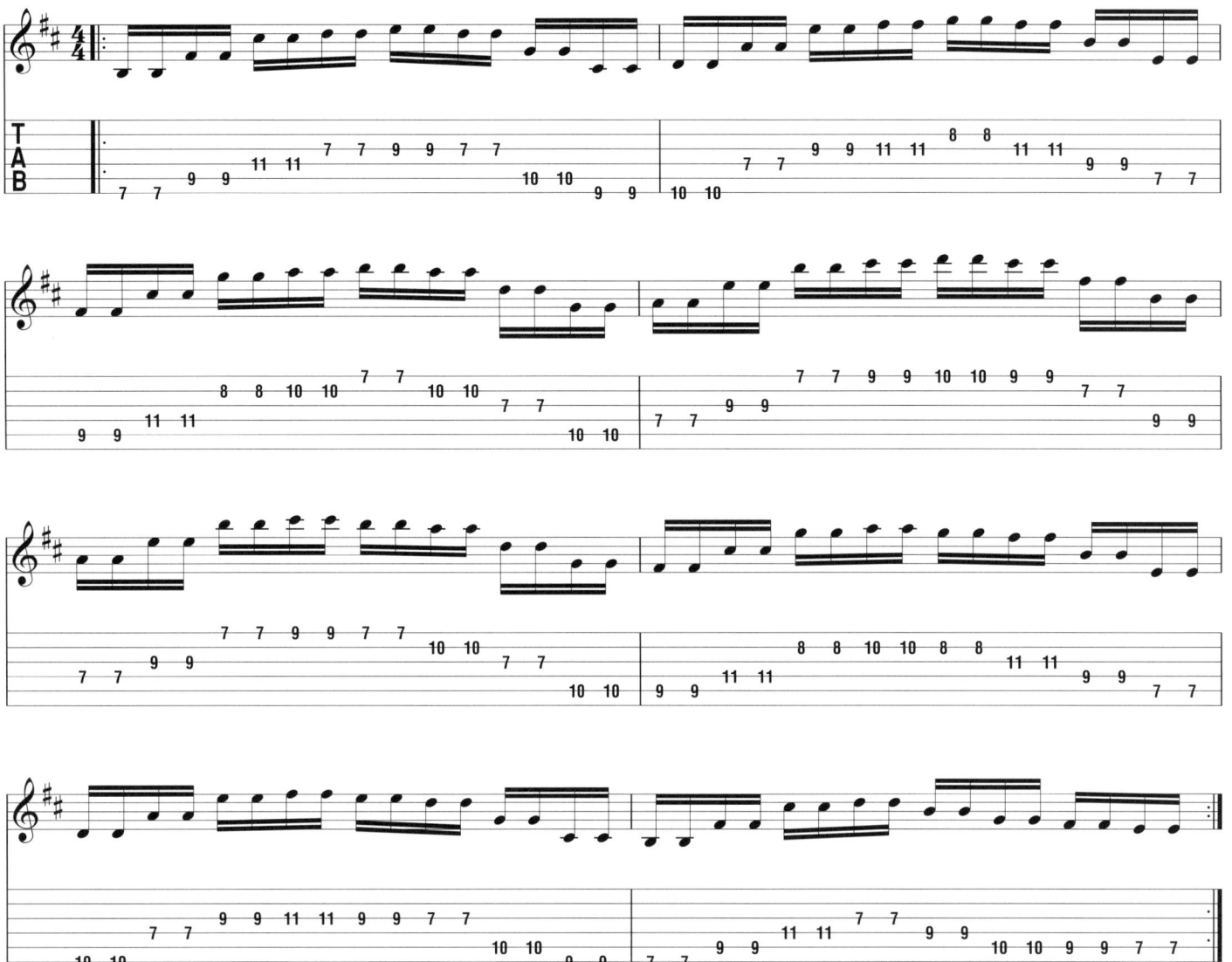

WAREHOUSE

Written by
David J. Matthews

w/Riffs A & A1 (both 2 times) and Fill 1
N.C.(Bm9)

Play 3 times

a - way.
(Sing 1st time only)

w/Riffs A & A1 (both 2 times)
N.C.(Bm9)
*Bkgd. Voc. Fig. 1

Play 4 times
(end Bkgd. Voc. Fig. 1)

(4th time:) Hey!   2. A

(Ooh.)
*Refers to cue notes only.

2nd, 3rd, 4th Verses
w/Riffs A & A1 (both 4 times)
w/Bkgd. Voc. Fig. 1 (4 times)
% N.C.(Bm9)

reck - less___ mind,_____ don't throw___ a - way___ your play - ful be - gin - nings.
3.4. *See additional lyrics*

(Gtr. III out)

You and___ I_____ will fum - ble a - round in the touch - es. And be sure to

Pre-chorus
N.C.

w/Riff B (3 times)

leave___ all___ the lights on so we___ can see the black cat chang - ing___ col -

Riff B (Gtrs. I & II)

(end Riff B)

let ring

```
|-----------------|-----------------|
|-----------------|-----------------|
|--7-7-7-7--7-7-7-7-7-|--7-7-7-7--7-7-7-7-7-|
|-5---------5---------|-3---------5---------|
|-----------------|-----------------|
|-----------------|-----------------|
```

ors.___ And we___ can walk un - der___ lad - ders.___ And

Fill 1 (*Two gtrs.)

*Violin (higher gtr.) and sax. (lower gtr.) arr. for two gtrs.

*Two gtrs. arr. for one.

Ooh,—— that's our——

Additional Lyrics

3. Hey, we have found
   Becoming one in a million.
   Slip into the crowd.
   This question I found in the gap in the sidewalk.

   2nd Pre-chorus:
   Keep all your sights on.
   Hey, the black cat changing colors.
   And you can walk under ladders.
   And swim as the tide choose to turn you. *(To Chorus)*

4. Shut up, I'm thinking.
   I had a clue, now it's gone forever.
   Sitting over these bones,
   You can read in whatever. You're needing to...

   3rd Pre-chorus:
   Keep all your sights on.
   Yeah, man, the black cat changing colors.
   When it's not the colours that matter,
   but that they'll all fade away.

   2rd Chorus:
   And I, life goes on.
   End of tunnel, TV set, spot in the middle.
   Static fade, statistical bit.
   Soon I'll fade away, I'll fade away.
   Oh, but this I admit.
   Seems so good, hard to believe an end to it.
   The warehouse is bare, nothing, it's all inside of it.
   The walls and halls have disappeared, they've disappeared. Well.
   My love, I'd love to stay here, *etc.*

SO MUCH TO SAY
From *Crash* (1996)

The opening track on the band's second major-label release, *Crash*, offers up a tighter, more focused ensemble sound and a clear progression from their earlier work. Every phase of the music has moved forward, as the songwriting, arranging, production values, and performances are all more sophisticated, sharply defined, *and* accessible than ever before. "So Much to Say" shows off the band's funk, rock, and blues inclinations with crystal clarity, and it eventually reaped the boys a Grammy Award for Best Rock Vocal Performance. Well deserved, indeed.

THEORY

Harmony

In some ways, "So Much to Say" is quite similar harmonically to some of the other songs we've examined so far. For instance, Dave's opening guitar riff is constructed primarily with notes and chords derived from the A Aeolian mode and provides the foundation for much of the tune. The A minor sound of this section changes to A major during the song's bridge, with the new chord actually functioning as V in D, closely paralleling the harmonic movements of "The Best of What's Around." And there's more: Take a look at the main riff that's first heard in its complete form when Matthews begins to sing.

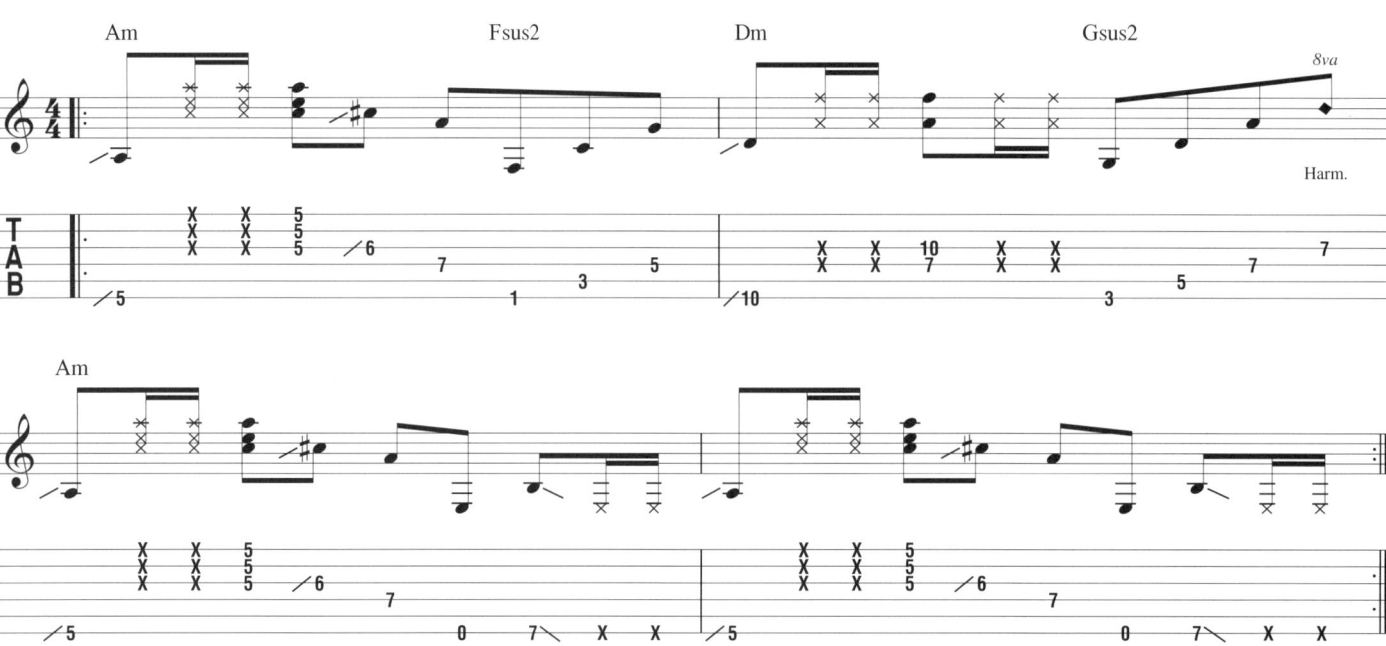

Two things stand out here. First, there are the Fsus2 and Gsus2 chords constructed with two consecutive 5th intervals, which we hear in the main riffs to both "Satellite" and "Warehouse." It's an intriguing sound and one that Matthews clearly enjoys; he's resourceful enough to present it to us in a different way each time so that it always sounds fresh. Secondly, there's the Am chord that's closely followed by the note C♯ (the major 3rd), making the listener register the sound as more of an A7♯9 chord than a true minor chord. This quasi-dominant chord lends the song a bluesy quality that's a natural fit with Dave's largely pentatonic vocal melody. The juxtaposition of major and minor sounds above the same tonic is the defining harmonic element of the blues and goes back to the style's earliest days, when bluesmen with a rudimentary grasp of the guitar strummed open-position major chords and sang minor pentatonic melodies above them, echoing the African songs their enslaved forebears brought to America. The blues is such an important, wide-reaching influence on contemporary music that the conflict between major and minor has long ceased to be jarring or unusual; it is, in fact, the basic sound of rock 'n' roll (among countless other styles). When we hear "So Much to Say," with its C♯ over Am and its pentatonic melody, we don't say "that sounds wrong," we say, "that sounds like the blues." Our ears accept it because it's everywhere and we've heard it all of our lives.

Let's do a bit of Roman numeral analysis before we move on. We can think of "So Much to Say" as being in C major if we remember that A minor is that key's relative minor, and that the A Aeolian mode is built on the C major scale's 6th degree. However, a song like this is better understood if we treat Am as the i chord and relate the harmonies to that. "The Best of What's Around" also relies heavily on the A Aeolian mode but eventually winds its way to C major, which is clearly the I chord, and the song was analyzed from that perspective. "So Much to Say," on the other hand, steadfastly refuses to go to C, which makes it easy to call A the tonic. The chords that follow, then, must be interpreted as the VI (Fsus2), iv (Dm), and VII (Gsus2). With the arrival of the bridge, we get a sudden shift from the A minor tonality to a sequence of major triads that moves from A to D to G and back again to D. At first listen, it sounds like a bit of modal interchange—the A Aeolian mode becoming the A Ionian mode (A major). However, the A major chord reveals itself, upon closer examination, to be the V chord in the key of D, with D representing the I and G the IV chord. What we're left with is a V–I–IV–I progression in the key of D, but the key change is obscured by the more striking shift from A minor to A major.

Rhythm

"So Much to Say" isn't a particularly complex song rhythmically, and it doesn't need to be. Dave sets the tone with his propulsive opening figure and the song pretty much stays there, chugging along at a funky, medium-tempo pace. Matthews' songwriting style and the arranging style of the band in general often traces a fine line between highly danceable grooves and the more adventurous "feel" changes they clearly relish but are wise enough to limit. Too much adventurousness in a single song can bring a sense of schizophrenia to the music and disrupt its flow, making the total less than the sum of its elements. The boys carefully edit themselves, as "So Much" clearly demonstrates, and introduce a single rhythmically (and harmonically) contrasting section that is heard twice in just over four minutes. The new section, which bears the distinct influence of African pop, has more of an impact than it would if it were merely one of a handful of differing grooves coming at us. Matthews uses shifting accents to break up the steady stream of strummed 16th note barre chords in this section, returning to a device he used to great effect in "Warehouse." Here, he uses a basic 3–3–2–3–3–2 scheme to break up the 16th notes, although he does bring some additional variety to the riff by ending every other measure with two eighth notes that begin on beat 4. Try tapping out the phrase slowly with heavy accents as indicated, and then take it to your guitar and work it back up to speed. The 16th notes go by fairly quickly at this tempo (115 beats per minute), so your right-hand strumming technique will get a fairly vigorous workout as well.

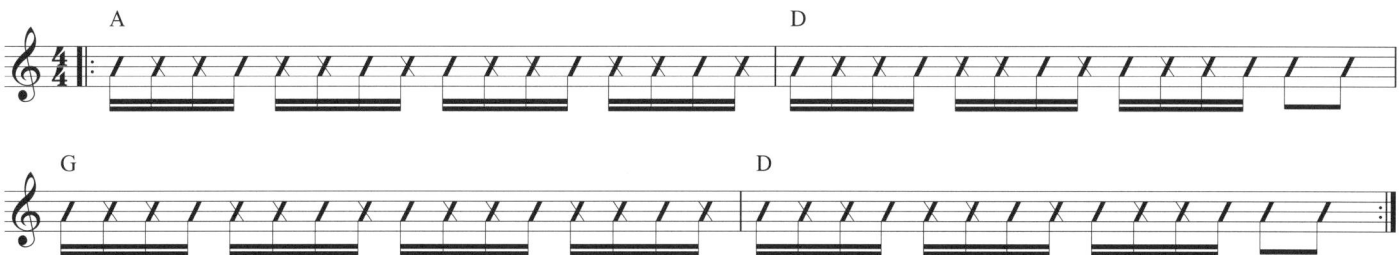

Scales

The chords and single-note lines of "So Much to Say" are based primarily on the A Aeolian mode, with notable exceptions derived from the A Mixolydian mode (the "C♯" in the main riff and outro solo) and the D major scale (the chords of the bridge). Our examination of "Warehouse" included an in-depth look at the (B) Aeolian mode; now let's take a quick look at the two most common fingerings for the mode in A on the following page.

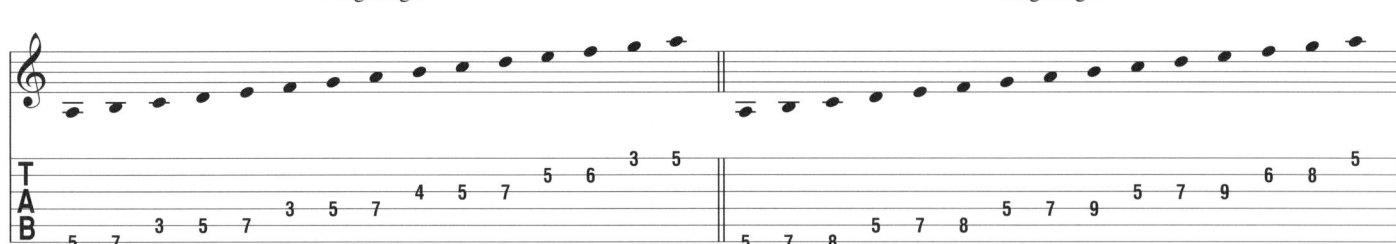

Fingering 1   Fingering 2

The C♯ that keeps popping up in the song's main riff hints at the A Mixolydian mode, shown below in a three-notes-per-string fingering beginning on the low E string (refer to the earlier discussion of "What Would You Say" for two other fingerings). The short guitar solo under the outro in the tune's final moments combines Aeolian pitches with Mixolydian tones played over Am, giving it more of a dominant 7th flavor.

Composition

"So Much to Say" is very much in the mold of some of Dave Matthews' earlier funkified jam tunes such as "What Would You Say," and employs many of the same compositional techniques. If anything, it demonstrates Matthews' growing sense of economy in terms of the use of his ideas and a more organic arranging style by the band. As mentioned earlier, the group limits the number of different sections and grooves, and the song is that much stronger for their restraint. Dave sets up a nice vamping riff and the band builds from there, creating interest through the use of variable dynamics and timbres, particularly from the saxophone and violin. LeRoi's use of the baritone sax really expands the register and overall sound of the band, especially during the song's bridge, where he functions as a second bass player and fattens up the bottom end of things substantially. Another wrinkle at work here is the addition of subtly layered electric guitar throughout the song (shown as Gtr. 2 in the music). It first enters with the bass and drums, playing a fairly simple double-stop line that reinforces the middle-register aspects of the song's main riff. It functions in much the same way during the bridge, and then is joined by an additional electric during the coda that spins off into some tasty solo lines, building intensity in the section without ever stepping completely into the foreground. The overdubbed electrics are just one of a handful of elements contributing to a texturally rich sound, and indicate the band's growing comfort in the studio and willingness to take advantage of its technical possibilities.

However, the heart of Dave Matthews Band is always Dave's voice and acoustic guitar, and that remains true on "So Much to Say." Once more, his opening riff remains the central compositional element. Matthews also revisits some favored devices heard in earlier tunes, such as the transition from a minor tonality to a major one, and the use of chord voicings made up of consecutive perfect 5th intervals (the Fsus2 and Gsus2 chords) such as those found in "Satellite" and "Warehouse." In addition, the blues influence that occasionally found its way into his earlier work really steps into the limelight here, particularly in his jagged vocal lines. The South African–turned–American Southerner clearly has an affinity for rural acoustic blues, giving this über-eclectic ensemble another gritty texture to explore.

TECHNIQUE

While much of what happens technically in "So Much to Say" (funky strumming patterns, muted tones, barre chord riffing, etc.) should be familiar enough to you from the songs previously explored in this book, let's take a closer look at how to play the main riff (shown in an earlier example and in the complete song transcription to follow).

You'll notice that the many slides indicated in this part don't necessarily begin or end on a specific note. These should be played from a few frets below the targeted pitch in the case of ascending slides, and moving down to a few frets below in the case of those that descend. For example, the riff's opening 5th-fret A should be played with your middle finger sliding up from the 3rd or 4th fret to the target tone; follow up by using your ring finger for both the muted notes and the barred G, B, and high E strings immediately after. Use your ring finger for the C♯ as well, and then play the A on the D string's 7th fret with your pinky. Jump down to play the final three eighth notes (Fsus2) in the measure with your index finger, middle finger, and pinky on the low E, A, and D strings, respectively. In the second measure, slide up to the D on the low E string's 10th fret with your ring finger; the double stop on the D and G strings should be played with your index finger and pinky. For the final four notes in the measure (Gsus2), use your index finger, middle finger, and pinky to mimic the fingering of the previous measure two frets higher, but add a 7th-fret harmonic on the G string with your pinky as well.

A *harmonic*, if you're unfamiliar with the term, is a bell-like tone that is created through one of several techniques. Harmonics can come in two varieties: *natural harmonics*, which we'll discuss here, and *artificial* or *pick harmonics*, which are created by striking a string with both a pick and a bit of the flesh of the thumb and/or index finger simultaneously. A natural harmonic is created by laying a fret-hand finger lightly on a given string directly above the fret metal, (rather than the wood between the frets), and then picking the note without pressing down on the string with the fret hand. Apply any real left-hand pressure and you'll get nothing—your touch needs to be light as a feather. The ease of creating harmonics and the volume you'll get out of them varies greatly from guitar to guitar (generally, the better the instrument, the better the harmonic response) and is also affected by things such as string height and age, amp volume, effects, and more. Most guitars produce their clearest, most audible harmonics at the 5th, 7th, and 12th frets, but there may be many others all over your instrument's fingerboard at varying levels of audibility. Try the exercise below, which includes harmonics at the three previously specified locations on all six strings and, if you're able, compare the response of different guitars. Cranking your amp up or adding distortion to an electric should also really help. Once you're done, do a little scouting around on your axe and see if you can find any harmonic "sweet spots" that really jump out at you.

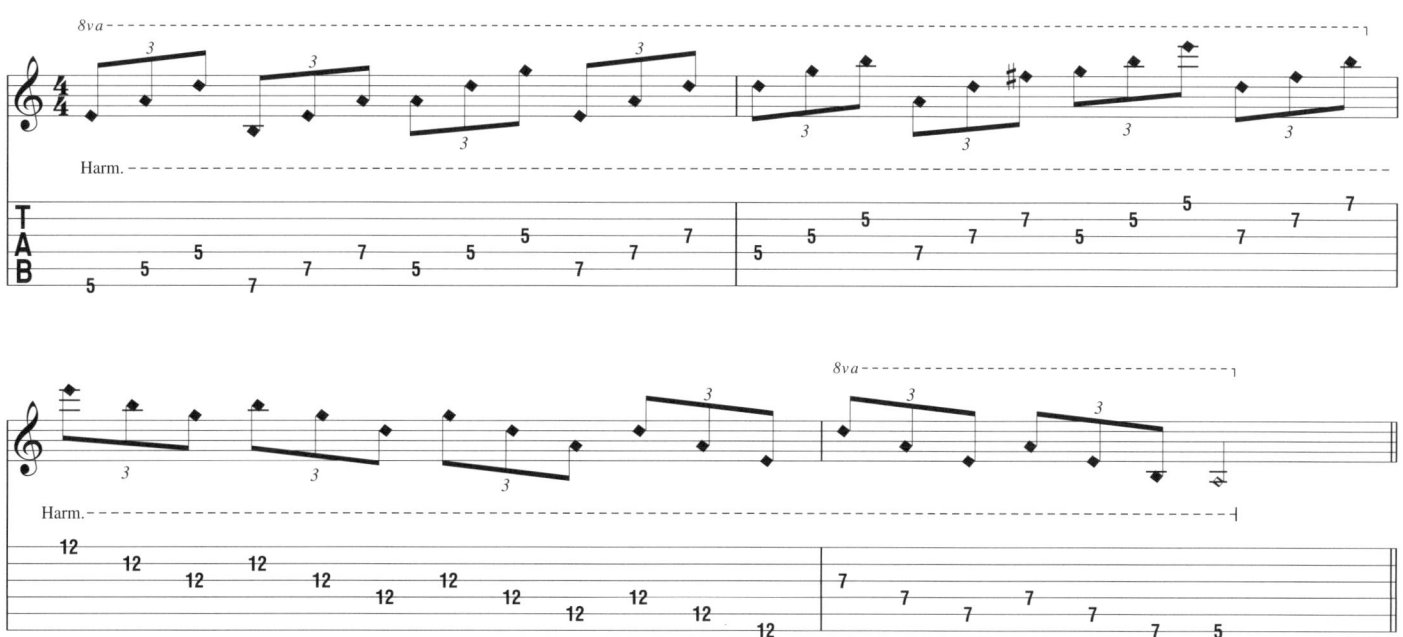

Let's move on and take a peek at the short electric solo that weaves its way in and around the coda jam toward the end of the tune. The entire eight-measure statement is shown below.

Begin by sliding up the D string with your ring finger. By using your pinky and ring finger for the last two notes in the measure, you'll put yourself in good position for the open-string licks that follow. Take the F on the B string with your ring finger, and then pull off and down to the E at the 5th fret (middle finger) and the open B string. Use your index finger for the B on the G string (4th fret), slide up the D string with your middle finger, and then finish out the measure with your index finger on the B string's 5th fret. Play the hammer-ons in the third and fourth measures with your index and middle fingers, using the index finger to barre the D and G strings in measure 4. Execute the pull-off at the end of measure 5 with your middle finger, putting yourself in position to play the Es that follow (B string, 5th fret) and the slide down the G string with your index finger. The long slide up the D string to the 14th fret and all subsequent 14th-fret pitches should be played with the ring finger. All in all, it's not a particularly difficult solo, but it demands a carefully considered fingering approach to enable the clean execution of all of its fairly unusual moves. The use of open strings creates a unique sonority, particularly when open string pitches are closely followed by identical tones on fretted strings. The close juxtaposition of notes a half step apart (E and F, B and C) results in some nicely clashing "rubs" as well. Not many guitarists would take such an unorthodox approach to solo lines, and the overall effect is musically intriguing as well as thought provoking from a guitarist's technical viewpoint. After all, how often do you move to a lower string to play a higher pitch?

SO MUCH TO SAY

Written by
David J. Matthews, Peter M. Griesar,
and Boyd Tinsley

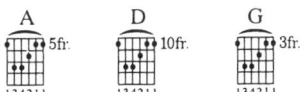

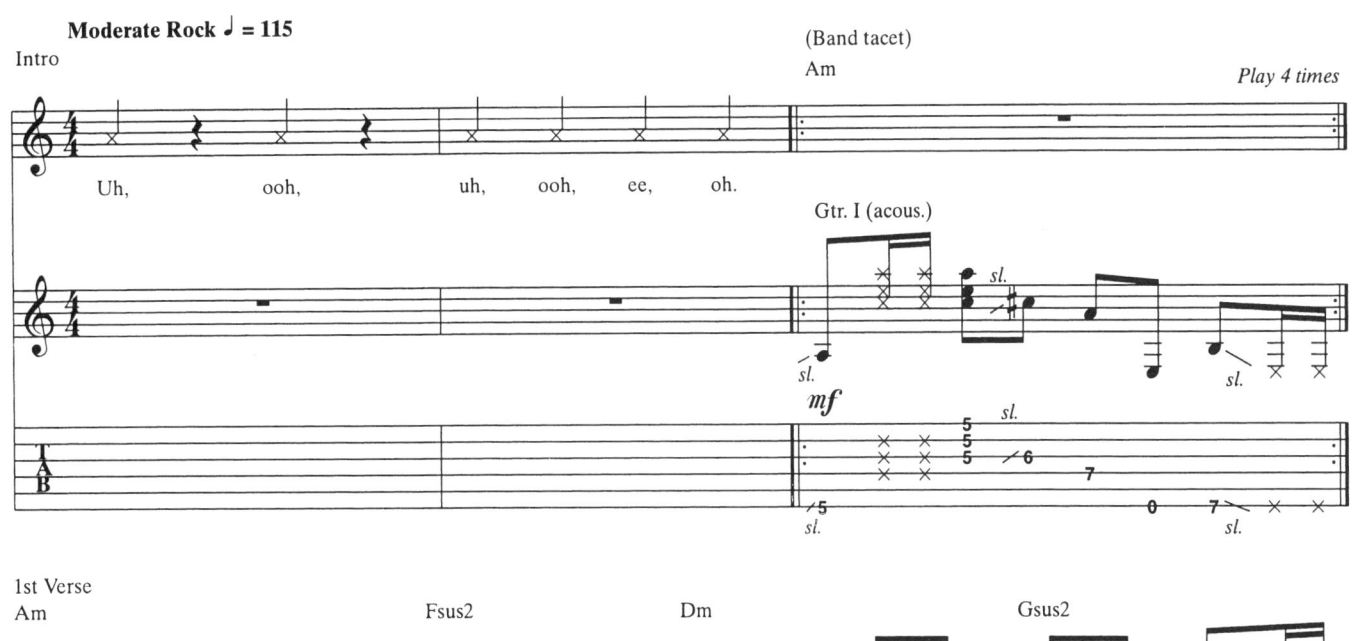

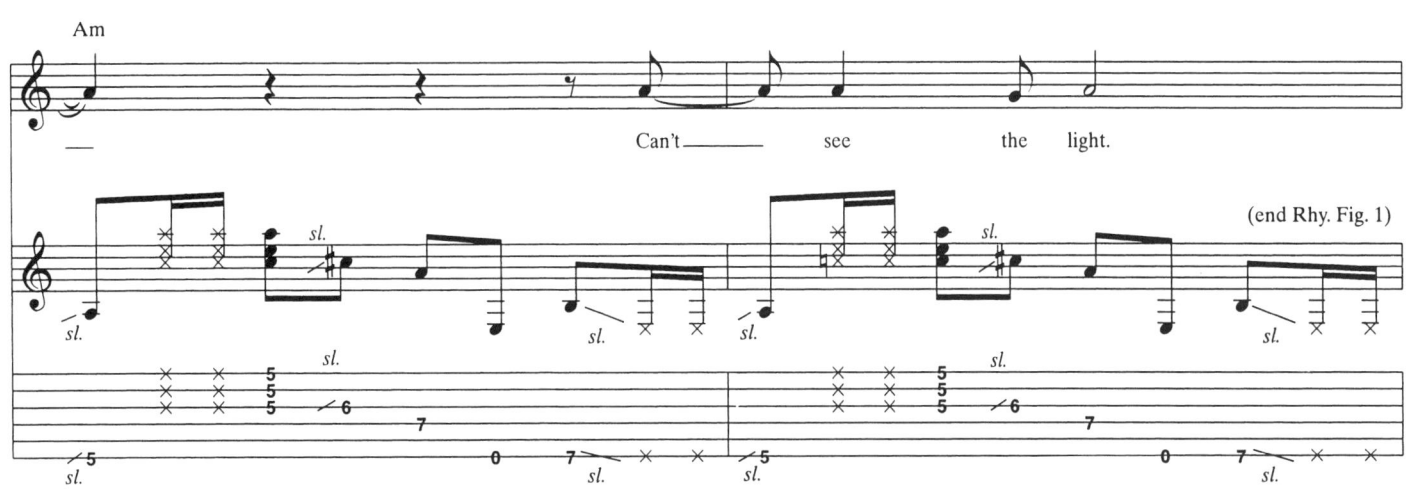

w/Rhy. Fig. 1 (5 times)

And my heav-en is a nice house in the sky. Got cen-tral heat-ing

and I'm al-right. Yeah, yeah, yeah,

can't see the light. Keep it locked up in-side.

Don't talk a-bout it. T - T - Talk a-bout the weath-er.

(Band in)

Yeah, yeah, yeah,

*Riff A (**Gtr. II)

* Play w/slight variations ad lib. when recalled (throughout).
** Elec. w/clean tone

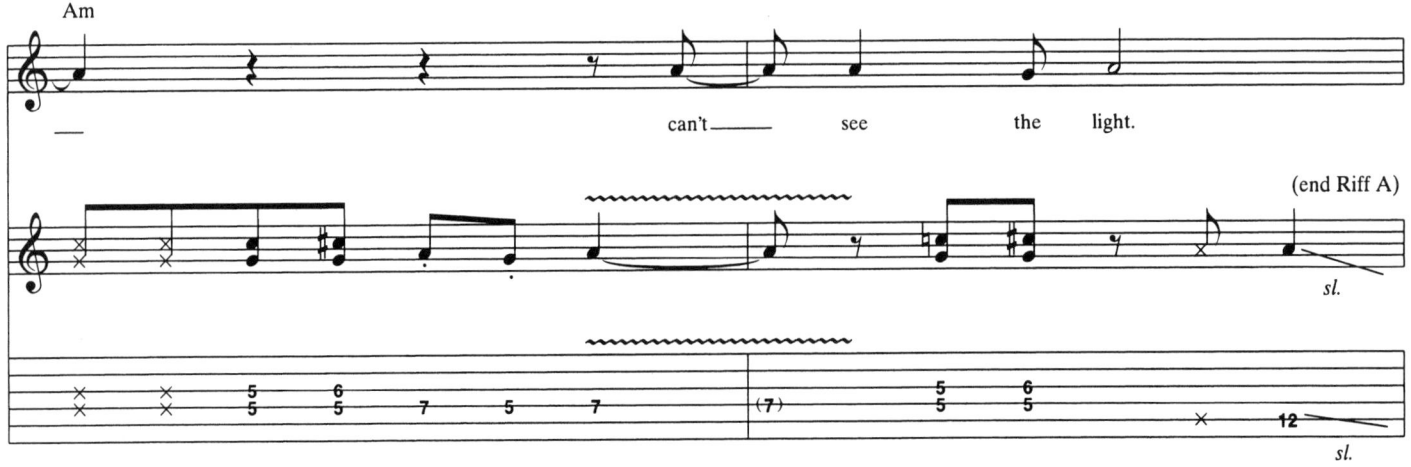

can't see the light.

(end Riff A)

65

(Resume Riff A)

Fsus2 Dm Gsus2 w/Fill 2 Am

Tread - in' trod - den trails for a long, long— time,— time, time, time,— time,— time,

Bridge

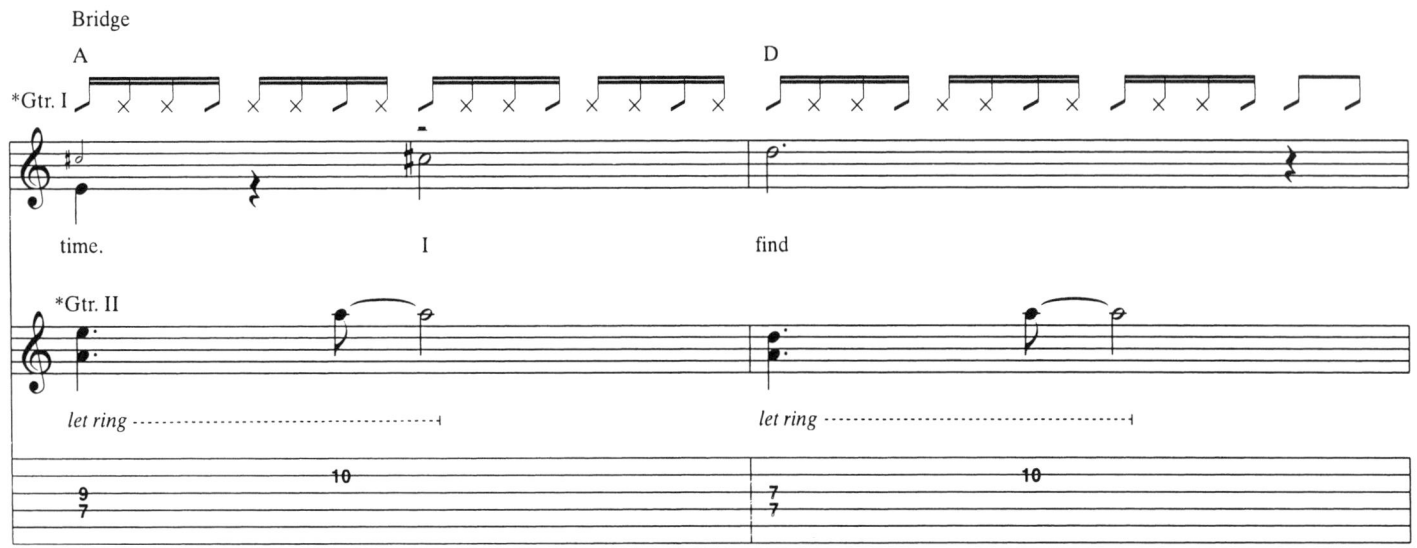

*Gtr. I

A D

time. I find

*Gtr. II

let ring

* 2nd time both gtrs. play w/slight variations ad lib.

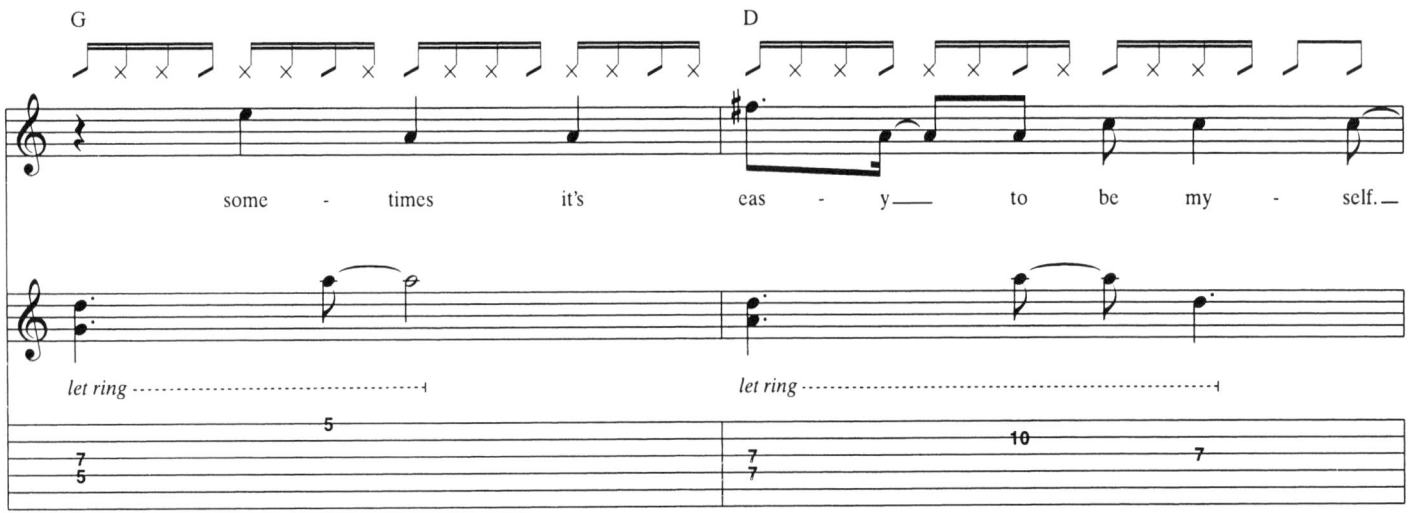

G D

some - times it's eas - y— to be my - self.—

let ring let ring

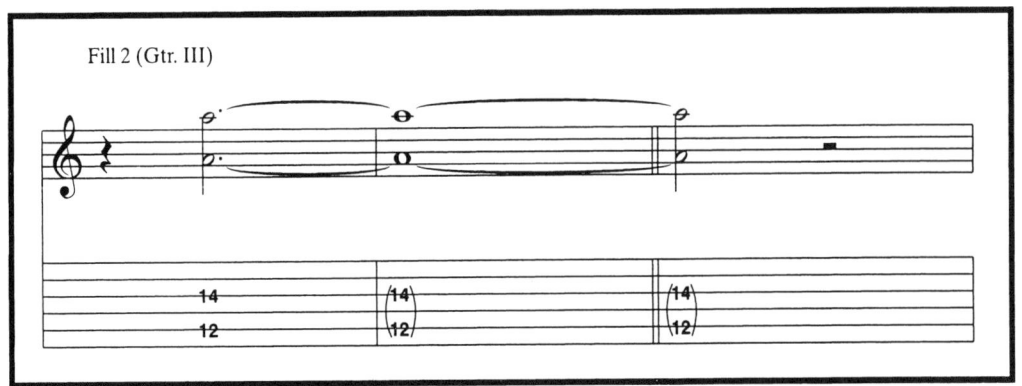

Fill 2 (Gtr. III)

66

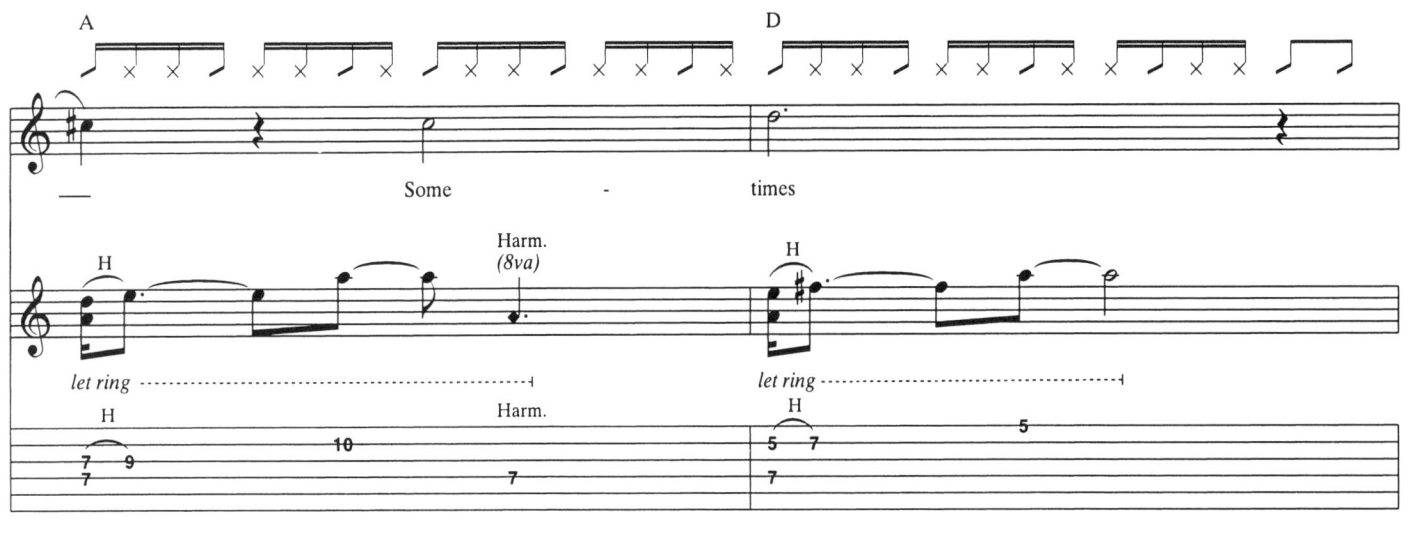

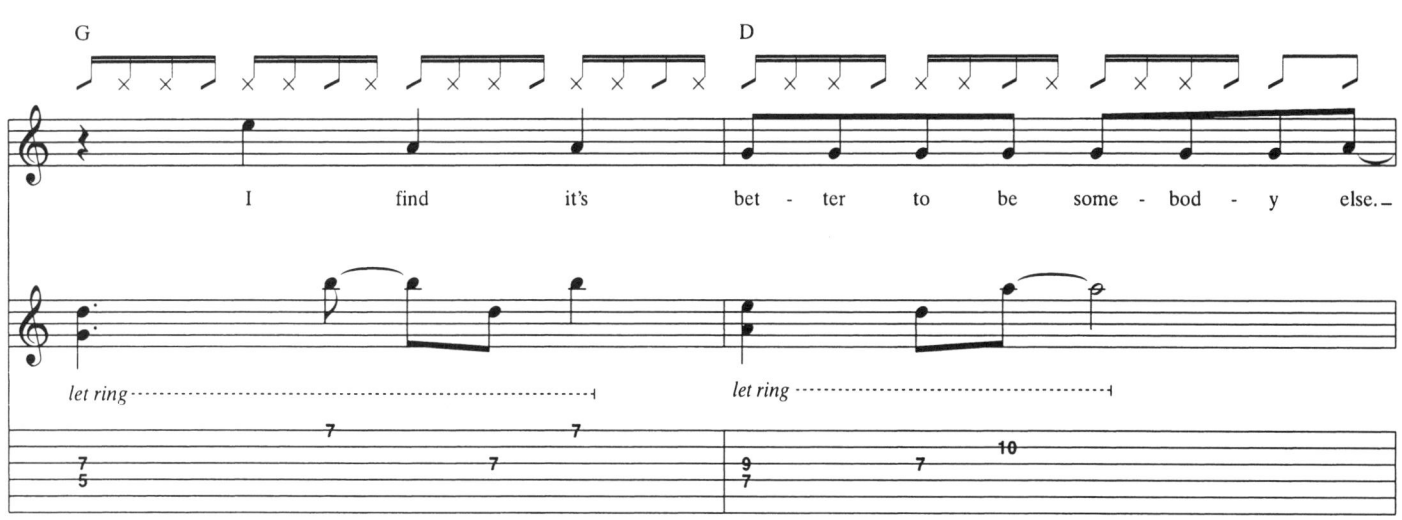

w/Rhy. Fig. 1 and *Riff A (both last 2 bars only)
w/Fill 1

3rd Verse
w/Rhy. Fig. 1 and Riff A (both 4 times)

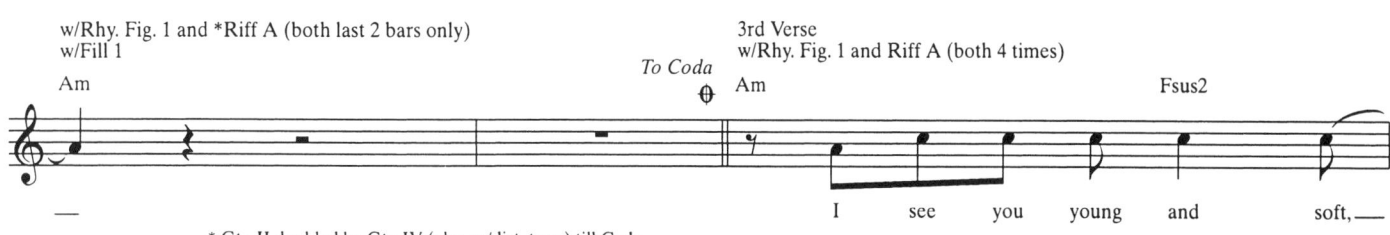

* Gtr. II doubled by Gtr. IV (elec. w/dist. tone) till Coda.

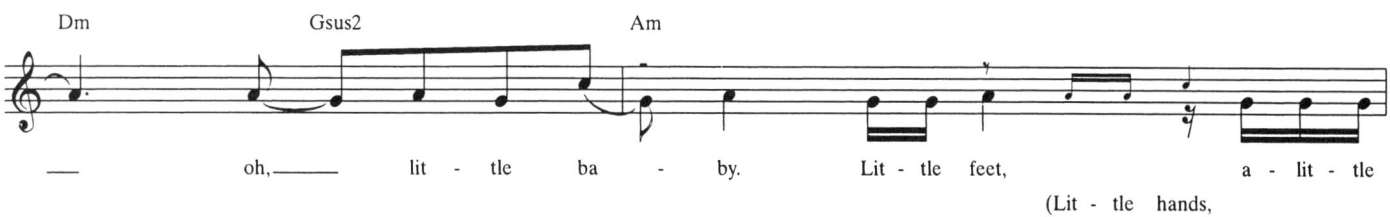

Dm　　　Gsus2　　　Am

words— creep up in - side,— creep in - to your mind,— yeah.———

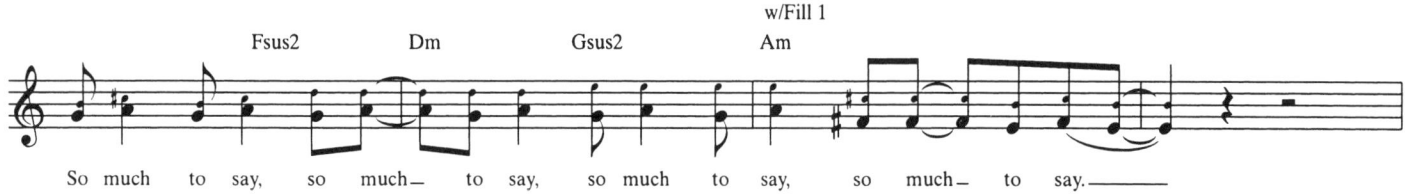

w/Fill 1

Fsus2　Dm　Gsus2　Am

So much to say, so much— to say, so much to say, so much— to say.———

w/Fill 1

D.S. al Coda
%

Fsus2　Dm　Gsus2　Am

So much to say, so much— to say, so much to say, so much— to say.——— 'Cause

w/Rhy. Fig. 1 (4 times)
w/Riff A (Gtr. II: 4 times; Gtr. IV: 2 times)
Coda

w/Fill 1

Am　　Fsus2　Dm　Gsus2　Am

So much to say, so much— to say, so much to say, so much— to say.———

Fsus2　Dm　Gsus2

— So much to say, so much— to say, so much to

w/Fill 1
Am

say, so much——— to say.

w/Fill 1

Fsus2　Dm　Gsus2　Am

So much to say, so much— to say, so much to say, so much— to say.———

Gtr. IV

CRASH INTO ME
From *Crash* (1996)

The gently undulating rhythms and lovely harmonies of "Crash Into Me" combine to mask a dark lyric about the illicit desires of a Peeping Tom. In many ways a quintessential Dave Matthews composition, "Crash" was nominated for a Grammy Award in 1998, one of five such nominations for the band's second major-label release.

THEORY

Harmony

"Crash Into Me" is almost completely diatonic, remaining in the key of E major throughout the song, with a D/F♯ chord serving as the lone exception. This chord, heard only at the end of the song's chorus, represents the ♭VII chord in the key of E and can be viewed as a *borrowed* harmony, a temporary diversion from the home key—in this case, derived from the harmonized E Aeolian mode. Otherwise, the analysis is quite simple. C♯m7 is the vi chord, Asus2 is an open-sounding, suspended form of the IV chord that omits the major 3rd, E5 and E5/B are open-ended forms of I, again in an "incomplete" guise that omits the major 3rd, and E/G♯ is the tonic triad in 1st inversion (i.e., the major 3rd is the lowest chord tone). These strong, basic materials provide an evocative canvas for a haunting, deceptively complex composition.

Rhythm

"Crash Into Me" has a steady, consistent rhythm that's predominantly based on 16th notes, with the occasional eighth note or dotted rhythm helping to break things up, if only momentarily. These simple rhythms are far from boring, however, and instead create an insistent, gradually deepening intensity that draws the listener into the dark world of the voyeur who serves as the song's somewhat misguided protagonist. The tune's flowing rhythms are interrupted during the chorus, with the introduction of shifting time signatures that move from measures of 5/4, 3/4, and 6/4 back to the original 4/4 groove and a final measure of 2/4. It's essential to count (out loud or in your head) during these meter shifts to ensure that you always know what beat you're on and where "1" is. It's a relatively simple matter here, as there aren't any ties or over-the-barline phrases to further obscure the metric shifts. Merely add or subtract a beat (or two) from each measure of 4/4 as indicated and you'll be in good shape. The measure of 2/4 immediately preceding the return to the verse sections simply slices the 4/4 groove in half, so dropping beats 3 and 4 from the end is an easy matter. Take a look at the first three measures of the chorus in the example below.

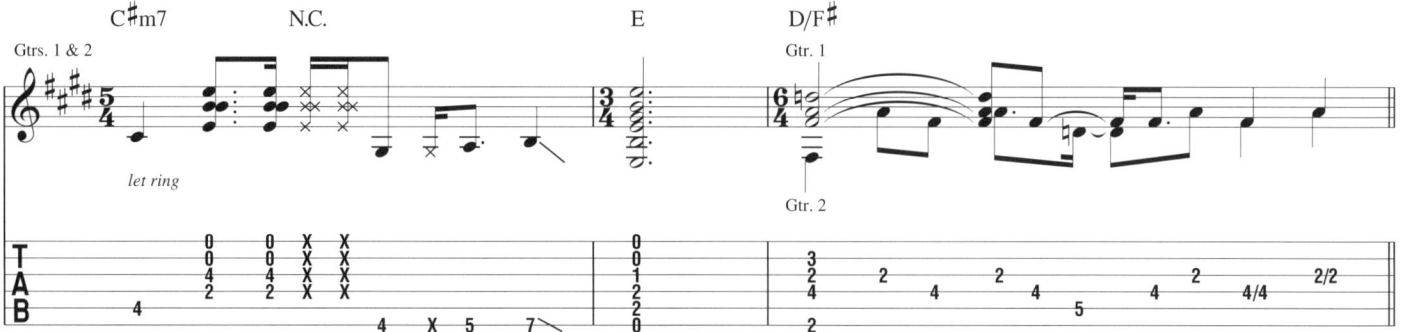

You may have noticed that the combined beats of measures 1 and 2 is eight, which is the same number of beats you'd find in two measures of 4/4 time. Play through the example while you tap out a steady quarter note pulse with your foot and you'll see how these two measures could be easily interpreted in 4/4 time. You can just plow through them and think of the big open-position E major chord that begins the measure of 3/4 as landing on beat 2 of the second measure of 4/4. But once you get to the measure of 6/4, you'll have to be a bit more careful, as both guitars (stemmed in opposite directions in the notation) have a true six-beat phrase that should be counted out carefully during your initial play-through.

Scales

There's no real scale playing or single-note lines to speak of in "Crash Into Me," but the harmonies are clearly derived from the E major scale. The example below shows this scale in an open-position fingering closely related to the chord voicings in the song. This material will most likely be familiar to you but may be illuminating nonetheless as you'll find most of Matthew's chord shapes neatly contained within.

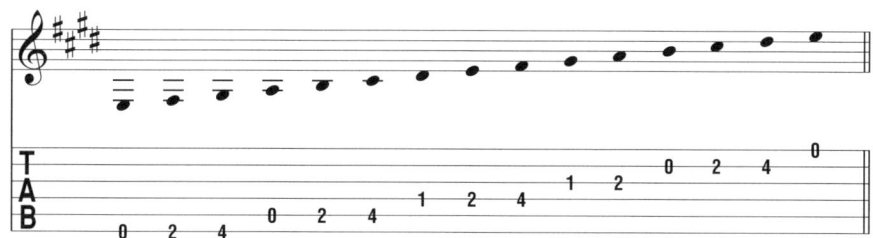

The E major scale fingering shown below begins on the A string, utilizes a three-notes-per-string approach, and encompasses the higher register, three-note chord phrases that are first heard after the chorus and before the song's second and third verses.

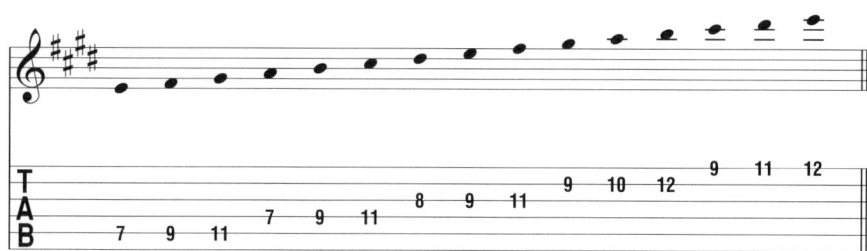

Composition

So what makes "Crash Into Me" such a compelling composition? The answer, at least to this author, lies in its emotional content. The overall mood of the piece—quiet, intense, and introspective—is a far cry from the party-down, good-time funk of "What Would You Say," "Too Much," and the other upbeat tunes in the band's catalog. The song may evoke different feelings in different listeners, but it's hard to deny its emotional punch, the result of a variety of disparate compositional devices. The most obvious of these is the use of simple, almost minimalist raw materials that are completely devoid of excess.

Rather than interjecting contrasting sections or rhythm section grooves, the band sets the mood of the song and sustains it throughout, casting a spell that draws us into its world completely. A sudden shift of harmony or rhythm would serve only to weaken that spell, so any such shifts have been wisely omitted. There is also the shrewd pairing of tender, pretty music with deceptively dark lyrics, each keeping the lesser tendencies of the other in check, striking a balance while preventing the song from getting either too maudlin or too creepy. Once again, there is the arrangement and skillful playing of the rhythm section, with Beauford and Lessard letting their parts unfold. Add to that the subtle, rich textures provided by Boyd Tinsley's violin and LeRoi Moore's saxophone, and the whole effect is one of gradually mounting intensity. Of course, the use of one of Matthews' favorite compositional devices, upper pedal points, really glues the entire piece together. The example on the top of the next page includes the song's main riff, in which the upper four-note chord voicing (E, B on the G string, and the open B and high E strings) repeats over and over while the bass notes move up and down along the A and low E strings.

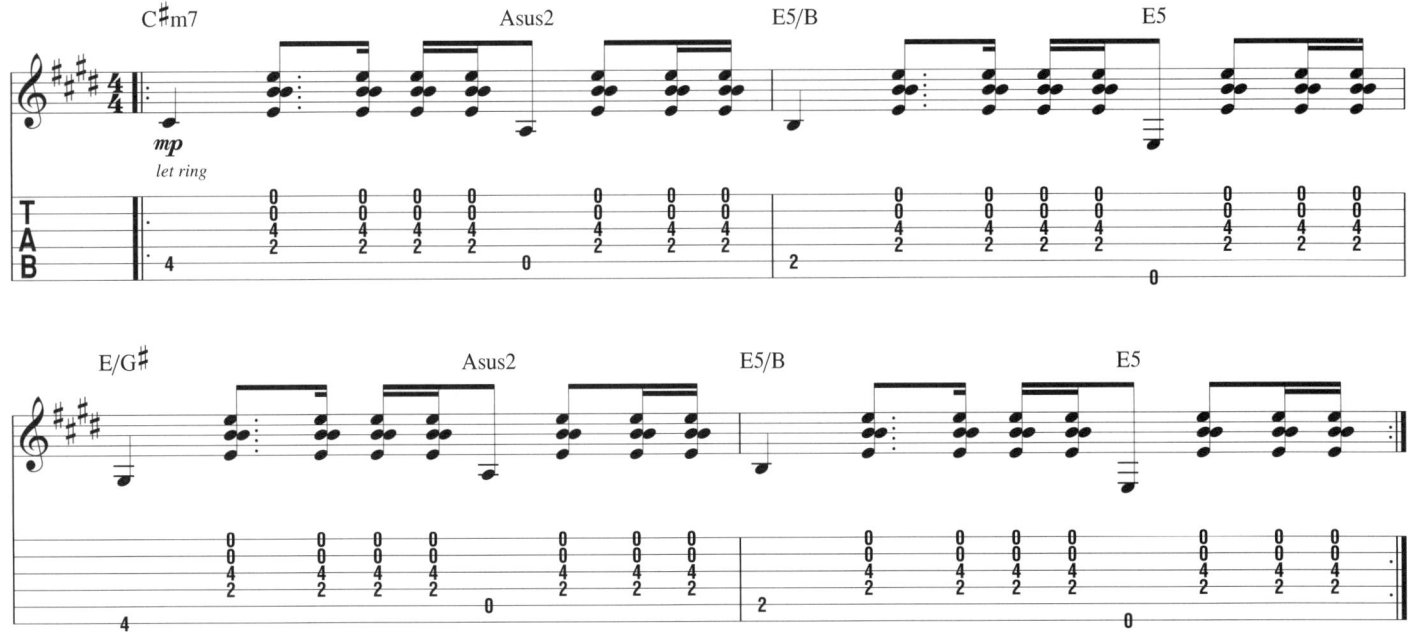

An upper pedal point layer is added immediately preceding the song's second and third verses. While there is some very slight variance in the pitches in this part, it still constitutes an upper pedal as the notes remain stationary the vast majority of the time.

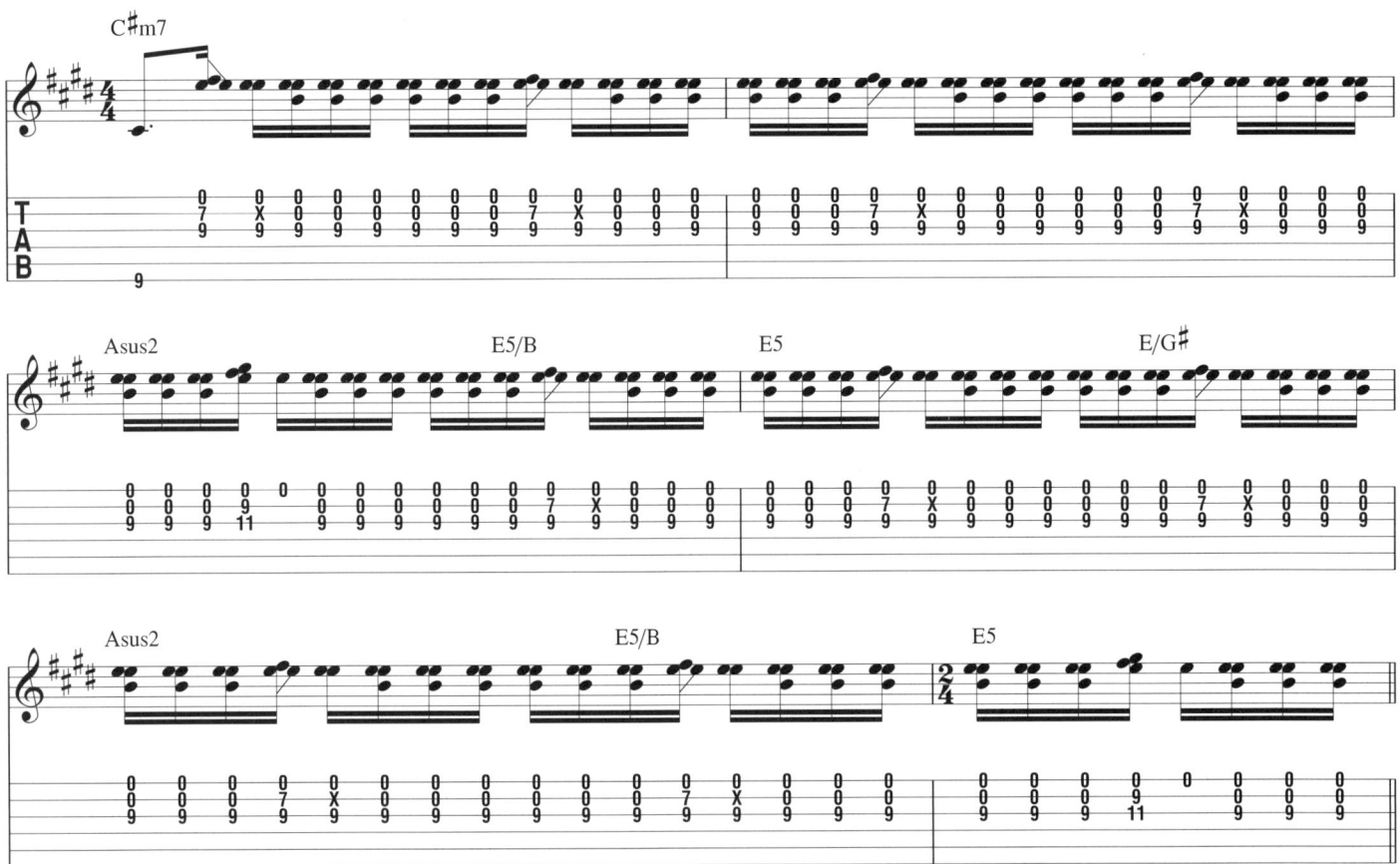

Pedal points can be found in various guises (single notes, a short repeated line, full chords) and in all styles of music. Matthews demonstrates some of their dramatic potential on "Crash Into Me" and has frequently returned to them in other compositions. They're an important stylistic component of his work and a unifying element in the band's repertoire.

TECHNIQUE

"Crash Into Me" is not a difficult song to play. Even by Dave Matthews Band standards, which value group interplay and compositional strength over flashy guitar licks, "Crash" keeps the instrument in a subservient role, providing a soft cushion for Matthews' voice and lyrics to float above. Nevertheless, let's talk briefly about some fingering considerations for the song's main sections.

The opening riff, which continues throughout the bulk of the song, is excerpted above. To play it, keep your index finger on the D string's 2nd fret and your pinky on the G string's 4th fret while using your ring finger to play the C♯ (A string, 4th fret) that begins the phrase. Simply lift your ring finger from the string and strike the open A string as indicated later in the measure. In measure 2, use your ring finger to barre the A and D strings at the 2nd fret to play the E5/B chord. You'll need to bend this finger backwards a bit at the first knuckle to ensure that the open B and high E strings are heard—an unusual technique to be sure, but one that's much easier to execute than it sounds. Return the index finger to its opening position on the D string for the E5 chord, leaving the slightest bit of fingertip on the A string to mute it. The E/G♯ chord in measure 3 calls for the same muffling technique, with the ring finger now added to the low E string's 4th fret to grab the G♯ bass note. Finish out the riff from there with a return to the Asus2, E5/B, and E5 chords played earlier. The overdubbed guitar part preceding the second and third verses and played on the top three strings (also excerpted above), should be played with the ring finger on the G string's 9th fret and the open B and high E strings ringing above. For the brief shift upwards in the third and sixth measures of this section, use your ring finger on the G string's 11th fret and your index finger on the 9th fret of the B string. The part shifts even further into the upper register during the song's outro.

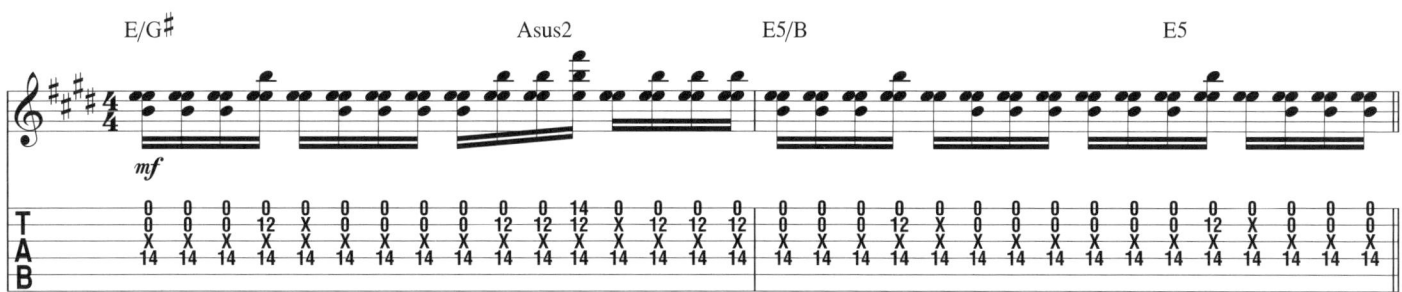

Play this part with your ring finger on the D string's 14th fret and flatten that finger ever so slightly to mute the open G string, which otherwise would serve as a seriously jarring disruption to the song's E major tonality. Use your index finger on the B string's 12th fret and your pinky on the high E string's 14th fret as indicated.

CRASH INTO ME

Written by
David J. Matthews

Additional Lyrics

3. Only if I've gone overboard,
Then I'm begging you
To forgive me, oh,
In my haste.
When I'm holding you so, girl,
Close to me.
Oh, and you come... *(To Chorus)*

TOO MUCH
From *Crash* (1996)

"Too Much" marks a return to the high-energy funk style of "What Would You Say," with a big step forward in terms of the complexity of the arrangement, the variety of textures from both the guitars and the other instruments, and the seamless fashion with which sections are sewn together. The transitions flow smoothly and organically into each other, shifting on the fly with all the ease and precision of a fine European sports car.

THEORY

Harmony

"Too Much" is played in an overall F♯ tonality and, while the key signature (six sharps) indicates F♯ major, the quality of the tonic chord veers between dominant and minor throughout. The guitars spend much of the tune riffing on an F♯5 power chord, interrupted at the end of most measures by an E7sus chord that serves no true harmonic function. This chord, comprised of the three lowest open strings and lasting for a single eighth note (the final eighth note in the measures in which it occurs) is way too brief to affect the harmony as more than a passing chord. Although we *can* call it ♭VII (suspended), it's really just a "guitaristic" slash across the open strings to break up a bit of steady power chord riffing.

The F♯5 power chord, lacking a 3rd or 7th of any kind (the real defining tones in any chord), is an open sound that basically serves as a thick base upon which a variety of melodic lines are built. The lines in Matthews' vocal are built on notes from the F♯ Dorian mode (F♯–G♯–A–B–C♯–D♯–E) and F♯ blues scale (F♯–A–B–C–C♯–E) which, when combined with the single-note muted guitar line underneath, result in an F♯ minor sound. The unison horn lines that pop up after the third verse combine the F♯ blues scale with notes from the F♯ Mixolydian mode (F♯–G♯–A♯–B–C♯–D♯–E), resulting in an F♯ dominant sound. There's a one-note difference between the Dorian and Mixolydian modes—the 3rd, which is lowered to A from A♯ in the former—and this crucial tone is all that's needed to change the overall sound from F♯7 to F♯m7.

"Too Much" has three truly separate sections, including the main riff built on the F♯5 power chord. There's also the four-measure intro that returns throughout the tune to break up the one-chord vamp, and a later section that features Boyd Tinsley's violin line in the lead role. The intro, played in the key of D, moves from D/F♯ (the I chord in 1st inversion) to G (IV) to Bm (vi) and later to B♭, a "borrowed" harmony taken from D minor, representing the ♭VI chord. The key change to F♯ that occurs in measure 5 (and numerous other places throughout the song) is achieved quite seamlessly, even if the jump from a B♭ chord down to F♯ is a bit unusual. One of the reasons such a change works so well is that the D (with F♯ in the bass, which helps) and Bm chords occur naturally in an F♯ minor tonality, which is essentially where the song goes. Although the main sections are more Dorian than Aeolian in nature (the difference being the 6th degree of each mode—D♯ in the former and D in the latter), the connection between the key centers of the intro and verse are close enough to satisfy the ear. When the band shifts abruptly to the key of A minor (note the key signature change) and puts the violin up front, a similar relationship occurs.

We've been hearing a lot of the F♯ blues scale up to this point, so when we now move to A, B, C, E, D, G, and F♯ bass notes, most of which are present in that scale, the effect is smooth and pleasing. A basic harmonic analysis of the new section gives us the i, ii, ♭III, v, iv, ♭VII, and vi chords in A minor, although neither guitar plays full chord voicings here. It's the *common tones* among the keys that really bring a sense of unity to the shifting key centers. The A Dorian mode, spelled A–B–C–D–E–F♯–G, shares five common tones with the F♯ blues scale (F♯, A, B, C, and E), making for an extremely logical and natural-sounding transition.

Rhythm

"Too Much" has a steady 16th note pulse throughout much of the tune, particularly in the muted single-note verse line (played by Guitar 4 in the full transcription). There's a fair amount of variety in this line and others, requiring a solid grasp of 16th note rests and dotted rhythms. With that in mind, let's take a look at another exercise designed to improve your facility with and recognition of these often challenging figures. Here, rests have been substituted for the muted 16th notes played in the song. Play these on any note or string you choose; tapping the rhythms out on a tabletop will work just as well. Eventually, you'll want to bring these to the instrument, if only to get your pick to cooperate with the broken phrases on the page.

Scales

"Too Much" combines F♯ Dorian, Mixolydian, and blues-scale notes, and shifts to the A Dorian mode in an instrumental section. Play through the examples below to familiarize yourself with these fingerings.

Composition

"Too Much" employs many of the same compositional devices found in earlier Dave Matthews Band songs; they create a sense of continuity within the band's repertoire while clearly demonstrating the ceaseless evolution of their collective songwriting skills. While "Too Much" is primarily a one-chord (or *tonal-center*), jam-type tune, the band's approach to this kind of static funk is more sophisticated. Timbral and textural variety keep things interesting, with layered guitar parts, overdubbed horns, and unison lines popping up throughout. There's room here for instrumental passages, including the horn "shout" section that follows the third verse, and the violin lead during the A minor sections, but these sections are fairly brief in length and judiciously spaced throughout the song. The band continually dances on the fine line between radio-ready pop and more expansive jam band-style "stretching," giving the home listener a small taste of what they can do when turned loose on a live stage.

Matthews again re-uses earlier compositional material to great effect; the opening chordal phrase in D serves as a sort of "hinge" between song sections and key changes each time it returns. Interestingly, it's reduced to a single measure of 3/4 immediately preceding the second shift to A minor, a compositional technique sometimes referred to as *diminution*. If anything, this diminished transition keeps the listener on his or her toes and resists falling into a predictable pattern. At the end of the song, there's a nice call-and-response exchange between Matthews and the violin and saxophone, before the sax "shout" returns to mix with the vocals during the fade-out.

TECHNIQUE

The biggest technical challenge in "Too Much" lies in the steady 16th note part played throughout much of the song. While your right hand will need to keep up a constant stream of alternate picking, your left hand should be placed gently across the strings to muffle them where indicated. It's a more subtle move then it may seem at first. If you're too gentle about it, you'll hear harmonics and open string sounds; if you press down too much, you'll get actual pitches instead of the desired deadened, percussive attack. The following exercise simulates the part and its many variations to prepare you for the real thing. Press down to sound the notes indicated, and then release pressure but leave your fingers on the string to create the muted sounds represented by the "X" noteheads. Watch out towards the end, where three-note chords on the upper strings are added to the mix, really raising the difficulty quotient.

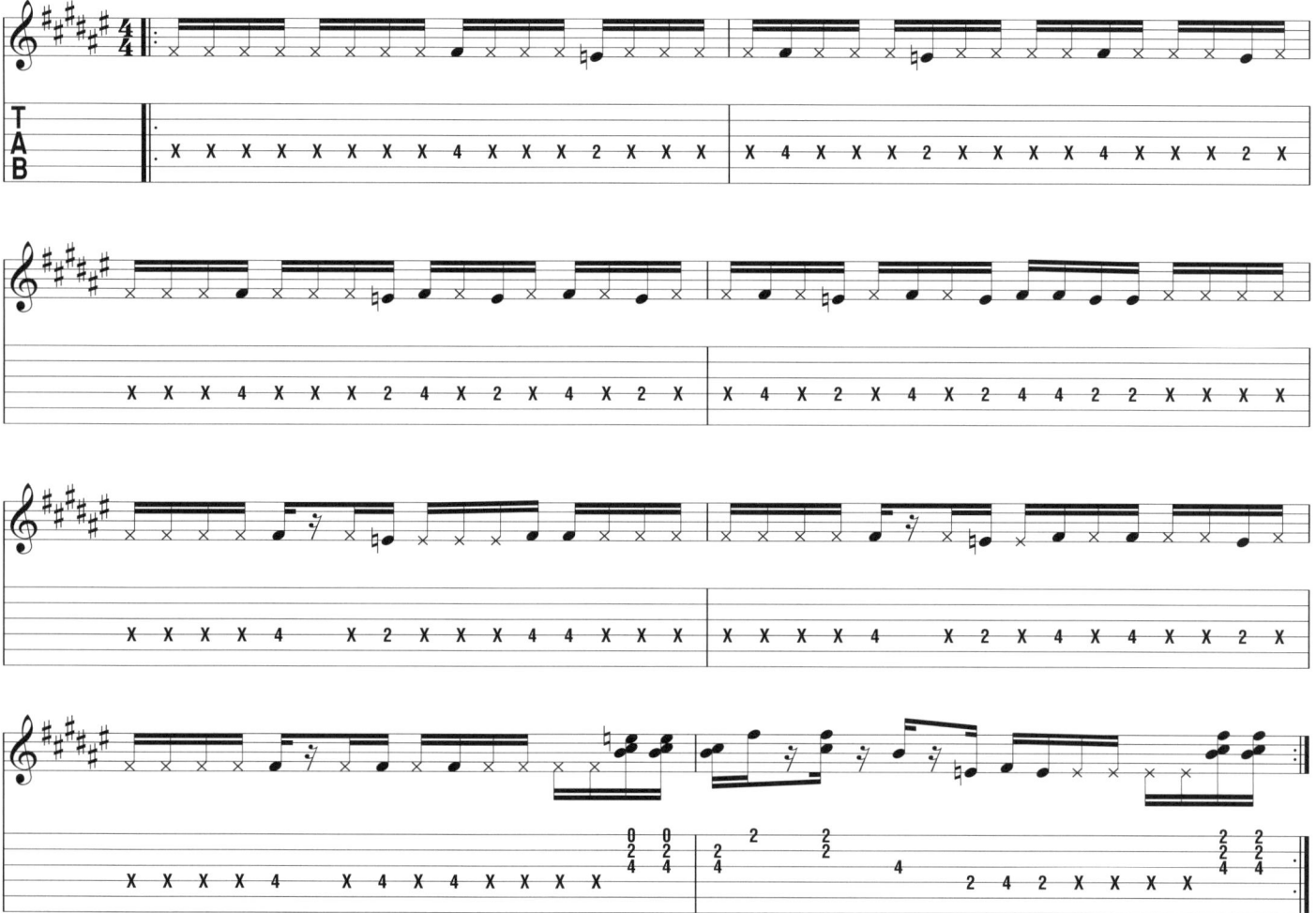

TOO MUCH

Written by
Dave Matthews Band

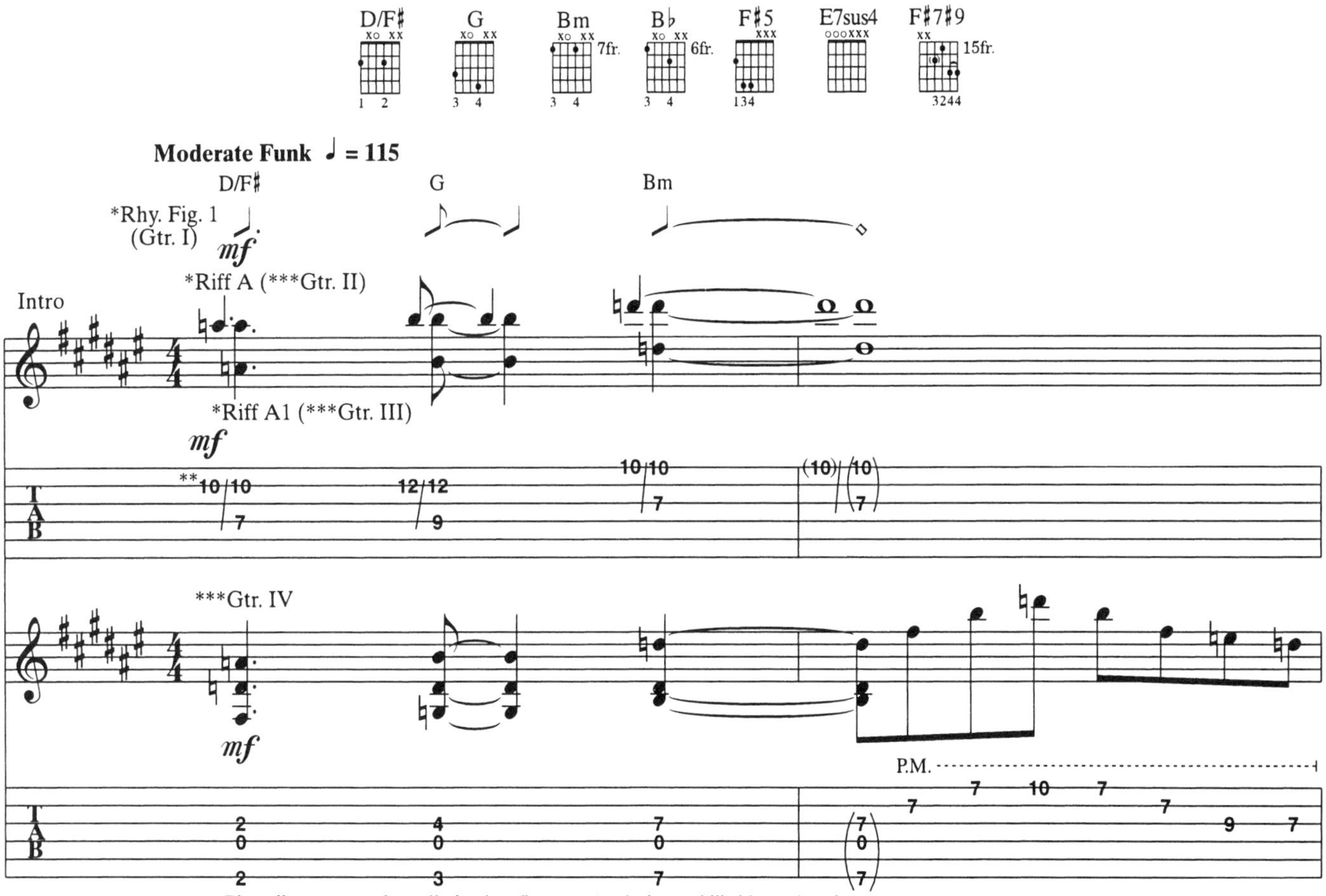

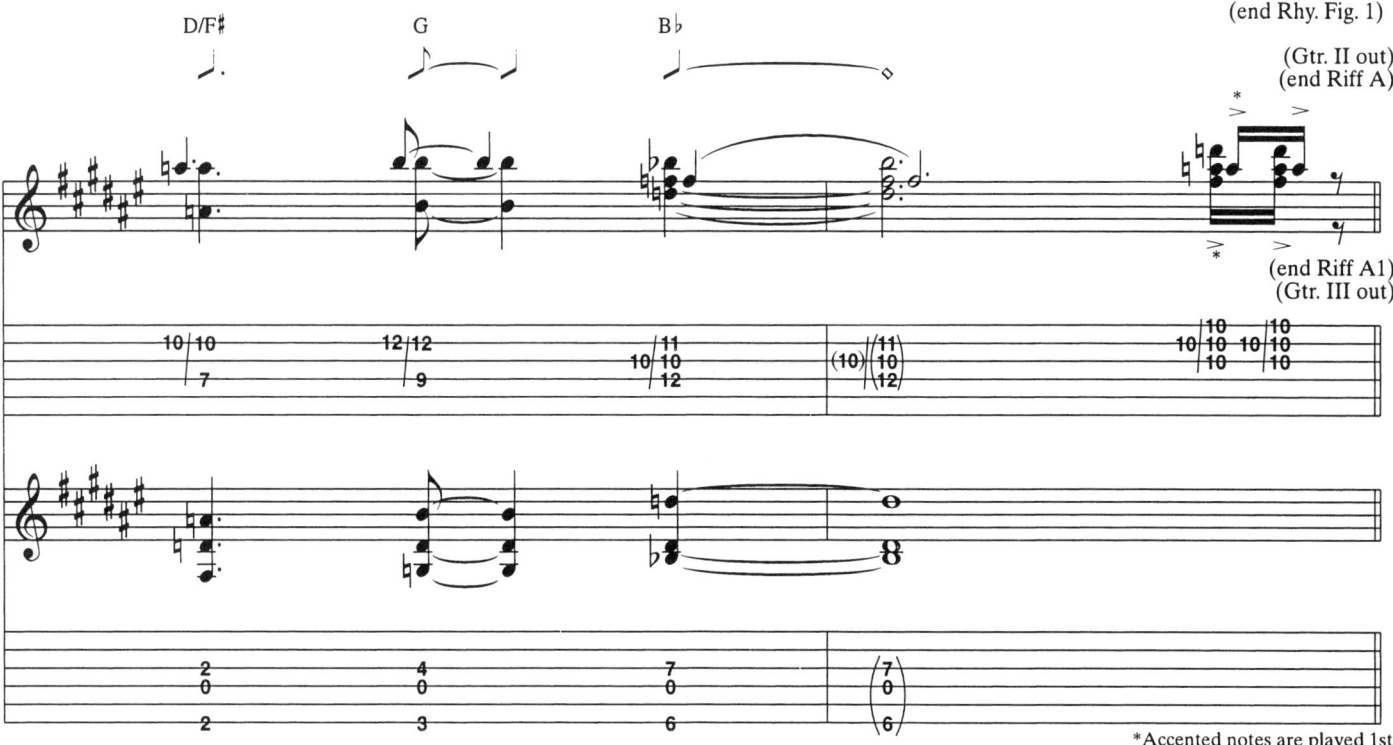

*Play all repeats and recalled guitar figures w/variations ad lib (throughout)
**Gtr. II to left of slashes.
***Gtr. II is violin arr. for gtr.; Gtr. III is horns arr. for gtr.; Gtr. IV is two gtrs. arr. for one.

*Accented notes are played 1st
time only; omit when recalled.

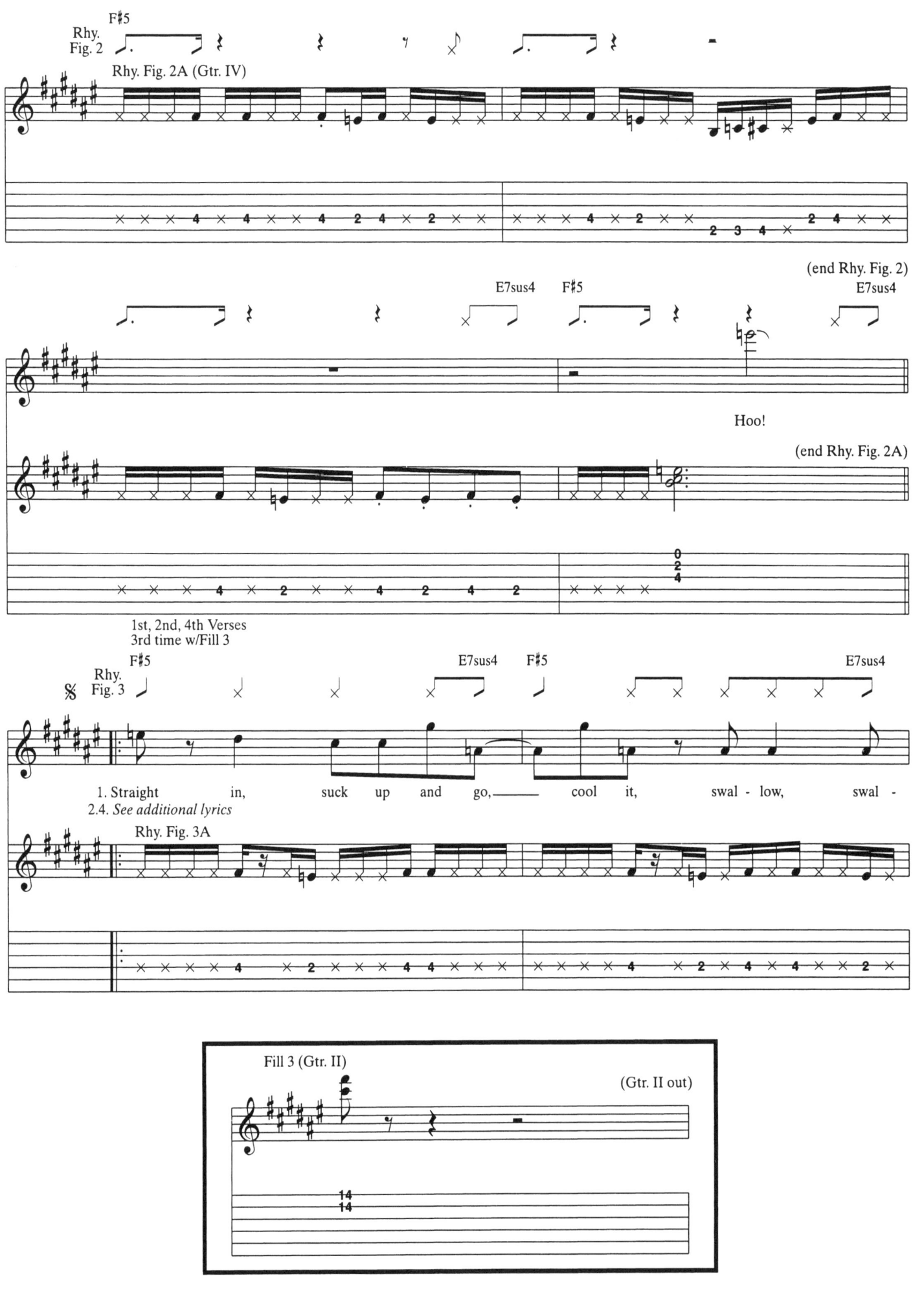

Fill 3 (Gtr. II)

(Gtr. II out)

85

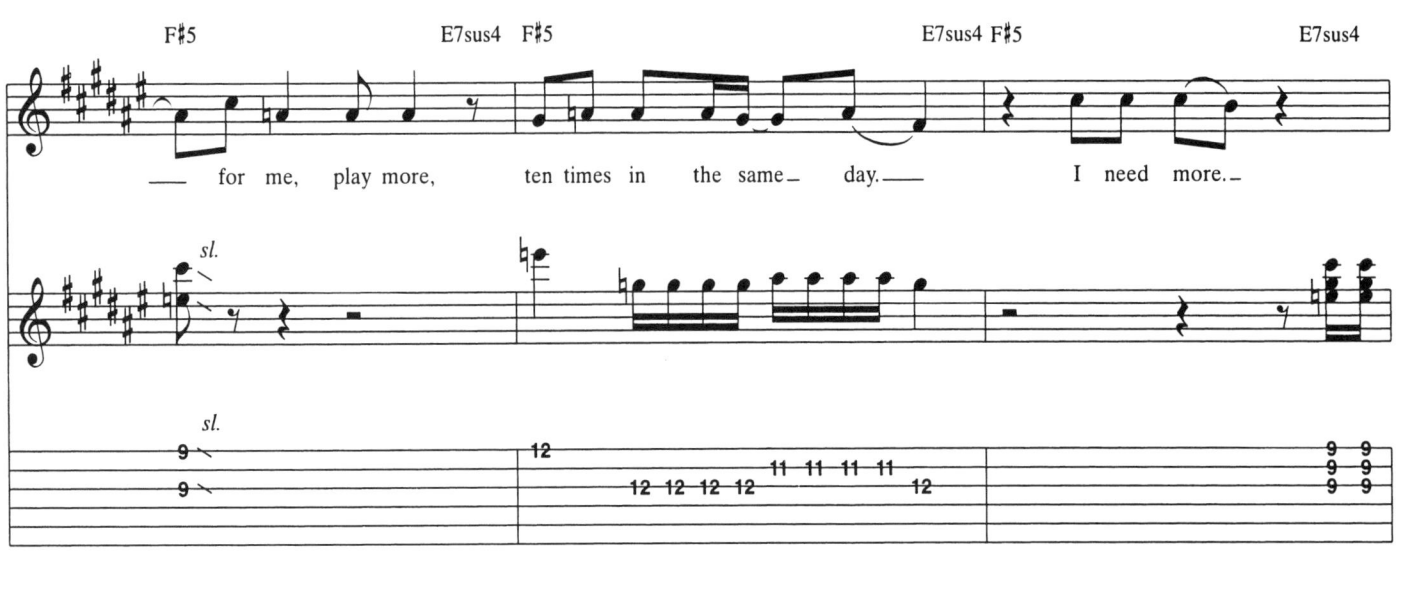

for me, play more, ten times in the same day. I need more.

I'm go-ing o-ver my bor-ders. Gon-na take more, more from you, let-ter by let-ter.

(cont. in slashes)

w/Rhy. Figs. 3 & 3A

Additional Lyrics

2. Oh, traffic jam, got more cars than a beach got sand.
   Suck it up, suck it up, suck it up,
   Fill it up until no more.
   I'm no crazy creep.
   I've got it coming to me because I'm not satisfied.
   The hunger keeps on growing. *(To Chorus)*

4. I told God, "I'm coming to your country.
   I'm going to eat up your cities,
   Your homes, you know."
   I've got a stomach full,
   It's not a chip on my shoulder.
   I've got this growl in my tummy
   And I'm gonna stop it today. *(To Chorus)*

RAPUNZEL
From *Before These Crowded Streets* (1998)

Now here's something different. "Rapunzel," packed with shifting time signatures, cycled dominant chords, and wailing soprano sax, surely ranks among the most sophisticated and jazz-influenced pop/funk ever committed to record. An amazing amalgam of influences and grooves, the song is a prime example of Dave Matthews Band at their heady best. Imagine seminal fusion supergroup Weather Report with Matthews up front, and it would probably sound something like this.

THEORY

Harmony

"Rapunzel" has three distinct sections in three separate keys. In the introductory 5/4 figure, recalled throughout the song, the band is really in C despite the key signature (one flat, the key of F). Here, the progression moves from Dm7 to F and G major triads, later bouncing back and forth between C and G/B chords ("I do/my best/for you"). The analysis is a simple one: Dm7 represents the ii chord, F and G the IV and V, respectively, while C is the I. G/B is simply the V chord in 1st inversion. As the verses begin, we shift to the key of G for a sequence moving from G7 (I7) to C7 (IV7) to F9 (♭VII7) and back to C7. Although these chords are not the usual "quality" (G and C would normally be major chords in this key) and F9 is non-diatonic, the progression makes sense on a few different levels. First, it's similar to a blues in that the I and IV are dominant chords; a quick analysis of Matthew's vocal melody reveals it to be comprised almost entirely of notes from the G minor pentatonic scale, strengthening the section's blues flavor. Secondly, the chords move through the *cycle of 4ths*, a common progression in which the harmonies continually resolve up a 4th interval. G7 becomes the V of C7, which becomes the V of F9, and so forth. The cycle stops at F9, reverses itself back to C7, repeats, and then returns to the C to G/B sequence first heard in the intro. Interestingly, these chords have different functions if we're thinking of G as the tonic; instead of I–V movement in C, it's IV–I in G.

The third section of the song, played in 6/8, shifts to the key of F, with a progression that moves from Dm (vi) to B♭ (IV) to Csus2 (V). Alternately, we can look at it as a modal sequence in F's relative minor key, D, and it's corresponding mode, D Aeolian. From that perspective, the chords represent i, ♭VI, and ♭VII, respectively. It's really a case of six of one, half a dozen of the other, as the passage has a distinctly minor sound while still consisting of chords belonging to the key of F major.

Rhythm

Most Dave Matthews Band songs have a crucially important rhythmic aspect, and "Rapunzel" is certainly no exception. In fact, in terms of rhythm, it's the most complex that we've examined so far. With its shifting time signatures and broken 16th note figures, it's a bit intimidating at first glance (and listen). But it doesn't have to be. Take your time analyzing each section, be clear about where in each beat each note and chord falls, count out the odd time signature measures, and you'll be fine. Let's take it a section at a time, beginning with the intro in 5/4.

Note that each measure is preceded by a 16th note that falls on the "a" of beat 4 (final 16th) and is tied over the barline. The 16th and eighth note rhythms in these measures are relatively uncomplicated, although you'll need to be on your toes for beats 4 and 5, where muted notes alternate with fretted double stops falling on the "e" of beat 4, the "a" of beat 4, the "e" of beat 5, and the "a" of beat 5 (tied over into the next measure). The final measure of this section shifts to 6/4 (simply add a beat) and gets a bit trickier, as the repeated jumps from C to G/B really obscure which beat we're on. Starting on beat 2, there's a repeated grouping of two eighth notes heard four times, each separated by a single 16th note. Consequently, the groups begin on beat 2, the "e" of beat 3, the "and" of beat 4, and the "a" of beat 5, twice crossing the downbeat and necessitating the use of a tie. Count it all out carefully and you'll be okay. If rhythms like these are new to you, you'll have to be especially patient as you work your way through them. Don't just listen to the album and mimic it—really learn exactly where everything falls.

Moving on, the verses shift to 4/4 and find the band laying down a series of *tutti* "hits" while Carter Beauford keeps his groove going underneath and Dave sings above it all. These hits fall on beat 1, the "a" of beat 2, and the "a" of beat 4, with rests in the spaces between. In every other measure, the hit on the "a" of beat 4 is tied over to beat 1 of the next measure. What really complicates matters here is the interjection of a measure of 7/8 in the middle of the section. Not only do we have the return of the C-to-G/B eighth note phrase that goes over the barline, but we also have a *metric modulation* to deal with. A metric modulation occurs when the basic pulse of the music is altered midstream; in this case, the quarter note pulse of 4/4 becomes an eighth note pulse in the new time signature. Here's an easy way to count a shift like this: In 4/4, count not only the quarter notes, but the eighth notes in between ("1–and–2–and–3–and–4–and"). When you move to 7/8, each syllable in 4/4 will then equal a single beat in the new signature. In other words, a measure of 4/4 and a measure of 7/8 would be counted: "1–and–2–and–3–and–4–and–1–2–3–4–5–6–7," with all "ands" and numbers given equal time. Matthews' acoustic part is shown in the example below with the beats counted out above the staff; remember that if in 7/8 an eighth note takes up a single beat, there will now be two 16th notes per beat instead of four.

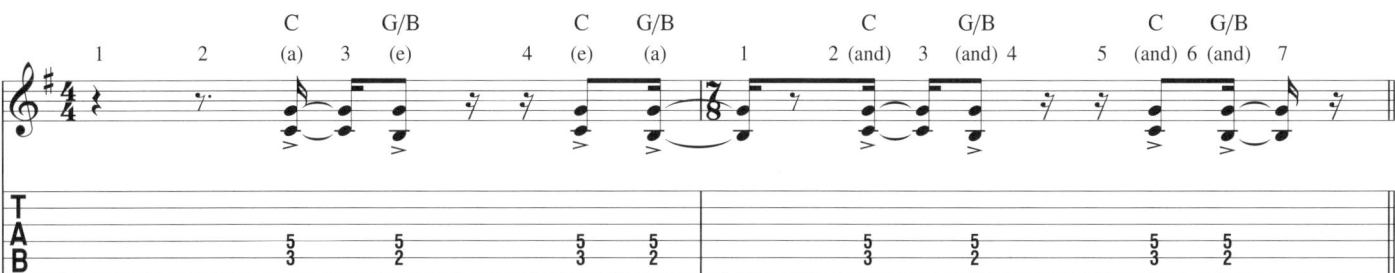

The bridge of "Rapunzel" moves to a 6/8 time signature via another metric modulation. Both of the times that this section comes up, we're coming from a measure of 4/4, so the eighth notes in that time signature become the basic pulse in 6/8. If you're counting quarter notes and the eighths in between when you're in 4/4, you shouldn't have much of a problem with this transition. The example below consists only of repeated "D" eighth notes and goes back and forth between measures of 4/4 and 6/8. Every note has exactly the same duration. Remember, the top number in a time signature tells you how many beats are in each measure, while the bottom number tells you the rhythmic value of a single beat. 6/8 = six eighth notes, 7/4 = seven quarter notes, etc.

Scales

"Rapunzel," like much of the Dave Matthews Band catalog, is less reliant on single-note lines and scalar figures than on funky chord strumming parts and overall tight ensemble work. Nonetheless, the opening intro figure is clearly based on the C major scale and its corresponding second mode, D Dorian. Both are shown below in three-notes-per-string fingerings that begin on the A string.

During the verses, Matthews sings notes derived primarily from the G minor pentatonic scale (G–B♭–C–D–F), but the band sticks to the dominant chord cycles described in the harmony section above. Note the use of incomplete chord voicings in this section; the guitars primarily play the 3rds and 7ths of the chords while the bass takes care of the roots below. The song's bridge is based on the D Aeolian mode, shown below in the A-string, three-notes-per-string fingering (a one-note difference from the D Dorian mode above), and in a similar scheme that begins on the low E string's 10th fret.

Composition

One compositional approach Dave Matthews frequently employs is the use of two or more closely related keys in the course of a single song, which goes somewhat against the grain of a more traditional songwriting approach. More commonly, a composer will move to the relative major or minor key, and then have a big transition (frequently in the bridge) that moves the song to a wholly unrelated key. In "Rapunzel," Matthews bounces around the keys of C, G, and F, often using chords that exist in multiple key centers. For example, C is the I chord in C, the IV chord in G, and the V chord in F. The C-to-G/B progression that harmonizes the lyric "I do my best for you" represents a I–V motion in the C major–based intro, and a IV–I motion in the G major–based verse. The Dm chord that begins the bridge is the vi chord in the key of F major, and the ii chord in the intro, etc.

We've observed Matthews writing this way in previous work, so it's no surprise that the trend continues here. These tendencies mark the evolution of both a single composer and an ensemble as well. Returning to previously used and favored techniques is not, in this case, a sign of lack of imagination but is in fact evidence of a highly intelligent, constantly developing musicality. While Dave Matthews Band is adventurous, eclectic, and all of the other things that are frequently used to describe them, they aren't a scattershot group of virtuosos toying with whatever strikes them today or tomorrow. Instead, Dave and the band have created a highly personal and unique sound that always comes *before* the more exotic trappings, complex arrangements, and expansive live experimentation. Of course, "Rapunzel" does put many of the band's most impressive facets on display. The nonpareil rhythm section is once more in the driver's seat, pushing the band smoothly through their most complex time signature shifts and modulations yet. Over-the-barline phrases that popped up sporadically in earlier works have assumed positions of prominence in the song. LeRoi Moore's soprano sax introduces a fiery new timbre to the ensemble sound. And, of course, there is the clever re-use of the song's best material, with the intro in 5/4 in particular serving as the central instrumental motif and "hinge" between the 4/4 grooves of the verse and the flowing 6/8 time of the bridge.

TECHNIQUE

The biggest obstacles to playing "Rapunzel" lie in its rhythms, metric modulations, and time signature shifts. If you've been diligent in breaking the song down from this perspective, you shouldn't have too much of a struggle when you actually pick up your instrument and try to play the song. While it isn't terribly demanding from a "guitaristic" standpoint, there are a few instances that bear closer inspection. First, take a look at the electric guitar part in the song's intro.

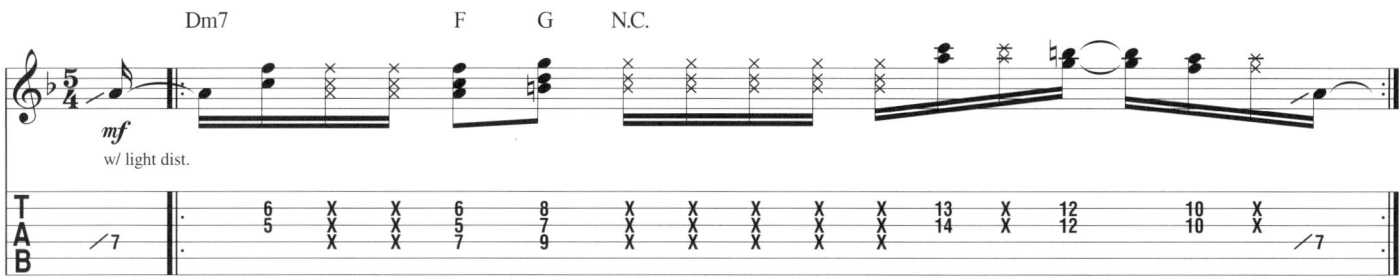

Play the opening slide with your ring finger on the D string, leave it there, and then complete the F and G triads (with their roots on top) by using your index finger on the G string and your middle finger on the B string. When you move up the neck on beat 4, use your ring and middle fingers on the G (14th fret) and B strings (13th fret), respectively, and then barre the strings with your ring finger (12th fret) and index finger (10th fret). In the 6/4 measure at the end of this section, use your ring finger to barre the G and B strings at the 5th fret (beginning on beat 2), and then barre the same strings at the 3rd fret with your index finger. With the barre in place, bring your middle finger down forcefully to perform the hammer-ons to the G string's 4th fret for each G/B chord. This move is repeated in the 7/8 measures of the verse as well.

Moving on to that section, play Dave's acoustic part (Gtr. 2) with your pinky taking the Gs on the D string's 5th fret. Play the 3rd-fret notes on the low E and A strings with your middle finger, flattening it every so slightly in the former instance to prevent the open A string from ringing. This will leave you in good position to stretch with your index finger down to the low E string's 1st fret to get to the root of the F9 chord; perform the same muting technique to silence the A string here. In the electric part (Gtr. 1) apply vibrato as indicated by rapidly and repeatedly bending the string up and down a very short distance while the note sustains; the wider and faster the bends, the more exaggerated the effect will be. In the song's third verse, the electric jumps into the upper register and applies micro-bends to three-note chords on the D, G, and B strings.

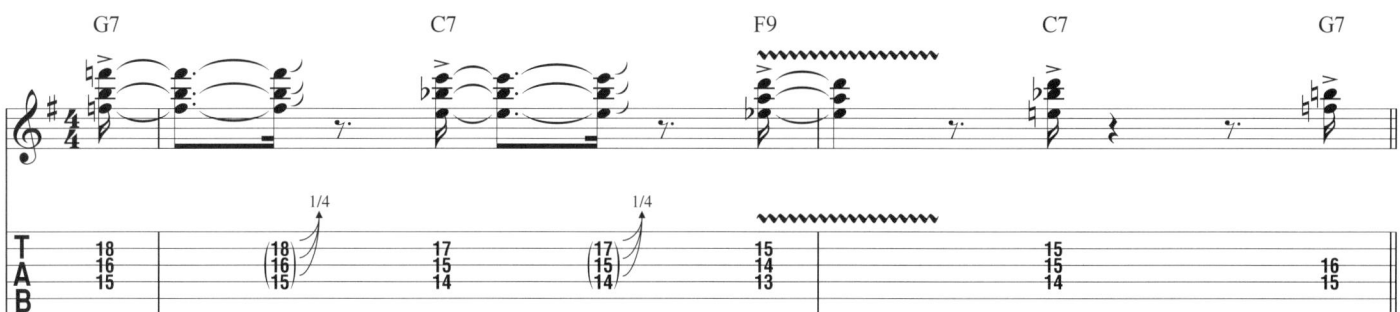

Play these figures with your index finger, middle finger, and pinky on the D, G, and B strings, respectively. Let the chords ring for the indicated durations before bending the strings toward the floor; pull down firmly enough to make the pitches rise a quarter tone (the Fs shouldn't fully reach F♯). Be sure to distinguish these bent chords from the vibrato-laden F9 that follows; at this tempo and register it's a subtle difference but an important one.

RAPUNZEL

Written by
David J. Matthews, Stefan Lessard
and Carter Beauford

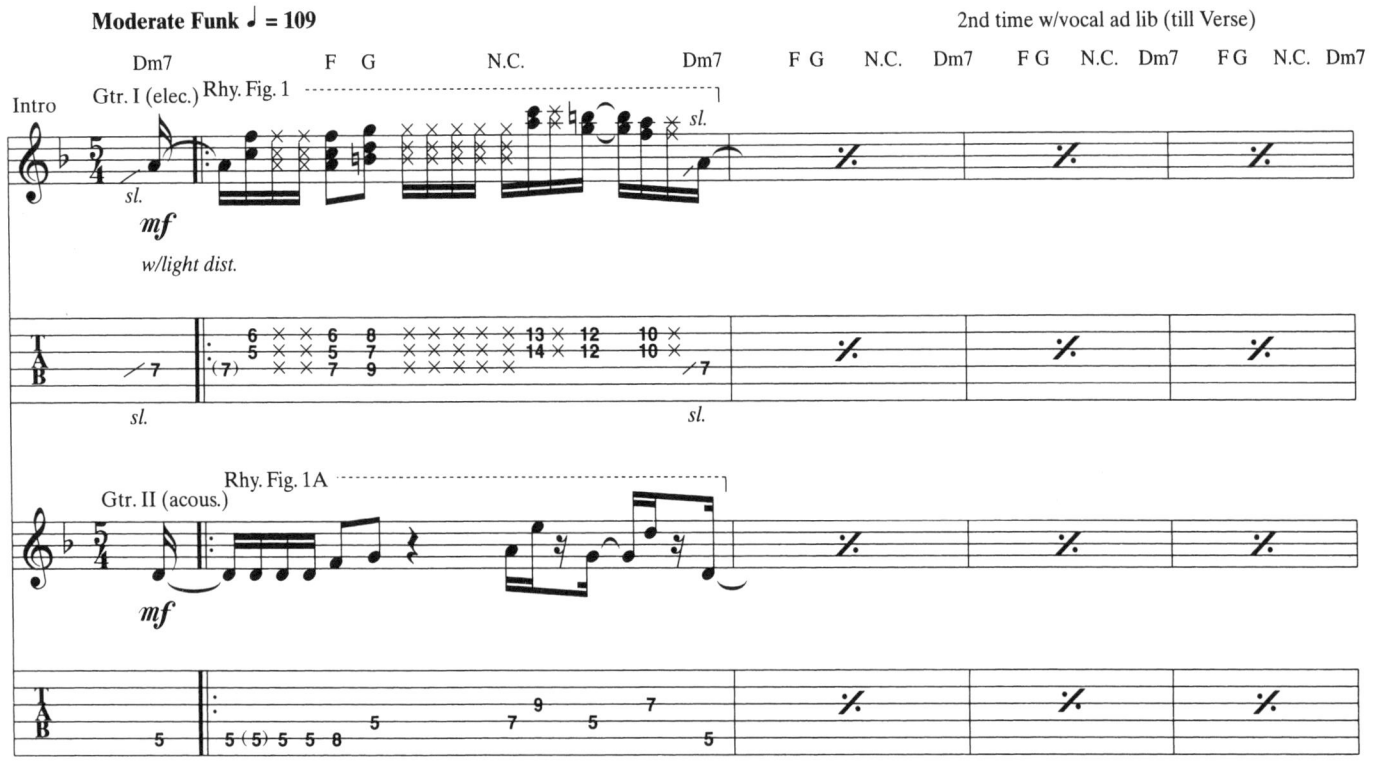

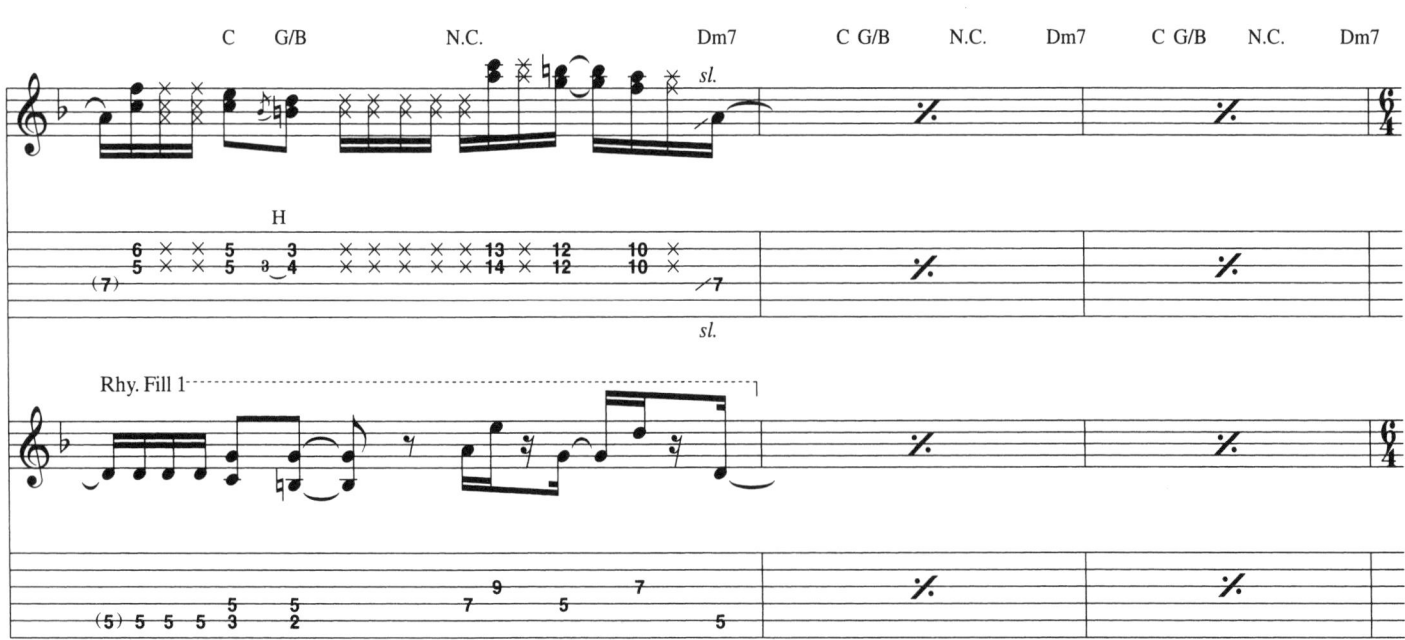

*Some chords implied by piano (throughout).

101

*Substitute muted strings in parentheses when recalled.

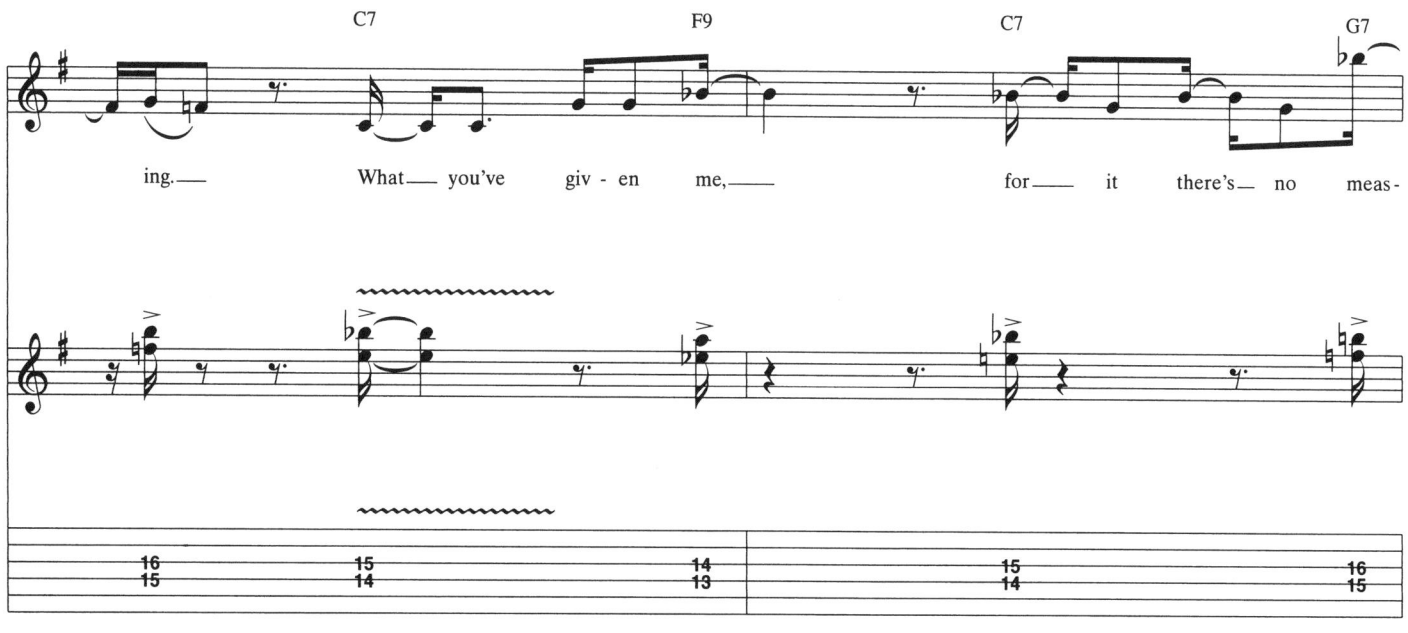

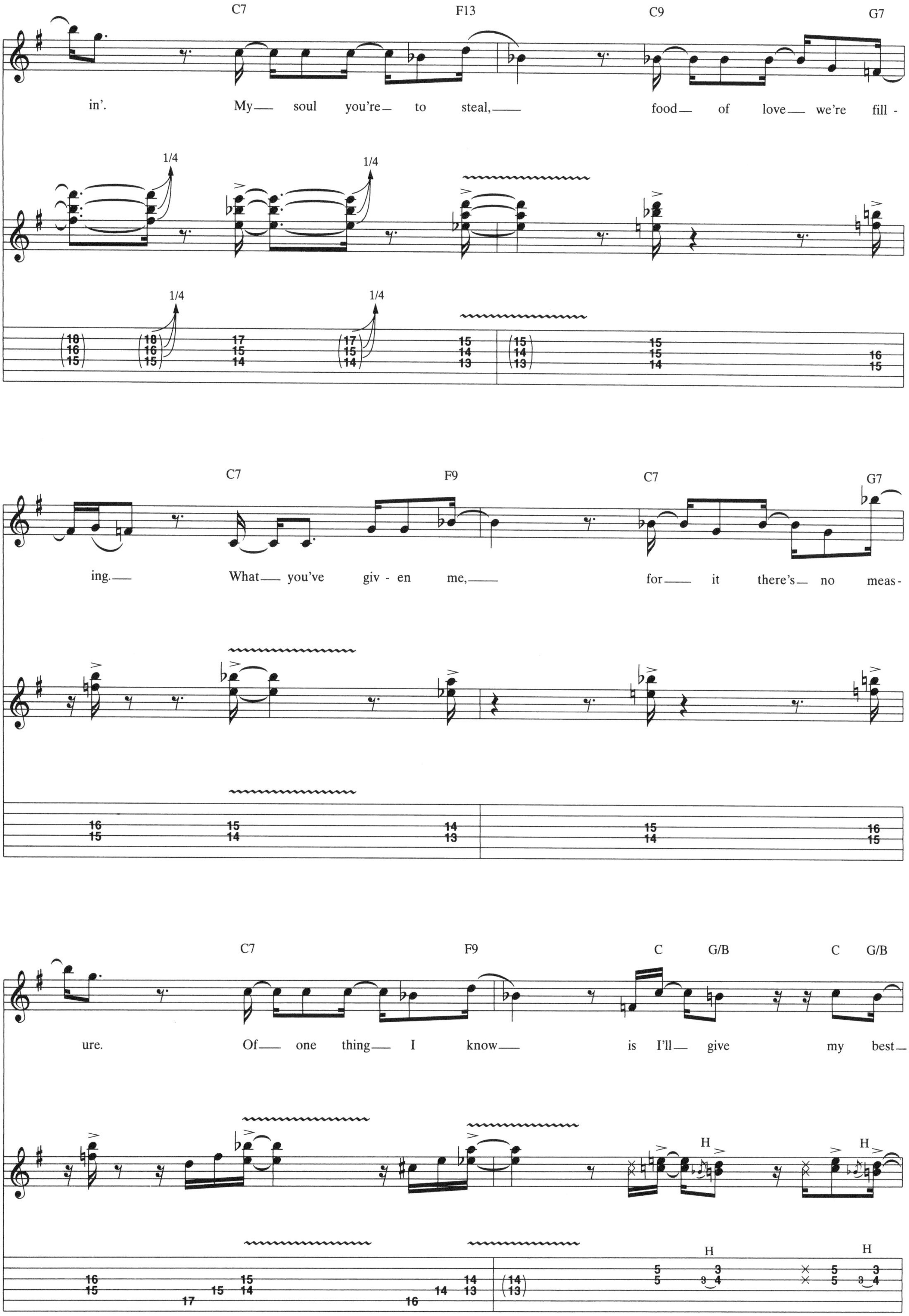

C7 F13 C9 G7
in'. My— soul you're— to steal,— food— of love— we're fill -
1/4 1/4
C7 F9 C7 G7
ing.— What— you've giv - en me,— for— it there's— no meas -
C7 F9 C G/B C G/B
ure. Of— one thing— I know— is I'll— give my best—
H H

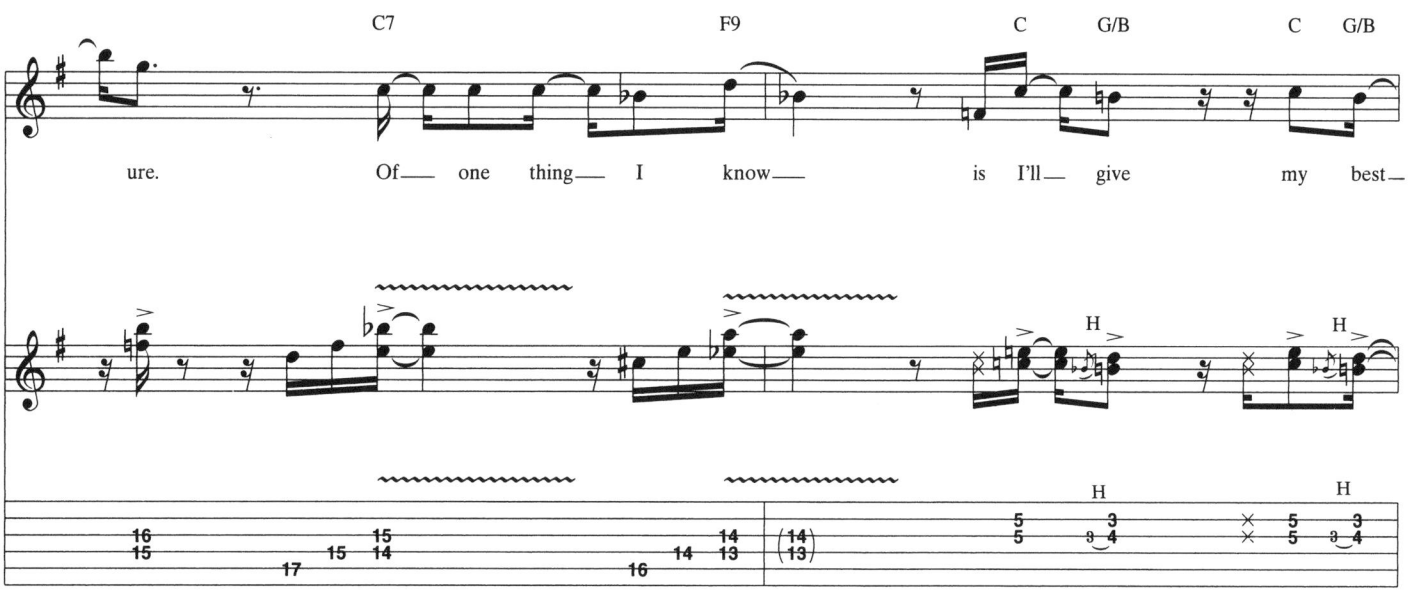

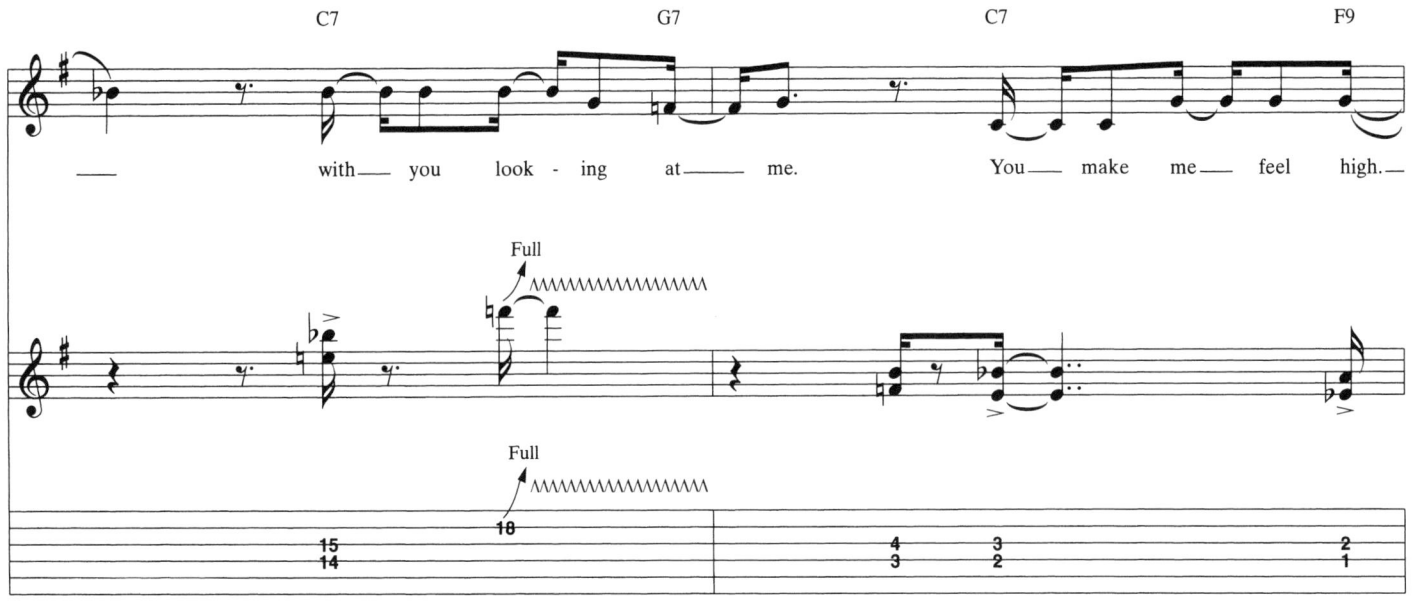

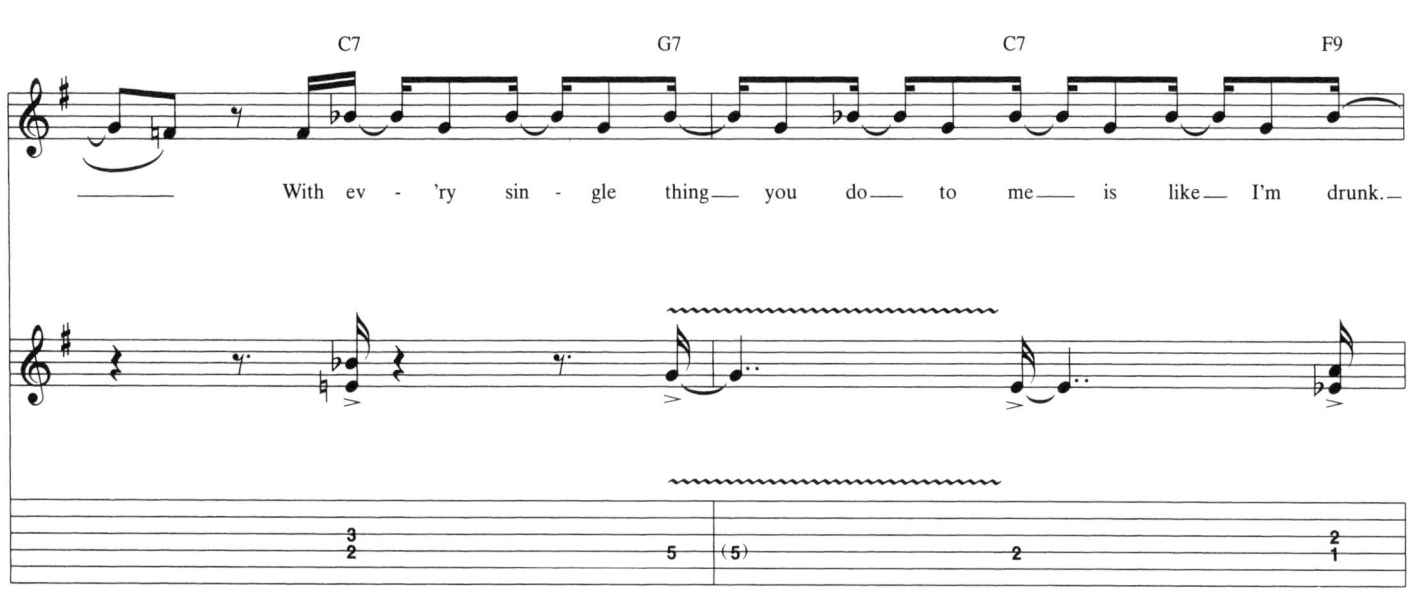

110

*Composite arrangement of both gtrs. (till end). Gtr. III is acous.

*Play w/variations ad lib when recalled.

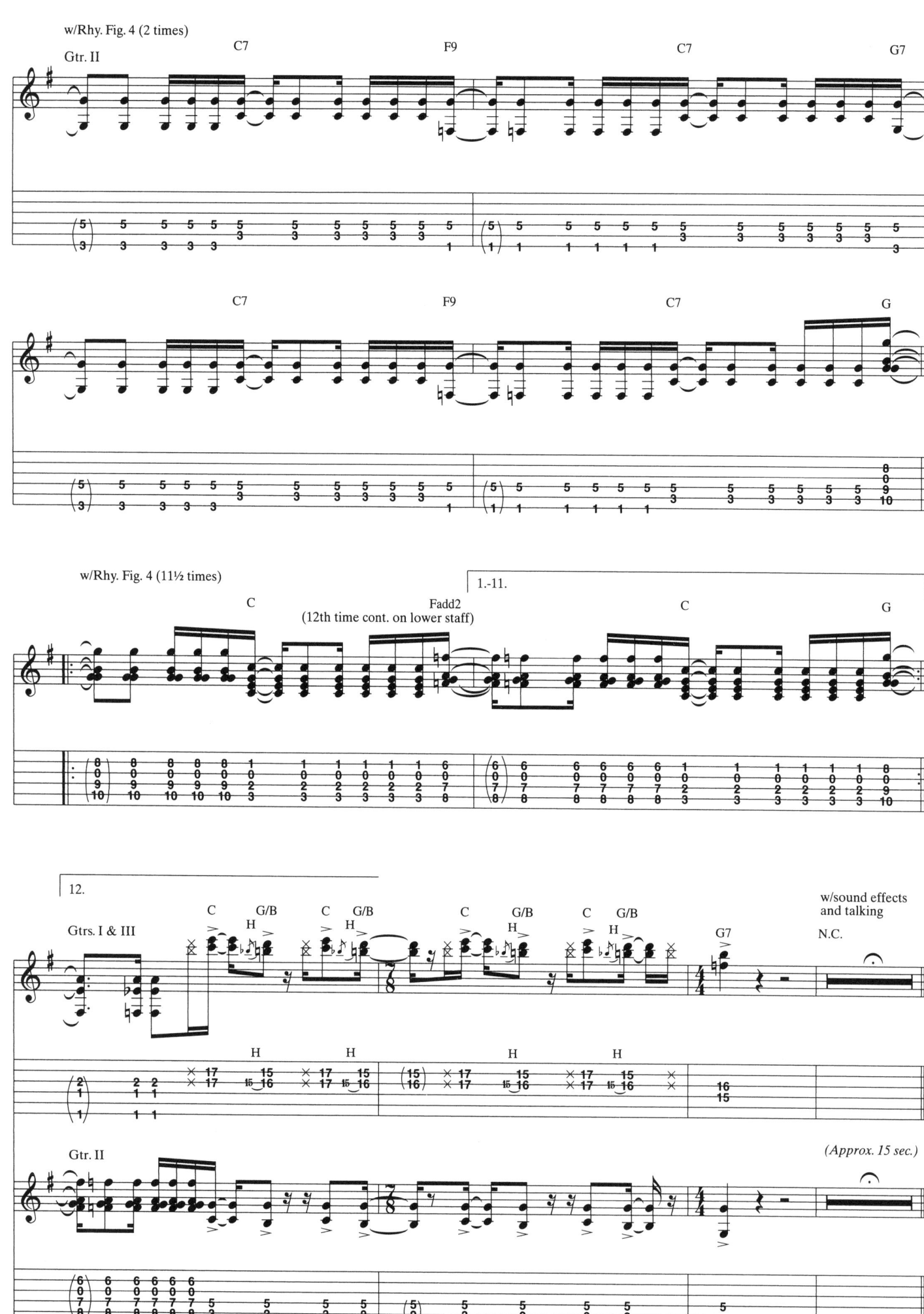

DON'T DRINK THE WATER
From *Before These Crowded Streets* (1998)

This scathing song, full of menace and fury, has a distinctly Eastern Indian flavor, even though it's clearly about the persecution and destruction of the Native American peoples. The use of virtuoso guest Bela Fleck's banjo gives the tune a bit of old-time, Wild West attitude as well.

THEORY

Harmony

"Don't Drink the Water" is notated in the key of D major (two sharps) but uses an open-ended D5 power chord as its tonic. The melodic lines in Matthews' vocal and in the banjo part (transcribed here as Gtr. 2) are derived from the D Mixolydian mode (D–E–F♯–G–A–B–C), giving the chord a dominant (and/or suspended) flavor throughout the song, although the occasional use of a bluesy F♮ gives things a temporary Dorian (D–E–F–G–A–B–C) sound. There are brief moments when the underlying harmony results in an Am/D chord, nearly synonymous with a D7sus4 chord, a sound borrowed from the key of G (the true home key from which the D Mixolydian mode is derived). During later sections of the song, the harmony shifts to G5 (the IV chord in D), and later Bm (vi). The vicious outro section includes both B♭ and B♭/D chords, the ♭VI chord in root position and in 1st inversion. This chord is borrowed from the D natural minor scale (Aeolian mode), a common enough practice and one we've seen in other Matthews compositions. On the whole, "Don't Drink the Water" is a simple song harmonically, with a droning, mostly static, modal feeling, and gains its complexity from other sources, namely the melodic lines and lyrics of Matthews' vocal.

Rhythm

This is also a simple song from a rhythmic standpoint, particularly in light of other Dave Matthews Band compositions, and that's clearly intentional. Nothing should distract from the power and fury of Matthews' voice and words on a song like this, so nothing is added that would. Drum fills, tricky over-the-barline phrasing, and fancy guitar licks are eschewed in favor of a fairly consistent backdrop that nevertheless does evolve by virtue of the slow addition of a variety of textural enrichments (banjo, strings, feedback-laden guitar tones, etc.). Rhythmic figures are almost always straightforward combinations of eighth and 16th notes, with the odd tie or dot popping up occasionally. The manner in which these are employed shouldn't create much difficulty if you've worked your way through this book up to this point—you've already seen many much more challenging phrases in earlier songs. Notice the use once more of subdivided 16th notes in the banjo part; in its first measure, the notes are divided into groups of three and one, with numerous subtle variations in the measures that follow.

Scales

As stated above, "Don't Drink the Water" is based almost exclusively on the D Mixolydian mode; the song's only real deviation occurs in the outro with the introduction of the B♭ and B♭/D chords that are borrowed from the D Aeolian mode. Of course, there is the odd F♮ sprinkled here and there in both the vocal and banjo parts, a bluesy pitch when played against the D7 backdrop. The fleeting presence of this note does not signify a true shift in scale or mode but is instead simply a borrowed pitch derived from the D Dorian mode (or blues scale, if you prefer). As we've already learned a variety of fingerings for these scales during our examinations of previous songs, let's concentrate instead on the D Mixolydian fingering employed in the banjo part. To play this part, you'll need to retune your guitar in open D tuning, dropping your low E string down a whole step to D, your G string down a half step to F♯, and your B and high E strings each down a whole step to A and D, respectively (note that the standard acoustic and electric guitar parts use a drop-D tuning in which only the low E string is lowered a whole step to D).

The example below doesn't show the mode in strictly sequential order; instead, all of the notes that are played on the D string are shown first, followed by those on the G, B, and high E strings. The occasional F♮ and other passing chromatic pitches are omitted.

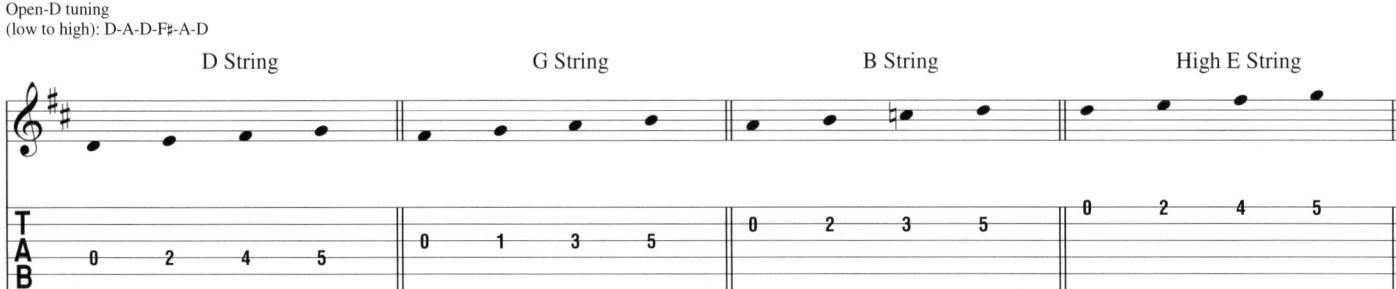

Overall, altered tunings can be more than a little disorienting, particularly if you've never used them before, so pay close attention to what you're doing and where each scale note falls (notice that whenever F♯ appears, it occurs on either the D string or high E string's 3rd fret). There's a brief instance in the eighth measure of the second verse in which the banjo plays a particularly exotic lick that's based on the G harmonic minor scale (G–A–B♭–C–D–E♭–F♯). Because we're hearing the droning D in both the bass and guitar parts below, it sounds even more unusual that it would played over a G bass note. The example that follows shows both the G harmonic minor scale in standard tuning and on the top four strings in the open-D tuning used by the banjo during the song.

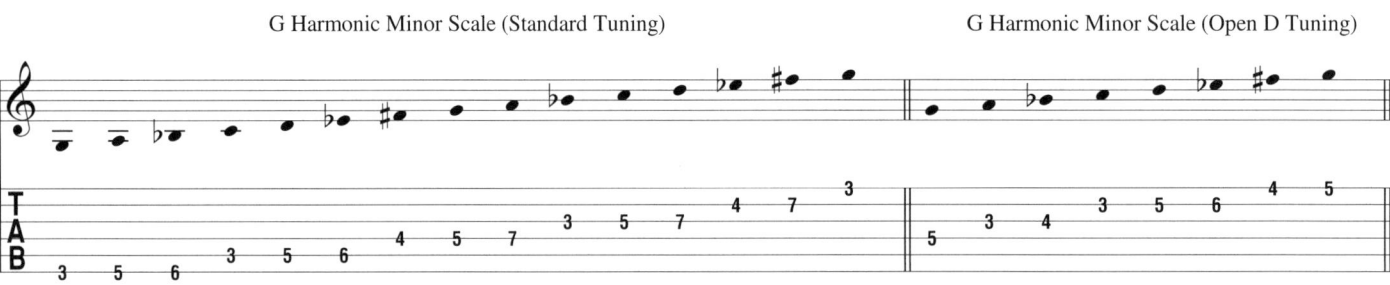

The next example is set up in the same way, but begins the scale on its 5th degree (D). There's no definitive terminology for the various modes of the harmonic scale, but let's call this one "Phrygian ♯3." It's identical to a Phrygian mode, except that its 3rd degree is raised a half step. The sound is extremely exotic and evocative of India; it's also very useful for soloing over an altered dominant chord. Although this mode is used only once (and fleetingly) in "Don't Drink the Water," it makes a strong impression, and combined with Matthews' quasi-Eastern vocal, serves to deepen the dark mystery of the song.

Composition

There are several new approaches employed during "Don't Drink the Water" that bear mentioning. First is the altered tuning employed by the various guitars, pushing the low E string down a whole step to D for added heaviness. The droning of this low pitch throughout adds significantly to the hypnotic, Indian-flavored feeling of the song. Next, there is the use of banjo as both an effective textural addition to the group sound and an important accompanying voice to shadow Matthews' guitar and vocal. Its ability to evoke the world of the Wild West, cowboys, Indians, and pioneer campfires is put to very effective use. Additionally, overdriven electric guitars come in and out, adding feedback-laden dive-bomb screams and kaleidoscopic harmonics. The band has clearly grown comfortable using the studio as a vital part of the compositional process by this time. Each new texture is exploited for maximum effect and is used to paint a complete, engrossing sonic landscape.

It's a very sophisticated song in its simplicity, with everything that's not completely essential stripped away to reveal the emotional core of the music. It sounds easy, but it isn't. This approach demands both the identification of that emotion and the willingness to share it unreservedly—the mark of both a mature songwriter and a confident band unconcerned with personal glories.

TECHNIQUE

The most challenging aspect of "Don't Drink the Water" is translating the banjo part to guitar. Aside from adjusting to the open D tuning, you'll need to use a (glass or metal) slide to recreate the part on your six-string accurately. Playing "bottleneck" slide is a subject that's worthy of an entire book on its own (and there are numerous fine publications on the subject), but there are some guidelines we can get into here without writing a Masters thesis in the process. First, select a guitar with fairly high action. When you wear the slide (on your pinky or ring finger), you'll place it gently on the strings just above the fret wire. Don't press down into the strings or your notes will disappear, replaced by an annoying whine. With a high action guitar, you're much less likely to hit the frets and cause this to happen. Next, flatten the fingers behind the slide so that they're lying across the strings, reducing excess noise. Go for a similar approach with your pick hand: Whichever fingers are not used to hold the pick or pluck the strings can be used for dampening purposes as well. Slide is an art and you'll need a fair amount of patience to build up your technique and especially your intonation. Staying in tune is particularly demanding at first, so proceed slowly and use your ears. Be exacting about it, and leave the slide at home until you have some semblance of skill with it. The banjo licks in "Don't Drink" have an added wrinkle, in that you'll constantly be switching between the slide and notes that are fretted normally. I strongly suggest wearing the slide on your pinky, as this will be the easiest (and least confusing) finger to repeatedly lift off and place onto the fretboard. Let's take a look at a sample measure from the song's verse in which this action is required.

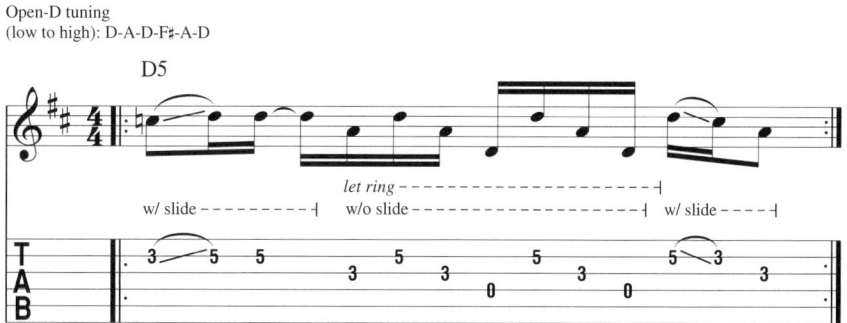

Begin the phrase by sliding up the B string with the bottleneck for the first three notes. Lift your pinky away from the neck, and then use your index and ring fingers to get to the notes on the G and B strings, respectively. On beat 4, return the slide to the neck and finish out the phrase. Don't worry if the whole process feels awkward at first—it *is* awkward. Loop the measure around on itself and repeat it slowly as many times as is necessary to gain a modicum of comfort with this process. There are numerous similar measures throughout the song, as well as many where you won't need the slide at all.

Try playing through the whole thing with the slide on your finger so it's handy when you *do* need it. A phrase like the one below is fairly tricky to execute while you're encumbered in this way.

Start the lick with your middle finger on the B string and your index finger on the G string's 1st fret. Execute the B-string pull-offs by lifting off *and* down with your middle finger, and then bend the G string at the 3rd fret with your ring finger while using your index and middle fingers to aid in the push. You'll need to hold your slide-laden pinky away from the neck while you slowly release the bend to finish out the measure. Again, it's an awkward, difficult technique, but an important one to master if you'd like to become a proficient slide player.

Moving on, there are some interesting sonic effects created by the two overdubbed electric guitars during the song. Guitar 3 makes two brief appearances, each time playing a single distorted, feedback-laden harmonic with the use of the whammy bar to slowly dive-bomb the note. The first harmonic is heard at the end of the second verse and should be played by placing your finger gently on the G string above the 7th fret. Pick the note without pressing down into the string with your fret hand, and then depress the bar slowly until the pitch descends an octave. The second harmonic occurs during the pre-chorus section following the third verse. The process is the same here, except that the harmonic that lies on the D string's 3rd fret should sound as a high A, and should be dropped only five whole steps down to B instead of a full octave. Guitar 4 (in drop-D tuning) has a more extensive role in the song, first entering a measure and a half before the start of the third verse. You'll need both distortion and wah pedals (the latter slowly opening and closing to sweep across the frequency spectrum) to recreate this part, a mixture of 16th notes using harmonics, fretted tones, and the open low E string.

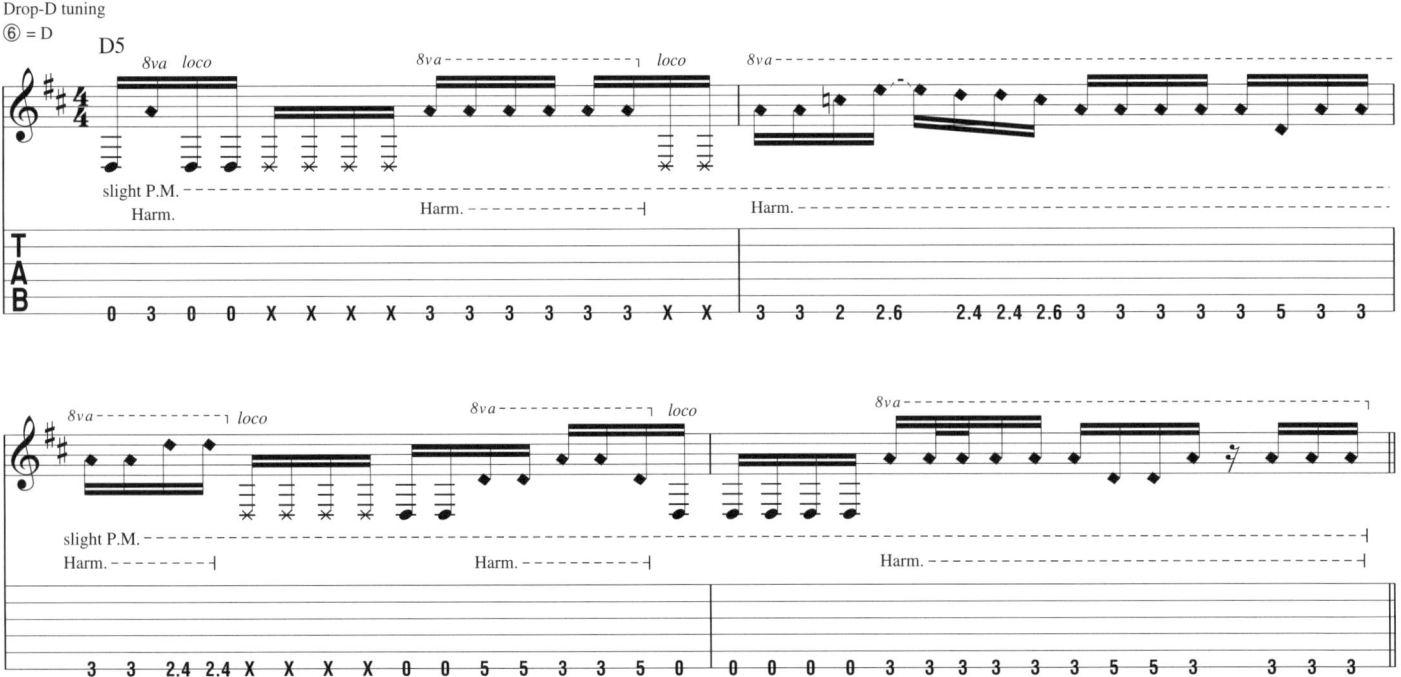

To play the excerpt (and much of the remainder of this part), employ a slight palm mute by resting the bottom of your hand gently across the low E string at the point where it meets the bridge saddle. Create the harmonics by laying a finger gently on the string above the indicated frets, a process that gets a bit tricky when there are numbers like "2.6" and "2.4" in the tab. While these are approximations, you'll need to do a bit of experimenting to find the exact spots on your particular guitar where the pitches required (C and D) can be heard. Fret these pitches in the correct octave (try the 1st and 3rd frets of the D string) so you know exactly what they should sound like, and then poke around a little bit on your low E string to see where exactly on the 2nd fret they can be created. A good amount of rich distortion or overdrive will really help them pop out audibly, as will an amplifier that's cranked up to a fairly high volume. Have fun!

A NOTE ON THE INTERLUDE

After "Don't Drink the Water" fades out, there's a brief interlude—played on twin, standard-tuned, acoustic guitars—that serves as an attractive segue to "Stay." The interlude is in the key of E major and moves among Esus2 (I), C♯sus2 (vi), and Aadd2 (IV) chords, ending on a sustained A5 power chord. There's a single beat of D5, the ♭VII chord in the key, but the fleeting nature of this harmony makes it more of a passing chord than a functional harmony. The lack of 3rds in most of these chords lends a very open-sounding aspect to the interlude. The bulk of the music is played in 5/8 time before shifting to 3/4 for the final four measures. Remember from our earlier discussion on metric modulation, that a single beat in 3/4 is equivalent to two in 5/8? If we were to count out alternating measures of each time signature, it would sound like this.

"1–2–3–4–5–1–and–2–and–3–and–1–2–3–4–5–1–and–2–and–3–and"

Both numbers and words should have equal durations, with the "ands" representing the eighth notes falling between the quarter notes in 3/4. From a technical standpoint, the interlude isn't particularly challenging; try playing the Esus2 and C♯sus2 chords in the Gtr. VI part by using your index finger to barre the top five strings, with your middle finger and pinky taking the notes on the D and G strings, respectively.

DON'T DRINK THE WATER

Written by
David J. Matthews

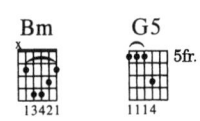

*All gtrs. except where otherwise indicated.

**Two acous. gtrs. arr. for one.

*Banjo arr. for gtr.
Open-D tuning (low to high): D A D F♯ A D

1st Verse
D5

Come out, come out, no——— use in——— hid - ing.———

Riff A

*w/slide
let ring
w/o slide   w/slide   w/o slide   w/slide

Rhy. Fig. 2

*Wear slide on pinky.

w/Riff A (6 times)

(Gtr. I)   (end Rhy. Fig. 2)

*w/Rhy. Fig. 2 (3 times)

Come now, come now,——— can you not——— see?———
*Play all gtr. parts w/slight variations
ad lib when recalled (throughout).

Pre-chorus
G5

So you will lay your arms down.

Gtr. II — Riff B

let ring

Rhy. Fig. 3 (Gtr. I)

w/Riff B (5 times)
D5

(Gtr. I)   (end Rhy. Fig. 3)

w/Rhy. Fig. 3
G5   D5

Yes, I will call this home.

2nd Verse
w/Rhy. Fig. 2 (2 times)
D5

A - way, a - way, you

Gtr. II

let ring

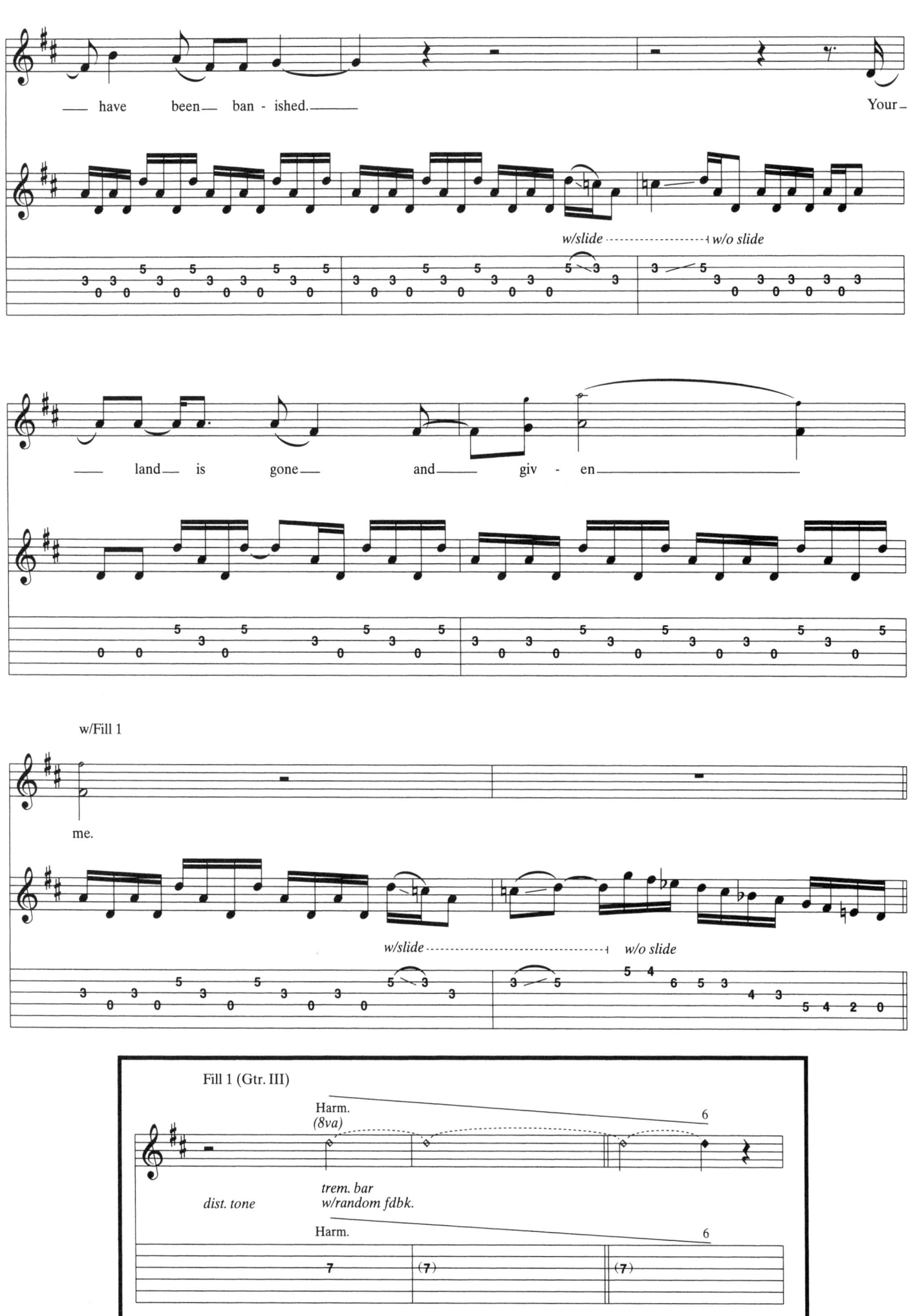

Pre-chorus
w/Rhy. Fig. 3 (2 times)

And here I will spread my wings.

let ring
w/slide

w/o slide *w/slide* *w/o slide*

Yes, I will call this home.

w/slide

w/o slide

Chorus
Bm
Rhy. Fig. 4
(Gtr. I)

What's this— you say?— You feel— a right to—

let ring

G5

(end Rhy. Fig. 4)

re - main?— Then stay and I will bur - y you.—

Full

grad. release

Full

w/Rhy. Fig. 1
D5

w/voc. ad lib (next 3 bars)

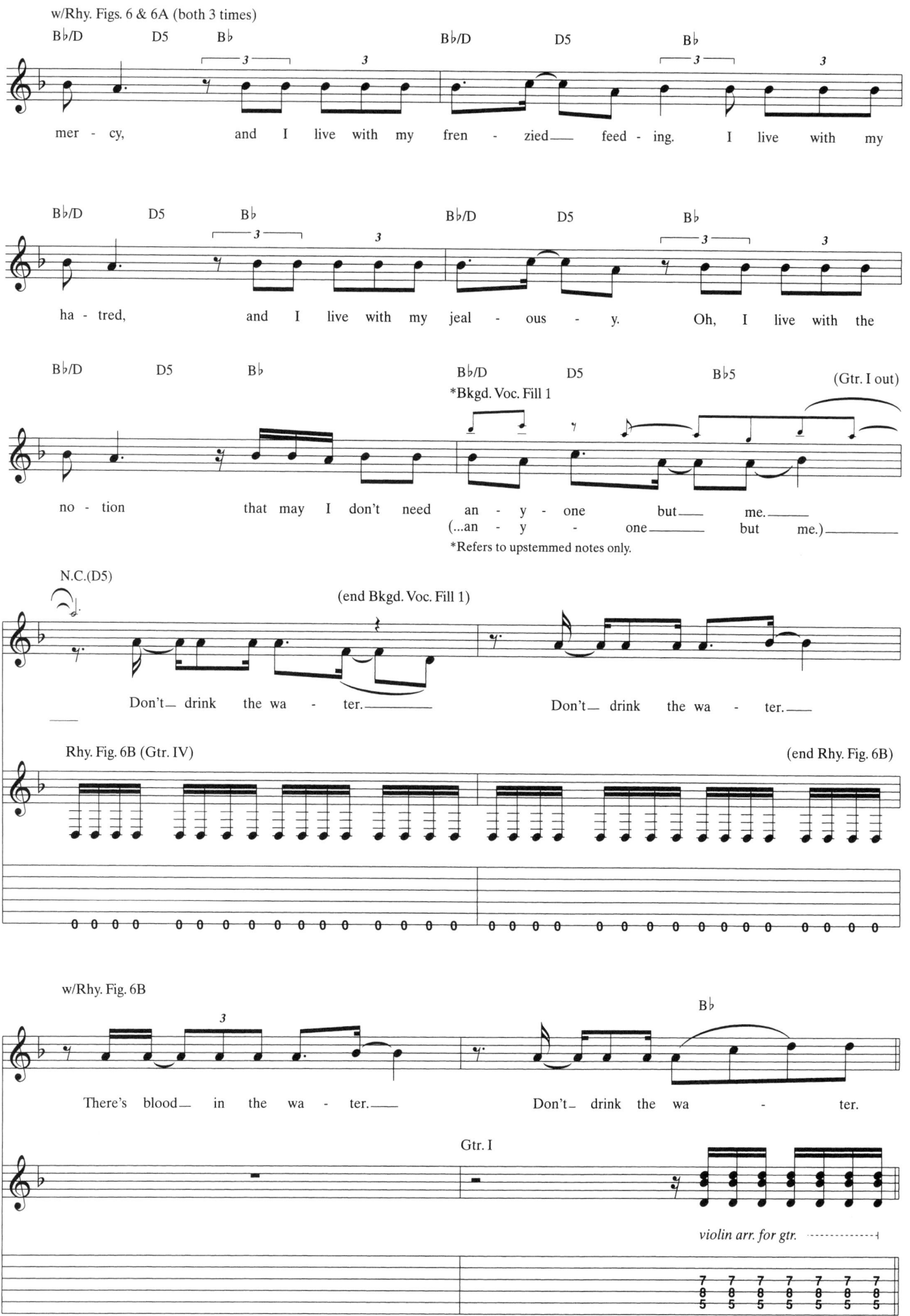

Segue to "Stay"

STAY (WASTING TIME)
From *Before These Crowded Streets* (1998)

Coming close on the heels of "Don't Drink the Water," "Stay" lightens the mood quickly with its free-wheeling, acoustic funk vibe and carefree attitude. Matthews clearly wants his listeners to think, but never too much to stop 'em from getting down and having some fun in the sun.

THEORY

Harmony

"Stay" is fairly uncomplicated harmonically, fittingly so for a song about the uncomplicated pleasures of a sunny afternoon. Played in the key of B♭ major, the song's main riff moves between B♭ (I), Gm (vi), E♭/G (the IV chord in 1st inversion), B♭7 (I7), and A♭ (♭VII) chords. The latter two shift the mode temporarily to B♭ Mixolydian, the 5th mode in the key of E♭. As we've seen numerous times before in Matthews' music, this kind of modal interchange (B♭ Ionian to B♭ Mixolydian) is one of his most favored harmonic devices. It's used very subtly here, as the B♭7 and A♭ chords are fairly brief in duration and don't give the listener a sensation of a true shift in key. In the chorus, the harmony moves from E♭maj7 (no 3rd), an open-sounding form of the IV chord, to an implied F chord, then to Fsus4 (both serving as the V in the key of B♭). The C5 power chord in this section functions as the ii, *sans* 3rds and 7ths (also a wide-open sound). That's pretty much the whole tune, except for a single-note riff played in octaves by the guitars and bass without chordal accompaniment. There is an implied harmonic sequence to this part, however, that seems to move from B♭7 (note the A♭ and D pitches in the sustained back-up vocals) to Cm (with a B chord serving as a chromatic connecter). The final two beats of the riff clearly imply E♭ (IV) moving up to F (V), with the E chord in between serving, similarly, as a chromatic passing chord.

Rhythm

If you've worked your way through this book up to this point, the broken 16th note figures you'll encounter in "Stay" shouldn't give you too much trouble. As always, it's simply a matter of examining each measure and counting it out carefully so you're sure where each note lies. The process is made that much easier by the relative scarcity of rhythmic variety in the song; there's only the two-measure opening riff, the longer chorus section, and the two-measure single-line second interlude mentioned above. About the only thing we haven't seen before is the use of a double dot to begin the chorus. A dot adds half of the rhythmic value of the dotted note to it, so a dotted quarter lasts for one-and-a-half beats—but a double dot repeats the process, adding half the value of the *dot* to the total equation. So, a double dotted quarter note like that which begins the chorus lasts for a quarter note, plus an eighth note, plus a 16th note. The total value of this note is one and three quarters beats, so the second time you strike the E♭maj7 (no3rd) chord, it falls on the last 16th note of beat 2 (the "a" of beat 2).

Scales

While "Stay" includes little in the way of single-note lines (the exception being the highly chromatic, non-scalar second interlude) the chords are based on the B♭ major scale (Ionian mode) and the B♭ Mixolydian mode. While we've looked at both during our discussions of previous songs, take a moment now to play through the three-notes-per-string fingerings shown here in the key of B♭. The only difference between the two is the 7th degree, which is lowered a half step from A to A♭ in the Mixolydian mode, allowing for the creation of both the B♭7 (B♭–D–F–A♭) and A♭ (A♭–C–E♭) chords. Aside from the implied chromatic passing chords in the interlude, these are the only deviations from diatonic harmony used in the song.

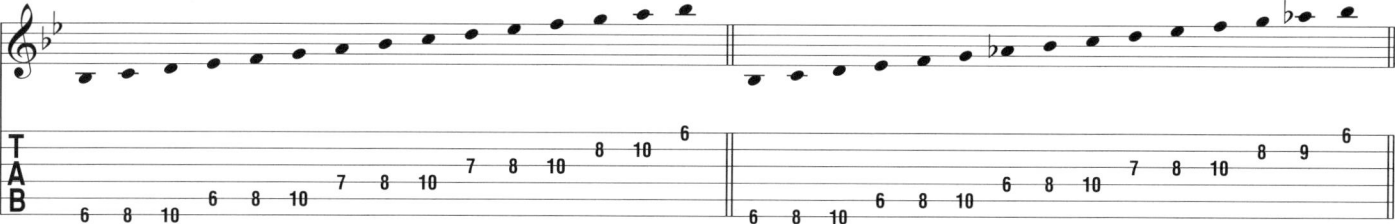

Composition

With "Stay," Matthews demonstrates a finely tuned ability, also present in his work on "Don't Drink the Water," to zero in on the essence of a song. He identifies the core emotion he wishes to express and makes it plain, trimming away any fat that could potentially obscure it. There's confidence in the song's simplicity and in the band's willingness to subvert their individualism for the betterment of the composition and its performance. While they often dazzle otherwise with all manner of tricky playing and turn-on-a-dime arrangements, they dazzle here by their professionalism and unerring support of their leader. Carter Beauford, for example, doesn't worry if we know he's a hell of a drummer (we do)—he just plays the perfect part for the song and helps carry us away to the relaxing, romantic scenario Matthews paints with his lyrics.

It's a simple song structurally, with verses and chorus in the same key (B♭), and no key-shifting bridge to speak of. Once again, Dave's two-measure acoustic riff is the true foundation of the music. The syncopated instrumental interlude does help to break things up nicely and reminds us just who we're listening to. The arrangement is further enriched by the presence of female back-up singers, lending a slick gospel/R&B touch to the proceedings, and by fat saxophone riffs and overdubbed chords created by LeRoi Moore.

Also, don't miss the very organic way in which the song's chorus expands to an unorthodox nine-measure length by the repetition of the word "stay" in a dotted quarter note rhythm that stretches across the barlines. After a conventional 16-measure verse, many songwriters would be content to follow up with a predictable, eight-measure chorus, but Matthews lets the song unfurl naturally instead of trying to force it into any type of preconceived architecture.

TECHNIQUE

Let's take a look at the two layered acoustic guitar parts that accompany the verses throughout the song. Both are shown in the example below.

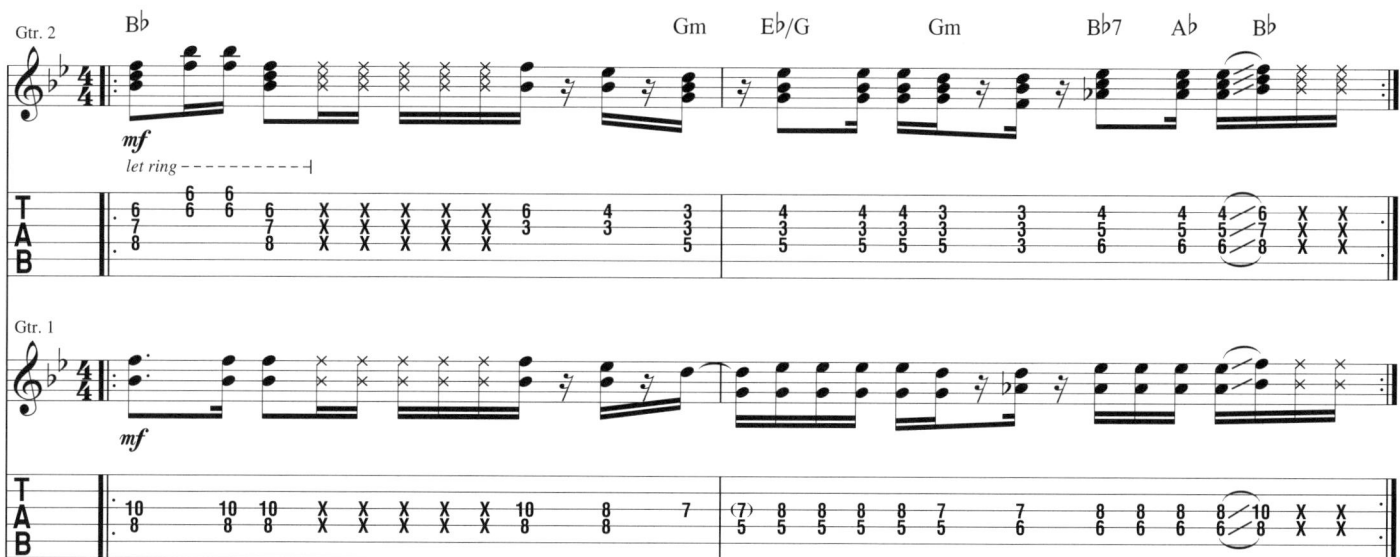

Start with Gtr. 1, the somewhat simpler part shown on the lower staff. Begin with a power chord shape, using your index and ring fingers on the D and G strings, respectively. Shift to an 8th-fret, index-finger barre where indicated, and then move down into 5th position to grab the final 16th note (D) of the first measure with your ring finger. This will put you in position to play all of the 5th-fret notes in measure 2 with your index finger while your pinky gets to the E♭s (G string, 8th fret) on beats 1 and 2. Return to the index- and ring-finger power chord shape on beat 3, sliding it back up to the starting position by pressing down firmly into the strings as you move up the neck. Notice that this is a slur slide, requiring you to pick only the first chord (A♭) and not the target chord (B♭).

The somewhat expanded part played by Gtr. 2 employs two- and three-note chords and fragments. Begin with your ring finger on the D string (8th fret), your middle finger on the G string (7th fret), and your index finger barring the top two strings at the 6th fret. As always, release pressure without lifting your fingers from the strings to create each of the muffled tones indicated by "X" in the notation. At the end of beat 3, use your index and pinky fingers to play the notes on the G and B strings, respectively. The final Gm chord in the measure should be played with the index finger barring these strings at the 3rd fret while your ring finger gets to the root on the D string. Add your middle finger to the B string to play the root of the inverted E♭ triad at the beginning of the second measure. Use your index finger for the 3rd-fret barre at the end of beat 2, and then return to the opening configuration for the A♭ triad that slides back to B♭ to finish the phrase. The guitar parts in the chorus should be fairly self-explanatory, but take care when performing the sliding octaves on the A and G strings that the open D string between cannot be heard (mute it with a flattened index finger). If you want a real challenge, try playing both the upper and lower parts in the second interlude at the same time—a real workout for octaves, 10ths, and other widely split intervals.

STAY (WASTING TIME)

Written by
David J. Matthews, Stefan Lessard
and LeRoi Moore

*Play all gtr. parts w/slight variations ad lib when repeated or recalled (throughout).
**Acous.

1st, 2nd Verses
w/Rhy. Figs. 1 & 1A (both 7½ times)

*Notes to right of slashes played by bass only (throughout).

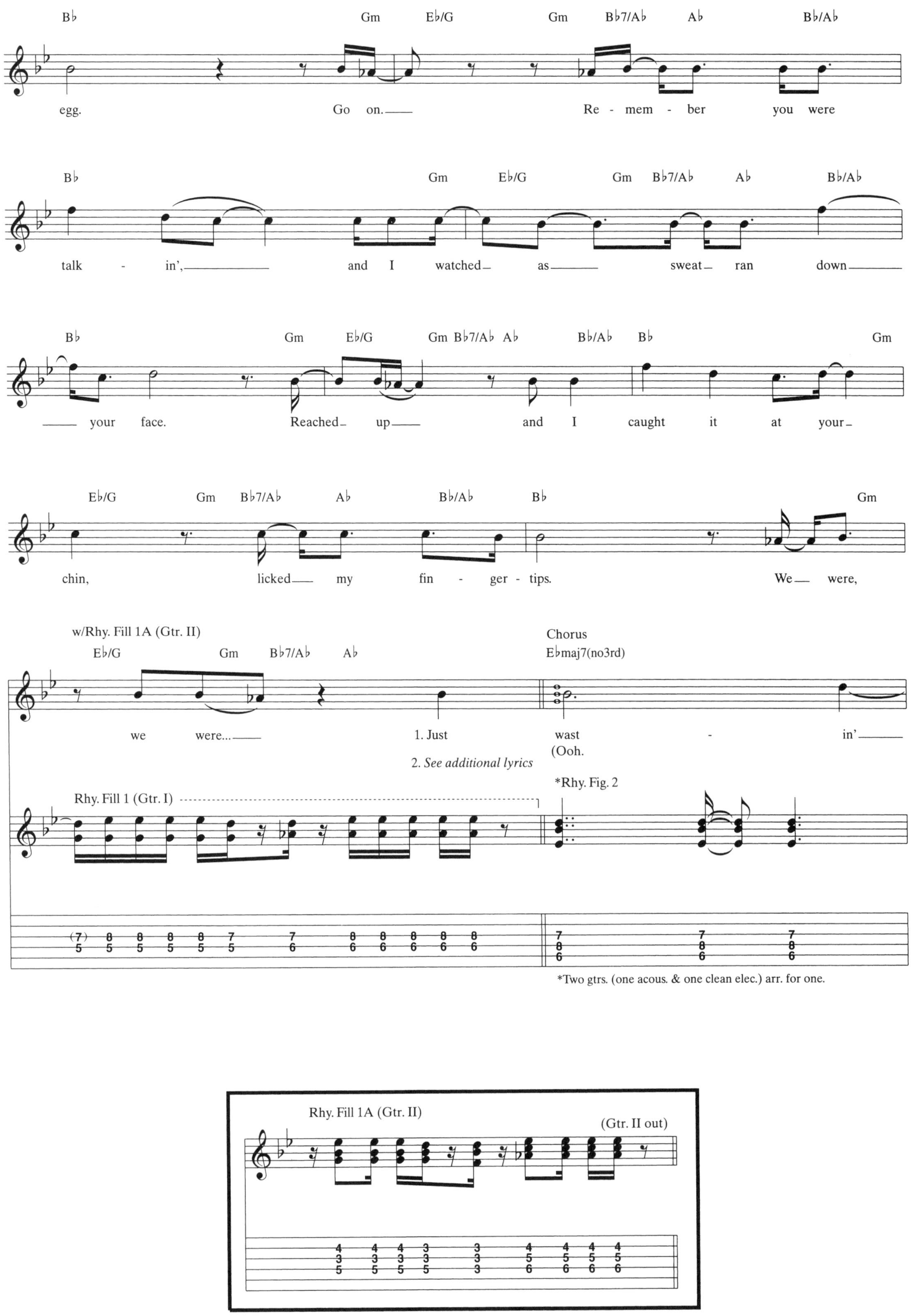

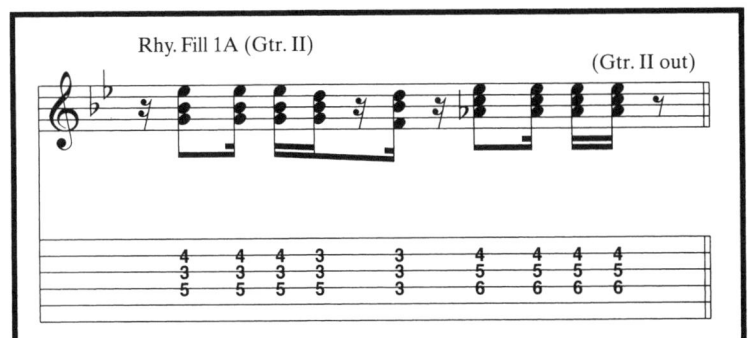

B♭ Gm E♭/G Gm B♭7/A♭ A♭ B♭/A♭
egg. Go on. Re - mem - ber you were
B♭ Gm E♭/G Gm B♭7/A♭ A♭ B♭/A♭
talk - in', and I watched as sweat ran down
B♭ Gm E♭/G Gm B♭7/A♭ A♭ B♭/A♭ B♭ Gm
your face. Reached up and I caught it at your
E♭/G Gm B♭7/A♭ A♭ B♭/A♭ B♭ Gm
chin, licked my fin - ger - tips. We were,
w/Rhy. Fill 1A (Gtr. II)
E♭/G Gm B♭7/A♭ A♭
Chorus
E♭maj7(no3rd)
we were... 1. Just wast - in'
(Ooh.
2. See additional lyrics
Rhy. Fill 1 (Gtr. I)
*Rhy. Fig. 2
*Two gtrs. (one acous. & one clean elec.) arr. for one.
Rhy. Fill 1A (Gtr. II)
(Gtr. II out)

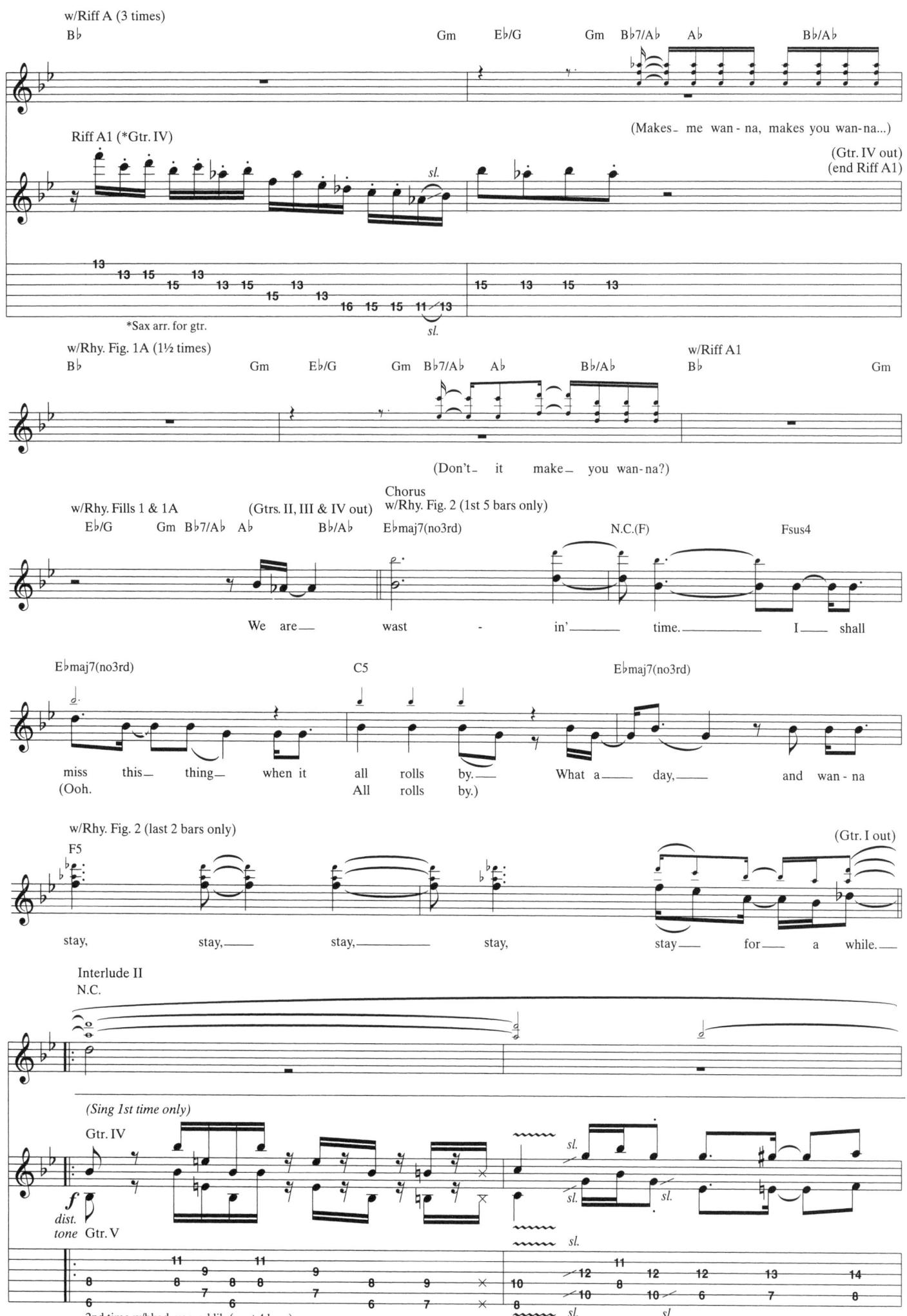

Additional Lyrics

2. Well, then later on the sun began to fade.
And then, well, the clouds rolled over our heads,
And it began to rain.
Oh, we were dancin', mouths open,
We were splashin' in the tongue taste.
And for a moment, this good time would never end.
You and me, you and me...

2nd Chorus:
Just wastin' time.
I was kissin' you, you were kissin' me, love,
From a good day into the moonlight.
Now a night so fine makes us wanna
Stay, stay, stay, stay, stay for a while. *(To Interlude I)*

THE SPACE BETWEEN
From *Everyday* (2001)

A huge hit from 2001's triple platinum smash *Everyday*, "The Space Between" is a classic pop power ballad with a distinctly Matthewsian touch. It's played on a baritone guitar designed by luthier Jerry Jones, so you'll need to tune all six of your strings down a perfect 4th (two-and-a-half steps) unless you're one of the very rare few who also have access to such an unusual instrument. Be prepared for a little weirdness from your conventional axe, however, as it's doubtless unaccustomed to such a slack setting of the strings. A heavier gauge will definitely help here, as will a little time to allow the instrument to "reorient" itself. Take care when tuning back up to standard pitch as well, as this may all prove to be a bit stressful for both strings and neck.

THEORY

Harmony

Please be aware that in both our discussion of this song and in the actual transcription, all music is shown or referred to as if it were played in standard tuning. In other words, the open-position A chord in the pick-up is referred to as A rather than the E chord it really is as a result of dropping each string down a perfect 4th. Put another way, if you put on the album and play along without retuning, your first change will be from E to Dsus2. Okay, now that we've gotten that out of the way, let's talk about the harmony.

"The Space Between" is in the key of D and uses just a few basic chords to get its message across. The A to Gsus2 progression that begins in the pickup and continues throughout the verse is simply V moving to IV (in a patented Matthews voicing that omits the 3rd in favor of the 2nd to give it more of a wide-open sound). In the chorus, D (I) moves to D/C♯ (the I major 7 chord in 3rd inversion, with its 7th degree in the bass), down to Gmaj7/B (the IV major 7 chord in 1st inversion, with the 3rd in the bass), up to A/C♯ (the V chord in 1st inversion). This gives us a strong, step-wise root movement that resists an overused pattern when it turns around and ascends back towards the tonic. At the end of the second chorus, note the change in key signature to one sharp (the key of G). The bridge that follows is really in E minor, the relative minor key of G, so the E5, D5, A/C♯, C5, and B5 chords in this section represent i, ♭VII, IV (again in 1st inversion), ♭VI, and V. Once again, the root movement is strong and scalar. The B♭5 chord at the end of the bridge represents the ♭V chord in E minor, with the D melody note sung by Matthews above it dovetailing nicely with the impending shift back to the key of D major—a skillful use of common tones.

Rhythm

"The Space Between" is one of the easiest Dave Matthews Band songs you'll encounter as regards rhythm. As always, take a moment to examine each section and be sure you know which beat each phrase begins and ends on. After all of the syncopated, broken 16th note figures that we've examined so far, this song should be a walk in the park. The verse riff simply repeats an eighth note phrase beginning on the third beat of every other measure which is tied over into the measures that follow, while the chorus accompaniment combines sustained chordal pads with a simple line of predominantly eighth notes. The syncopated octaves in the bridge go by slowly and should be a breeze after a white-knuckle workout like "Rapunzel."

Scales

The only single-note lines in "The Space Between" are those played by Ballard during the chorus and sung by Matthews throughout. Each is based strictly on the D major scale (D–E–F♯–G–A–B–C♯). The octave riff that accompanies the bridge is made up of notes from the E Aeolian mode (E–F♯–G–A–B–C–D), with the C♯ in the line serving as a passing, chromatic connector. This pitch can also be found in the E Dorian mode

(E–F♯–G–A–B–C♯–D). It should be readily apparent that there is a mere one-note difference between these two modes: the 6th degree. Both are favored choices (in addition to the minor pentatonic scale) for soloing over minor chords in a rock setting. The position of the 6th has a fairly substantial impact in the overall sound of the mode against a minor chord. Have an obliging friend strum an Em or Em7 chord while you play through these modes and you'll hear the distinct difference that one note can make. Both modes are shown in three-notes-per-string fingerings beginning on the low E and A strings in the example below.

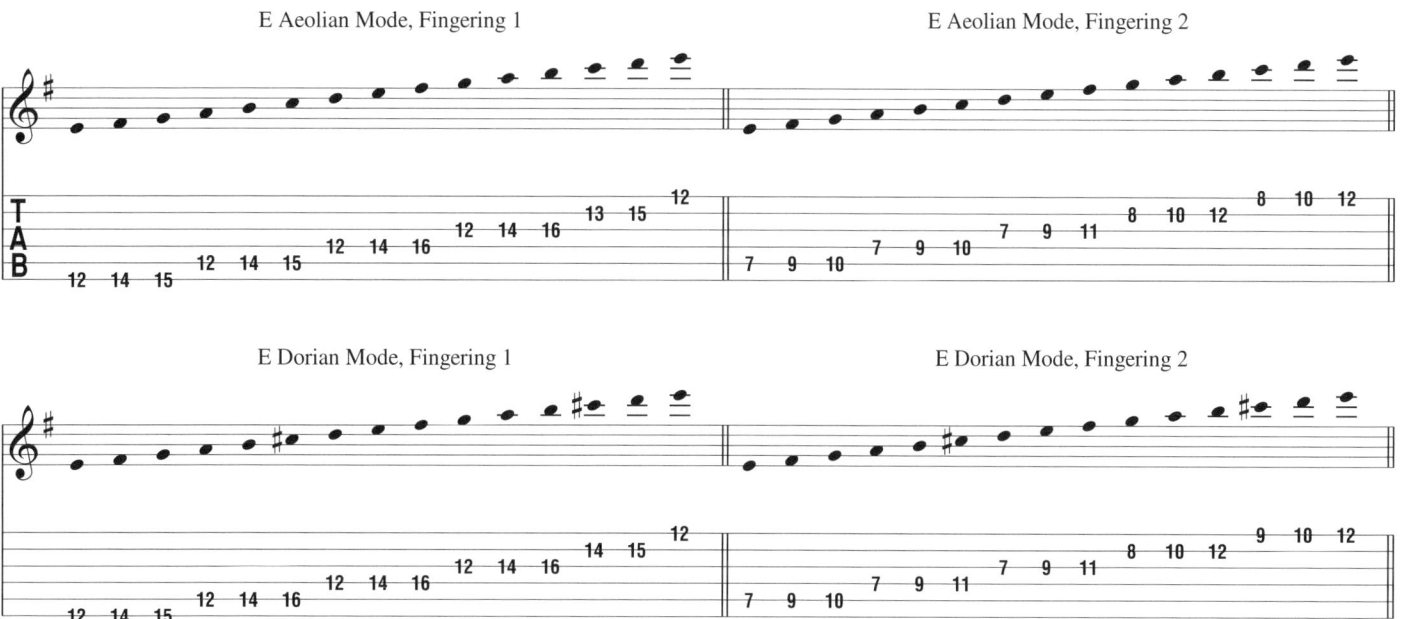

Composition

Contrary to the work of many bands and songwriters, Matthews and his mates have no problems with doing the occasional simple song, rather than upping the ante in terms of flashy arrangements and complex harmonic structures with each and every tune. Much like "Don't Drink the Water" and "Stay," "The Space Between" eschews the extraneous for a focused, emotional statement that's just about as direct as you can get.

Dave's very personal take on the traditional "power ballad" still includes a handful of wrinkles that help to separate it from other songs in this particular bag. From an arranging standpoint, there's the use of the baritone guitar—a real oddity—and the addition of keyboard parts. LeRoi Moore and Boyd Tinsley are mostly absent, which only helps to put Matthews' lonely voice and stark words into deeper relief (just because you have a violinist and a saxophonist doesn't mean that they have to be playing all of the time). One thing that stands out from a harmonic perspective is the key change in the bridge. While the transition to the key of the IV is common (which is what happens here if you look at the key signatures), moving to its relative minor is not. In other words, if we were to go from D major to a bridge in G major, no one would bat an eye. In "The Space Between," however, we're really going from D major to the key of E minor, which isn't something you hear very often. Traditionally, songs in a major key begin their bridge on the ii chord (D major moving to Em), but they're nearly always in the process of working themselves back to I. That's not the case here, as the E5 chord (the true i chord in the new key) descends to D5 and keeps going right past it, so the listener never registers the D as the tonic. It's yet another example of Matthews' wonderful quirkiness, which we've seen demonstrated time and again in his continued willingness to shift to unpredictable, non-traditional places in the harmony.

Because of the easy nature of the song, "The Space Between" should present little technical difficulty once yet get used to the slackness of your strings (if you've tuned down the full two-and-a-half steps, that is). For the verses, use a 2nd-fret, index-finger barre to play the A chords, and then play the root of the Gsus2 chord with your middle finger, flattened slightly to mute the open A string. Use a similar approach for the sustained D/C♯ and Gmaj7/B chords in the chorus. The tempo is slow enough that you should be able to play the single-note lines in this section, and then jump right back into the lower-register chords played by Gtr. 1 if you choose to. In the bridge, play the descending octave figures with your index finger taking the A-string notes (muting the open D string), and your ring finger or pinky—whichever is more comfortable—taking the notes on the G string. Notice that the slides here are *not* slur slides like those we've seen before, so be sure to pick both the notes at the bottom *and* the top of each slide.

THE SPACE BETWEEN

Written by
David J. Matthews and Glen Ballard

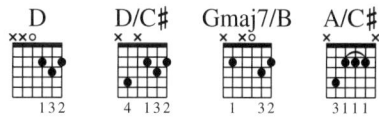

All gtrs.: Tune down 2 1/2 steps:
(low to high) B–E–A–D–F#–B

* Baritone gtr. arr. for standard gtr.; doubled throughout (music sounds a 4th lower than indicated).

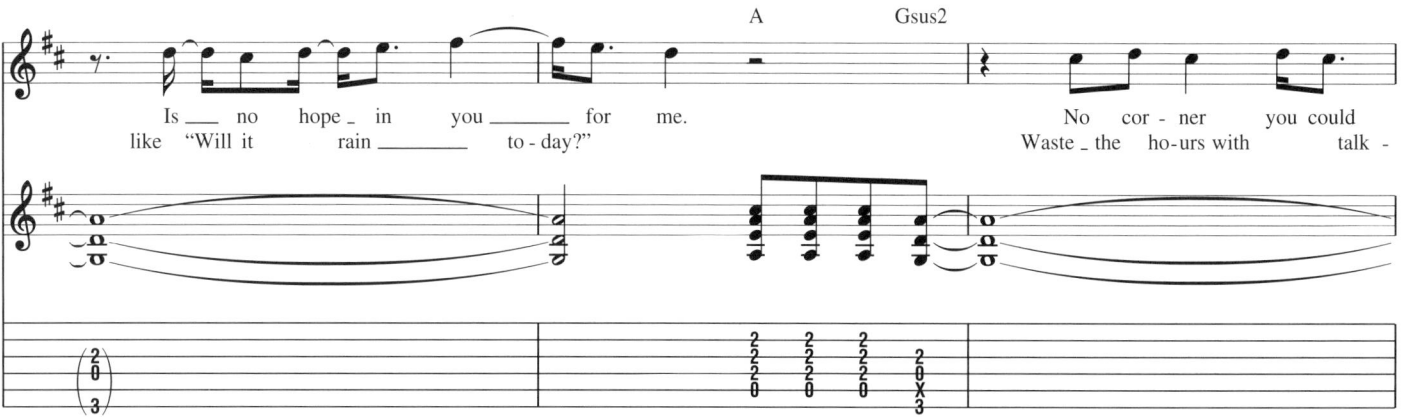

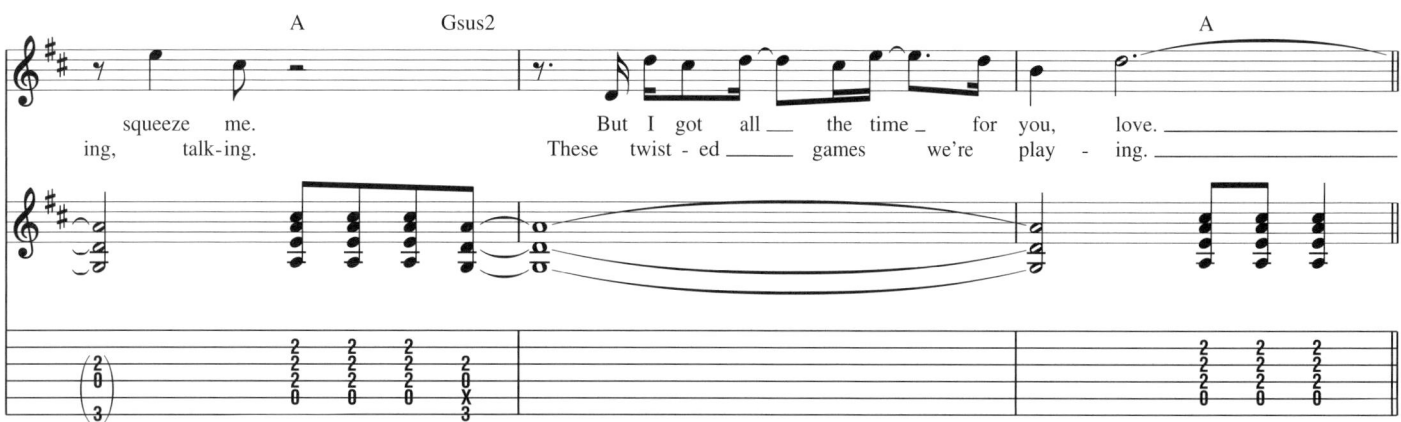

Bridge

Look at us spin-ning out in the mad - ness of a roll - er coast - er. You know you went off like the dev-il in a

Gtr. 4   Fill 1   End Fill 1

Gtr. 1

* Sax arr. for gtr.

Gtr. 4: w/ Fill 1

church, in the mid-dle of a crowd - ed room. All we can do, my love, is hope we don't take this ship down.

Gtr. 1

Chorus

Gtr. 2: w/ Rhy. Fig. 1 (6 times)
Gtr. 3: w/ Riff A (6 times)
Gtr. 1 & band tacet

The space be - tween where you smile and hide, that's where you'll find

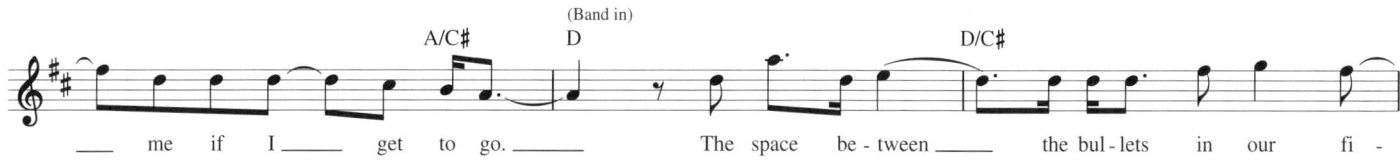

(Band in)

me if I get to go. The space be - tween the bul - lets in our fi -

Outro-Chorus
Gtr. 2: w/ Rhy. Fig. 1 (2 times)
Gtr. 3: w/ Riff A (2 times)
Band tacet

* Gtr. 5

* Bass arr. for gtr.

Repeat and fade

Gtr. 2: w/ Rhy. Fig. 1
Gtr. 3: w/ Riff A
Gtr. 5: w/ Riff B (4 times)

Gtr. 5: w/ Riff B (2 times)

GREY STREET
From *Busted Stuff* (2002)

A long-time staple of live performances, "Grey Street" had its official release on 2002's *Busted Stuff*. In keeping with much of the band's work from this period, it's a streamlined pop song that places Matthews front and center and stays away from the tricky transitions and more complex structures heard on earlier albums. Expansive jams showing off the group's virtuoso abilities have been mostly relegated to the live stage by this point, with their studio work showing off a more tightly focused sense of pop/rock craftsmanship than ever before.

THEORY

Harmony

"Grey Street" is in the key of D major and remains entirely diatonic throughout the tune. The verse moves back and forth between Bm, G, Aadd4, and D/F♯ chords, which represent the vi, IV, V, and I chords, respectively. The tonic chord (D) is played in its 1st inversion, with its 3rd degree in the bass, throughout this section. In the choruses, the harmony moves from Bm (vi) to A (V) to D (I) and G (IV), each played in familiar voicings that utilize the open strings whenever possible.

Rhythm

Because of the very basic construction of "Grey Street," there are only two rhythmic figures—those found in the verse and chorus—with which you'll have to acquaint yourself. Let's look at the verse first, shown in the example below as a series of rhythm slashes that allow us to put our full focus on this aspect of the music without concerning ourselves with nailing specific pitches on the fretboard.

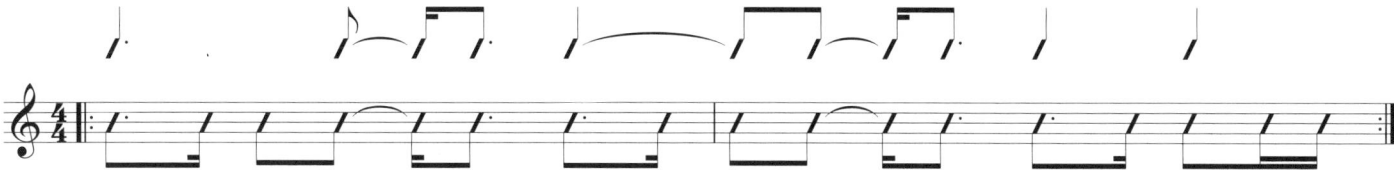

The first thing you may notice here is that the part is a little busier than the figure played by the rest of the band, which has more of a stuttering, stop-start feeling. That rhythm is shown above the staff to allow for easy comparison between the two parts. Before trying Dave's part on your guitar, tap out its rhythms slowly on a tabletop while tapping your foot in a steady quarter note pulse. Yes, we've done this before, but it's an invaluable way of getting to know exactly where each note falls in the measure, and it shouldn't be neglected unless you're such a wiz with 16th note and dotted rhythms that you read them perfectly the first time, every time. The rhythms in the chorus riff are simpler and less syncopated, with a single tie in the middle of each measure and no dots at all. The only thing to watch out for here is on beat 3, where the tie from the previous 16th note obscures the downbeat and the position of the eighths and 16ths is reversed.

Scales

"Grey Street" is yet another Matthews composition that stays away from single-note lines in favor of propulsive chordal riffs that support Dave's melodic vocals and poignant lyrics. All the materials here—chords and melody—are derived from the D major scale (D–E–F♯–G–A–B–C♯), which was examined earlier in our discussion of "Warehouse." Flip back to those pages for a bit of a refresher if necessary. You won't need to play the scale to get through "Grey Street," but it's always a good idea to have a grasp of the source material for any particular song you're learning.

Composition

Structurally, "Grey Street" is about as basic as a pop tune gets, simply alternating verses and choruses throughout. The song has neither a bridge nor a single key change, but it's still a highly personal statement and in many ways has more emotional impact by virtue of the dearth of instrumental distractions. It also marks another instance of Dave's use of pedal points, with the repeated note (D) placed on the inside of the harmony throughout the verses. This inner pedal tone, played on the open D string, rings out while notes move up and down on both upper (G) and lower (low E) strings, typical of Matthews' unique approach to chord voicings for guitar.

From an arranging standpoint, the use of violin and saxophone to augment the main instrumental line really thickens things up, making the band sound much bigger than just five men, while the 12-string guitar introduces a new sonic wrinkle to the mix. LeRoi Moore's use of both tenor and soprano saxophones adds further variety to the overall timbre palette. Also deserving of mention is the powerful use of repetition near the song's end; the material is strong, and picks up an almost elemental strength as it loops around on itself while the band ratchets up the intensity through Beauford's fills, Moore's wailing riffs, Lessard's highly varied bass figures, and Matthews' impassioned cries.

TECHNIQUE

Dave Matthews' use of a 12-string guitar on "Grey Street" helps to lend a brilliant, high-octave sheen to his parts, but they all work just as well on a conventional six string, and he has been known to perform the song live on that din-strument. The example below includes the two-measure riff he plays at the beginning of the song and through all of its verses. The chorus employs four very basic chord shapes and shouldn't present any particular technical difficulties.

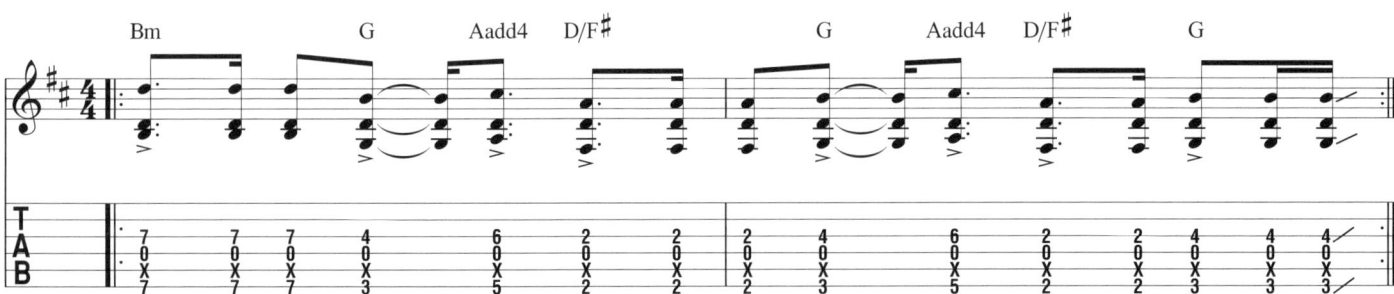

While there are a number of possible fingering choices here, Matthews plays the Bm shape with his middle finger on the low E string and his ring finger on the G string above. An identical arrangement is used for the D/F♯ chord, while the G and Aadd4 chords are played with the index and ring fingers on the low E and G strings, respectively. Throughout the riff, whichever finger happens to be on the low E string at the time is also recruited to mute the open A string. It should be noted that Matthews sometimes plays the Aadd4 chord by striking the open A and D strings while using his ring finger to get to the C♯ on the G string's 6th fret.

GREY STREET

Written by
David J. Matthews

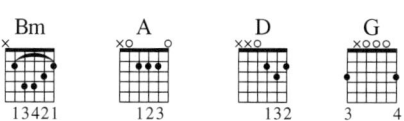

Intro
Moderately slow ♩ = 108

Gtr. 1 (12-str. acous.)

Rhy. Fig. 1

End Rhy. Fig. 1

(4th time:) 1. Oh, ___

Play 4 times

Verse

Gtr. 1: w/ Rhy. Fig. 1 (8 times)

look   at   how ___ she   lis - tens,   she ___ says   noth -
wish - es   it ___ was   dif - f'rent,   she prays   to   God ___
stran - ger, speaks ___ out - side her door, says, ___ "Take what

- ing   of   what   she   thinks.   She   just ___ goes
___ most   ev - 'ry   night.   And   though ___ she
you   can   from   your   dreams.   Make   them   as

stum - bling ___ through her   mem - o - ries,   star - ing   out ___
swears   it ___ does - n't   lis - ten,   There's   still   a   hope ___
real   as ___ an - y - thing.   Oh,   it -'d   take   the   work ___

___ on - to   Grey ___ Street. ___   And   she ___ thinks, "Hey. ___
___ in   her   it   might. ___   She   says, ___ "I   pray, ___
___ out   of   the   cour - age." ___   But   she ___ says, "Please. ___

© 2002 David J. Matthews (ASCAP)
International Copyright Secured   All Rights Reserved

153

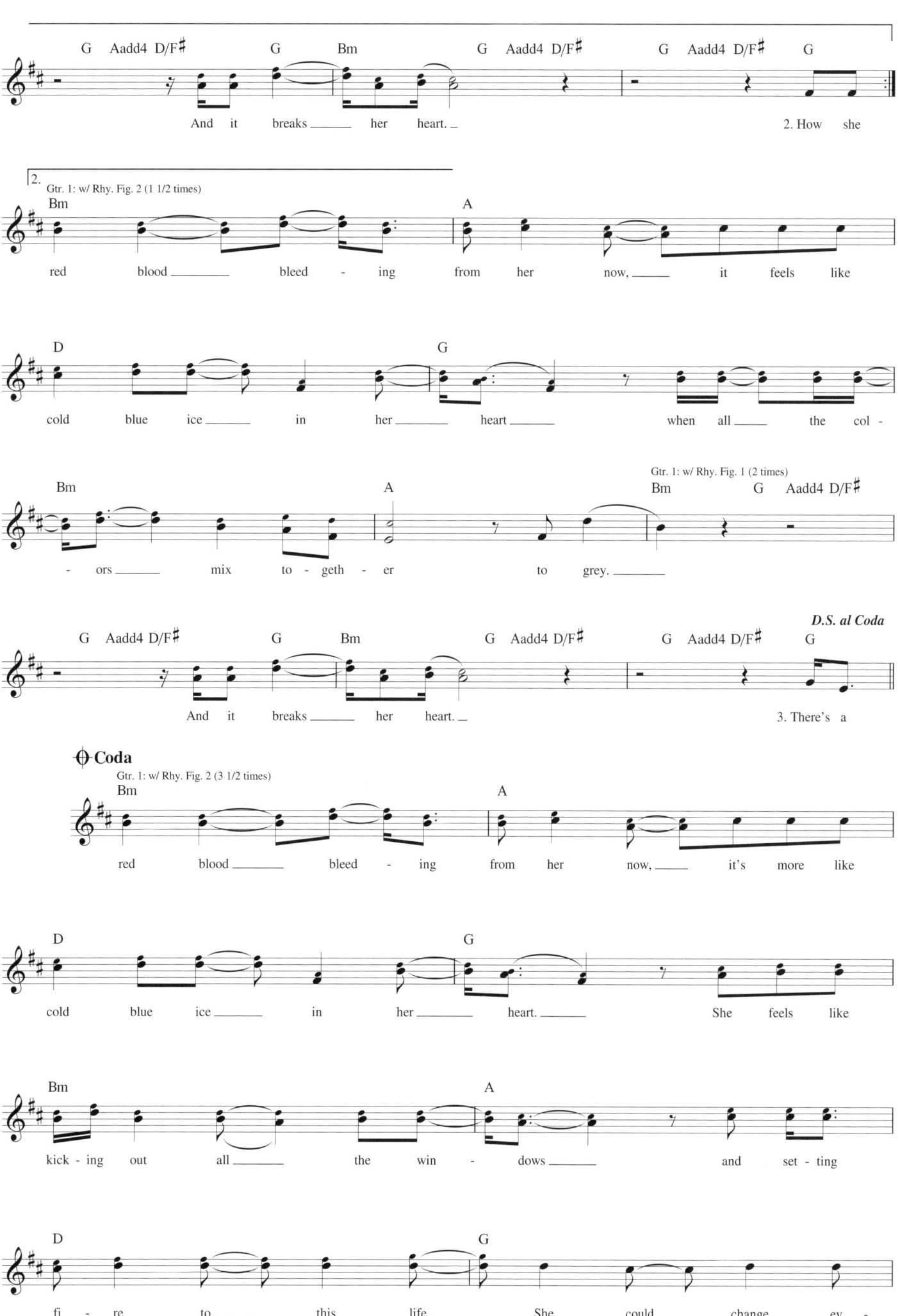

155

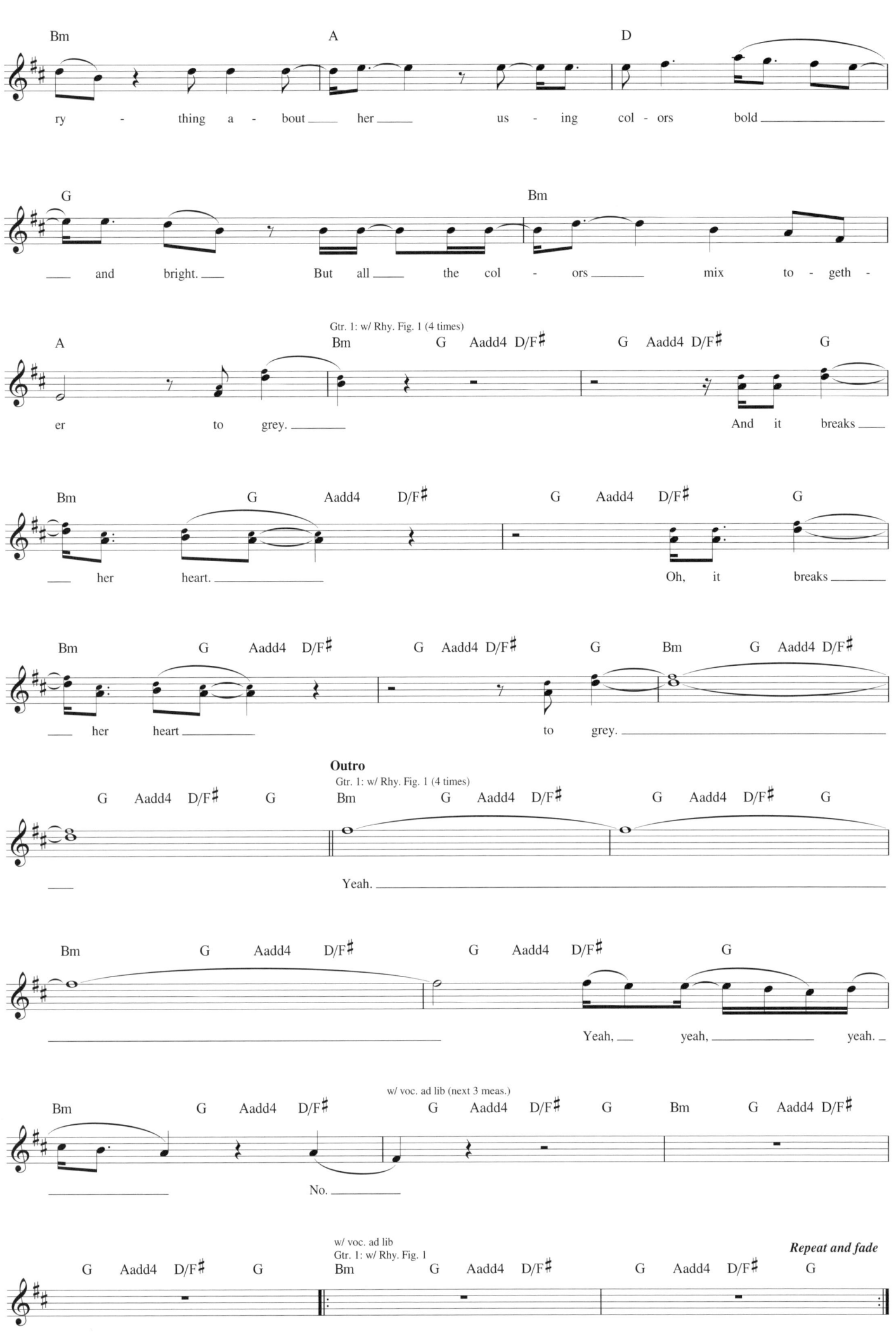

Outro

Repeat and fade

AMERICAN BABY
From *Stand Up* (2005)

"American Baby" is an intriguing mix of musical simplicity and a highly emotional, politically charged message. All in all, it makes for a tightly focused, effective song.

THEORY

Harmony

"American Baby" is written in the key of D major (two sharps) but avoids the tonic chord throughout the song, so it's also possible to look at it as being in B Aeolian (the relative minor key). If we take the former approach, Bm, A, and G represent the vi, V, and IV chords, with the briefly heard F♯m representing the III chord in D major. If we look at Bm as the tonic (i) chord, A, G, and F♯m represent VII, VI, and V, respectively. It's not entirely unusual to have this dual perspective on a song, because while all of the chords and melody notes can be found in the D major scale, we never hear a D major chord or the V chord (A) resolving up to the tonic. The first four tones of the single-note line that accompanies the bridge outline a Bm7 chord, reinforcing the Bm chord as the tonic in our ears. Either way, it's a harmonically basic song that includes primarily three chords.

Rhythm

"American Baby," with its consistent eighth note pulse, may be the easiest song in this book from a rhythmic standpoint. If you made it through the myriad time signature changes and metric modulations of "Rapunzel," or the highly syncopated 16th note figures of "Too Much," this one should seem like a walk in the park. Each eighth note phrase, including the verse riff, violin line, bridge accompaniment, and outro figure, comes in two-measure chunks that sometimes cross the barline but nonetheless allow for fairly easy digestion. Just count out each measure, watch out for ties and dots, and you'll sail through the song smoothly.

Scales

The D major scale and its 6th mode, B Aeolian, provide the source material for the chords and lines in "American Baby," and are explored in detail in the discussion of "Warehouse" earlier in this book. The song's bridge is built on the B Aeolian mode in its 2nd-position, A-string fingering, and begins with an *arpeggio* of a Bm7 chord. An arpeggio is simply the tones of any given chord (in this case, 1, ♭3, 5, and ♭7) played individually instead of simultaneously. On guitar we often play arpeggios by holding down a chord and plucking the strings one at a time while they are allowed to ring, but the notes can be played in a more discrete sequence as well. The exercise below starts with the Bm7 arpeggio that begins the bridge, and then continues multidirectionally through the various 7th chord arpeggios found in the mode. Stay strictly in 2nd position throughout (your index finger taking all of the notes on the 2nd fret, your middle finger taking those on the 3rd, etc.) except for the shift upwards for the first four notes in the fifth measure. Try applying the same set of permutations to any and all of the scales and modes you use, and you'll soon find yourself with an improved technical command and deeper understanding of these vital musical building blocks.

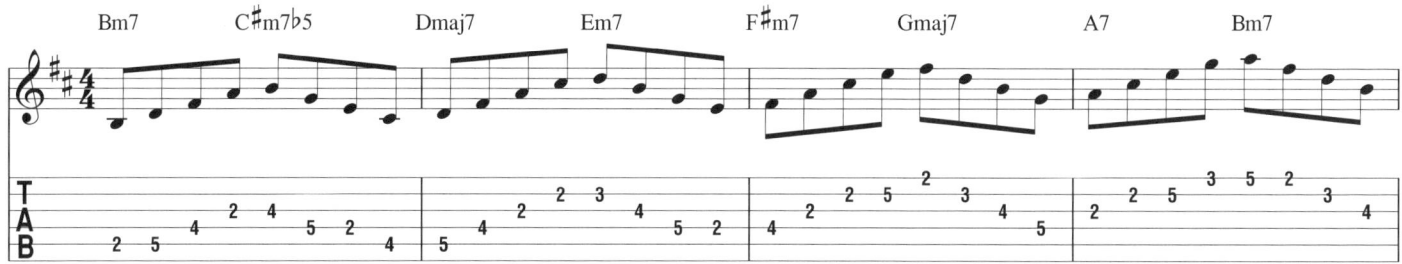

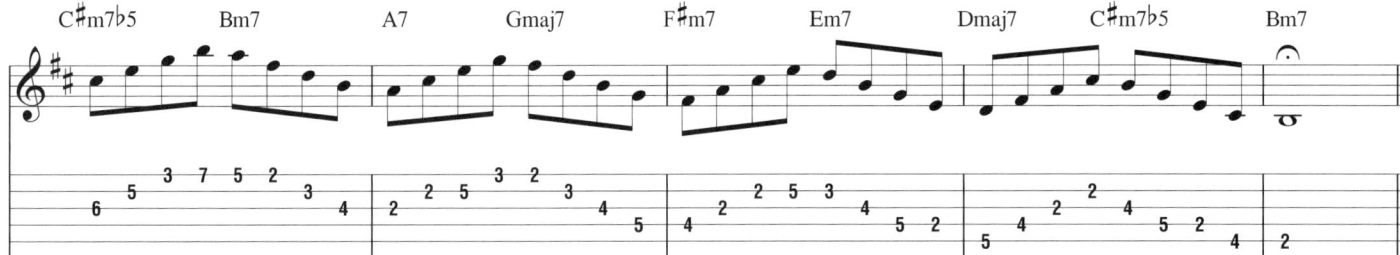

Composition

"American Baby" is one of the few songs in the Dave Matthews Band repertoire that doesn't rely heavily on one of Dave's acoustic riffs as the backbone of the piece, beginning instead with Boyd Tinsley's pizzicato violin line. There's a somewhat child-like, music box aspect to the motif that's suggestive of a certain wide-eyed innocence and American naiveté very much in keeping with the song's lyrics. It possesses many of the hallmarks of Matthews compositional style, including a bridge that stays in the same harmonic territory (B minor) as the rest of the song, the use of repetition to intensify emotion, and some typical chord voicings that omit some tones (mostly 5ths) in favor of others (the octave-doubled 3rds in the Bm, A, and G chords).

TECHNIQUE

"American Baby" isn't particularly hard to play and should be a fairly quick learn. The opening violin line has been transcribed for guitar and is easily played in the 7th-position B Aeolian–mode fingering covered earlier (see "Warehouse"). The main guitar riff in the verse is shown below and moves among G, Bm, and A chords.

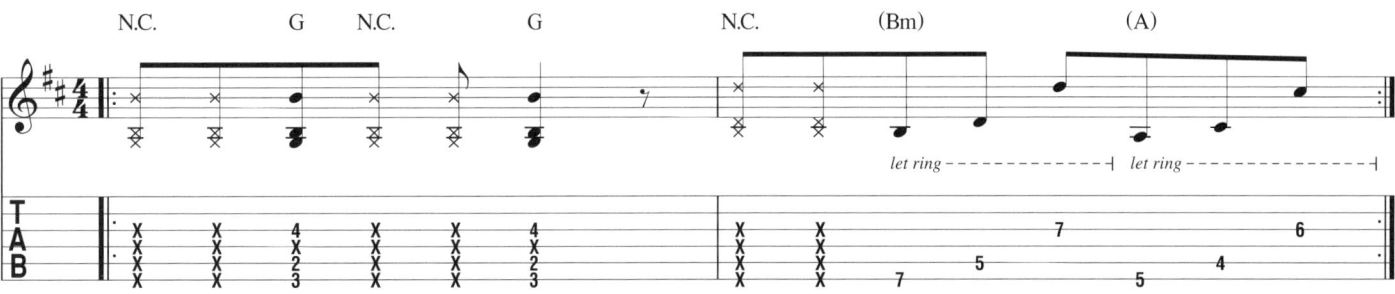

This is a typical Dave Matthews riff on a number of levels: the chords are "incomplete" (lacking 5ths but doubling the 3rds in octaves), muted tones lend shape and accent to the phrase, and there's an open string in the middle of everything that needs to be silenced. The G chord in the first measure and the A shape in the second should be played with your middle, index, and ring fingers on the low E, A, and G strings, respectively, while the Bm shape should be played with your ring, index, and pinky fingers. Be sure to allow each three-note sequence to ring out as you climb back down toward G in the second measure. The muted chords should be played by simply releasing pressure without lifting your fingers from the strings, while the D string should be silenced by your index finger throughout the phrase.

The chorus is a bit more ornately orchestrated, with the violin line (Gtr.1) joined by a smoothly distorted guitar (3) playing a repeated high F♯ that serves as an upper pedal point throughout the section. Meanwhile, the verse riff is transformed into a crunchy variation played by Gtr. 5 (retaining the same chord shapes from the earlier section), and twin guitars add a single-note lick to the mix. This odd little phrase, full of subtle rhythmic variations, should be played with your pinky on the 9th fret of the D string, allowing you to stay in position and use your index and middle fingers for the 6th- and 7th-fret G-string notes above. Play the entire bridge lick in 2nd position except for the middle finger slur slide up the B string at the end of the phrase; don't pick the E on the 5th fret.

AMERICAN BABY

Written by
Dave Matthews Band and Mark Batson

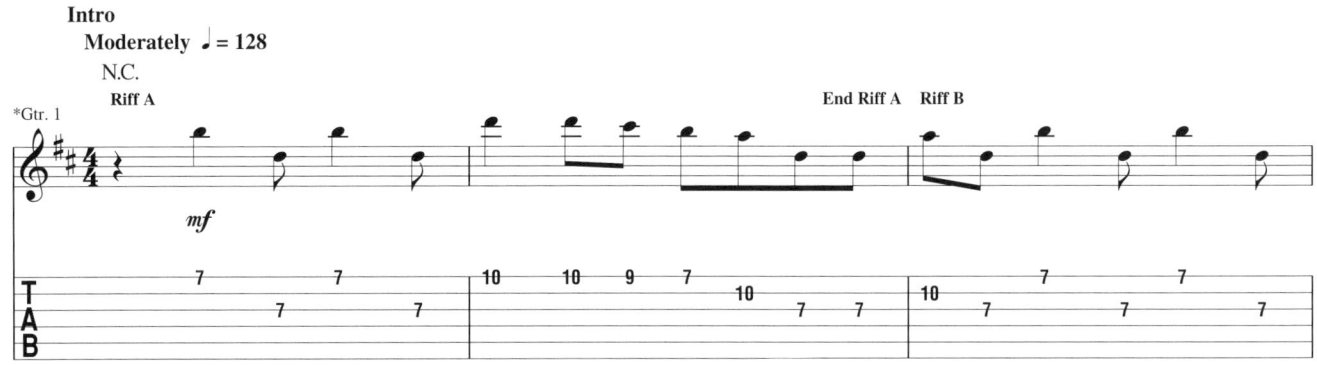

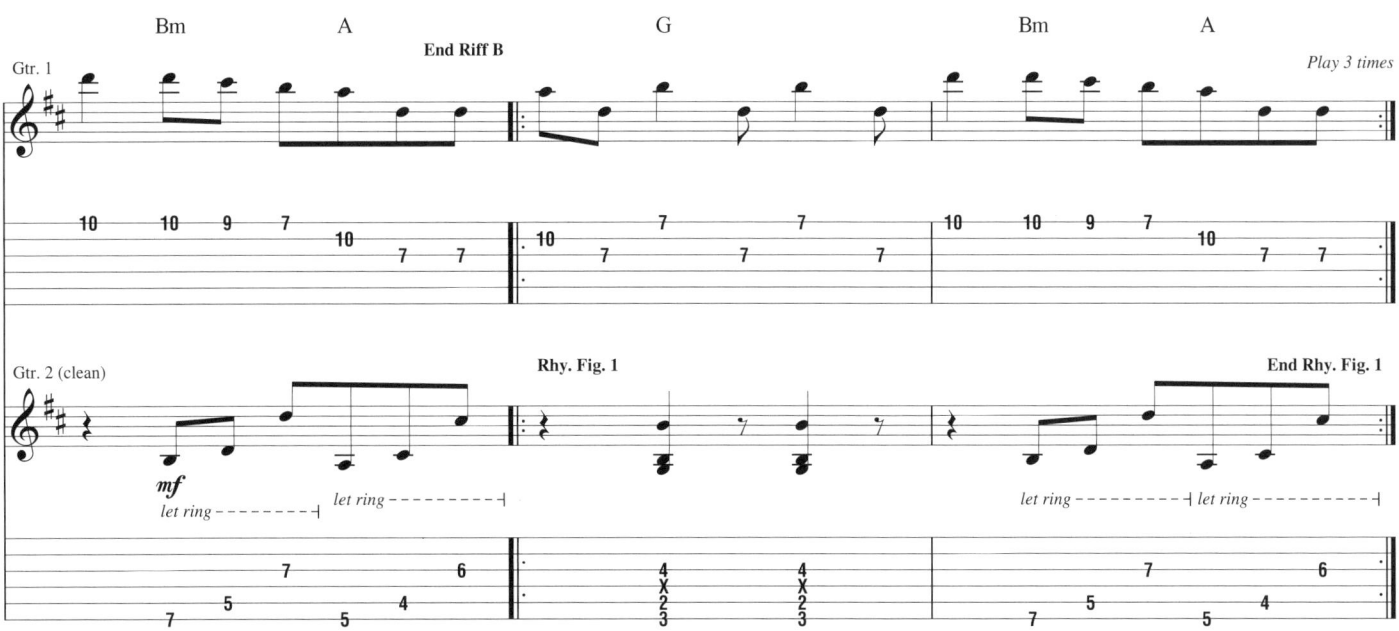

Verse

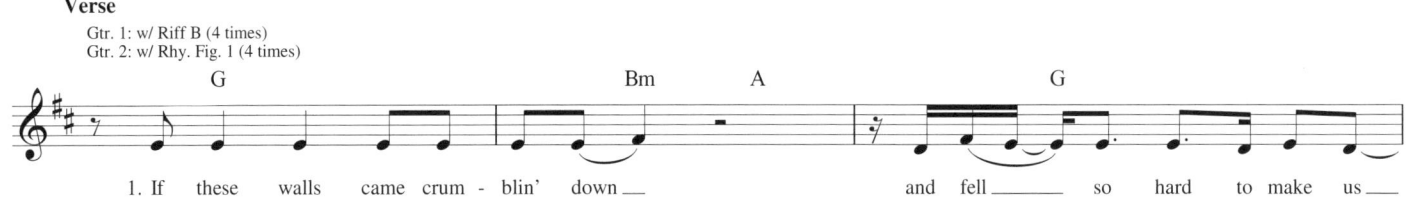

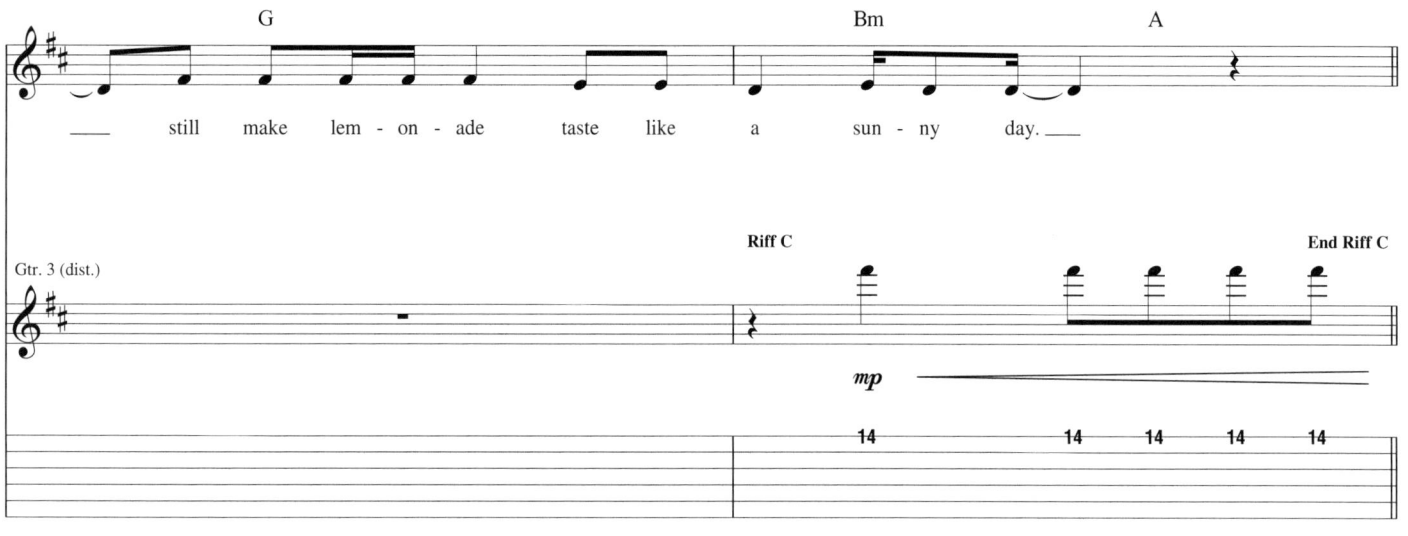

still make lem - on - ade taste like a sun - ny day.

Gtr. 3 (dist.)

Riff C

End Riff C

mp

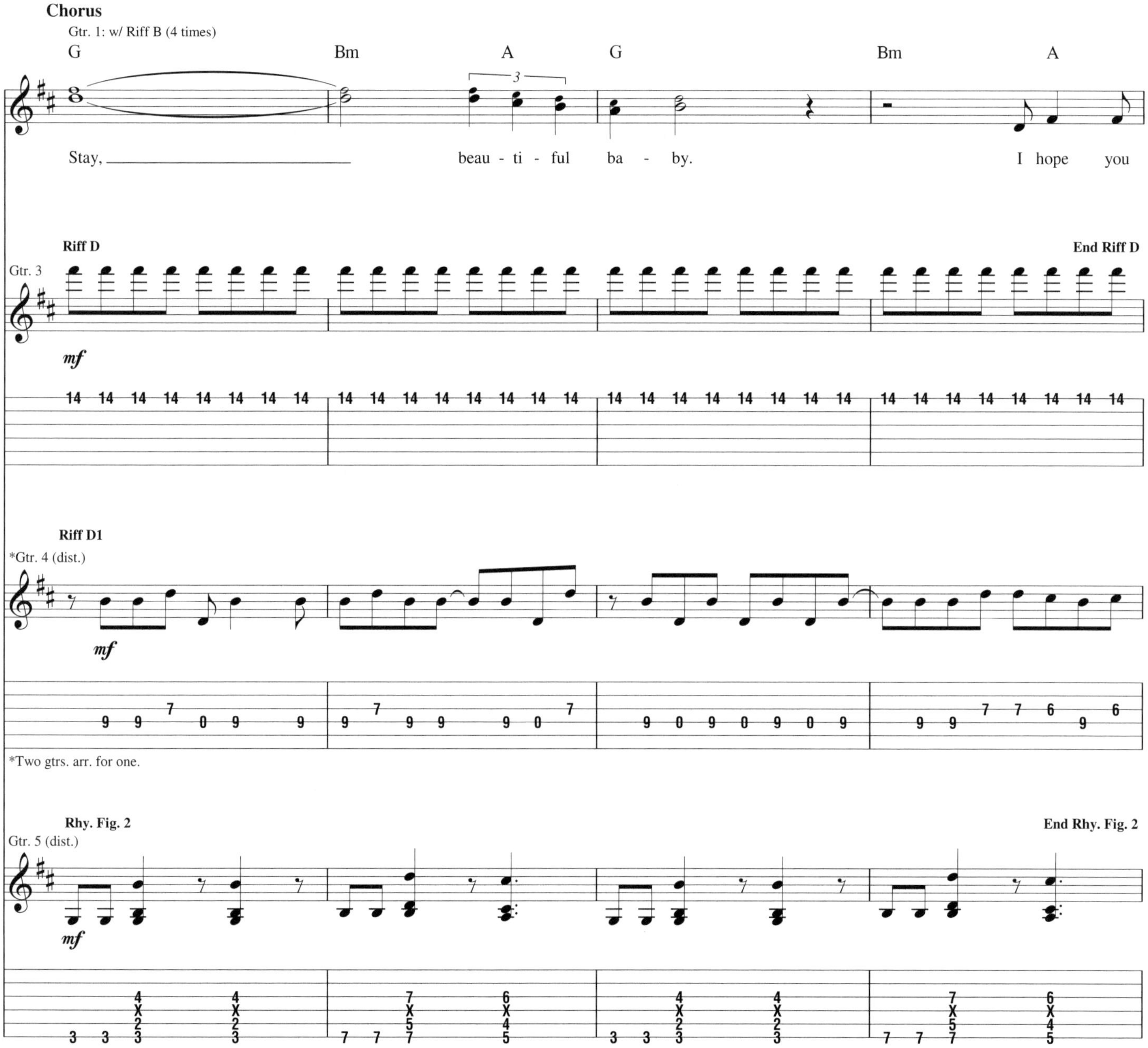

Chorus

Gtr. 1: w/ Riff B (4 times)

G   Bm   A   G   Bm   A

Stay, _____ beau - ti - ful ba - by. _____ I hope you

Riff D

End Riff D

Gtr. 3

mf

Riff D1

*Gtr. 4 (dist.)

mf

*Two gtrs. arr. for one.

Rhy. Fig. 2

End Rhy. Fig. 2

Gtr. 5 (dist.)

mf

Gtr. 3: w/ Riff D
Gtr. 5: w/ Rhy. Fig. 2
G Bm A G Bm A
stay, A - mer - i - can ba - by, A - mer - i - can
Gtr. 4
End Riff D1
Verse
Gtr. 1: w/ Riff B (4 times)
Gtrs. 3, 4 & 5 tacet
G Bm A
ba - by. 2. No - bod - y's laugh - ing now.
Gtr. 3
Gtr. 4
Gtr. 5
Gtr. 2
let ring
let ring
Gtr. 2: w/ Rhy. Fig. 1 (1 1/2 times)
G Bm A G
God's grace lost and the dev - il is proud. But I've been walk - ing for a

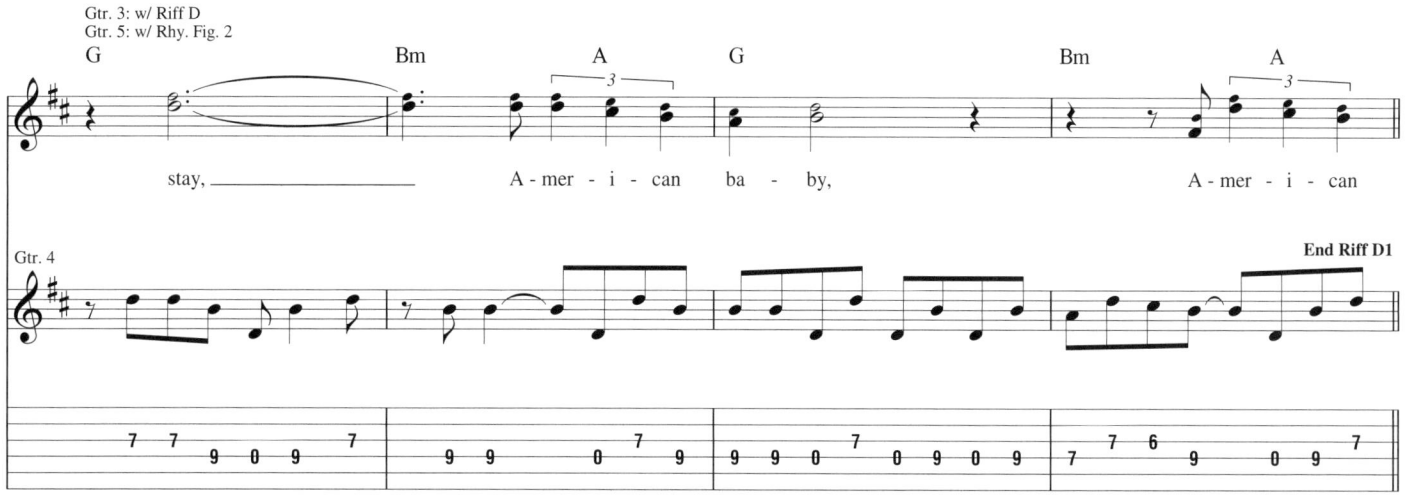

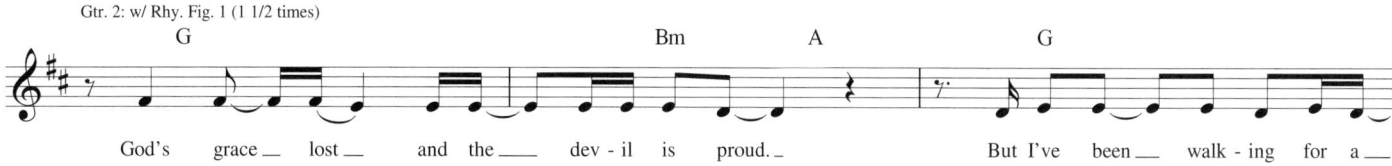

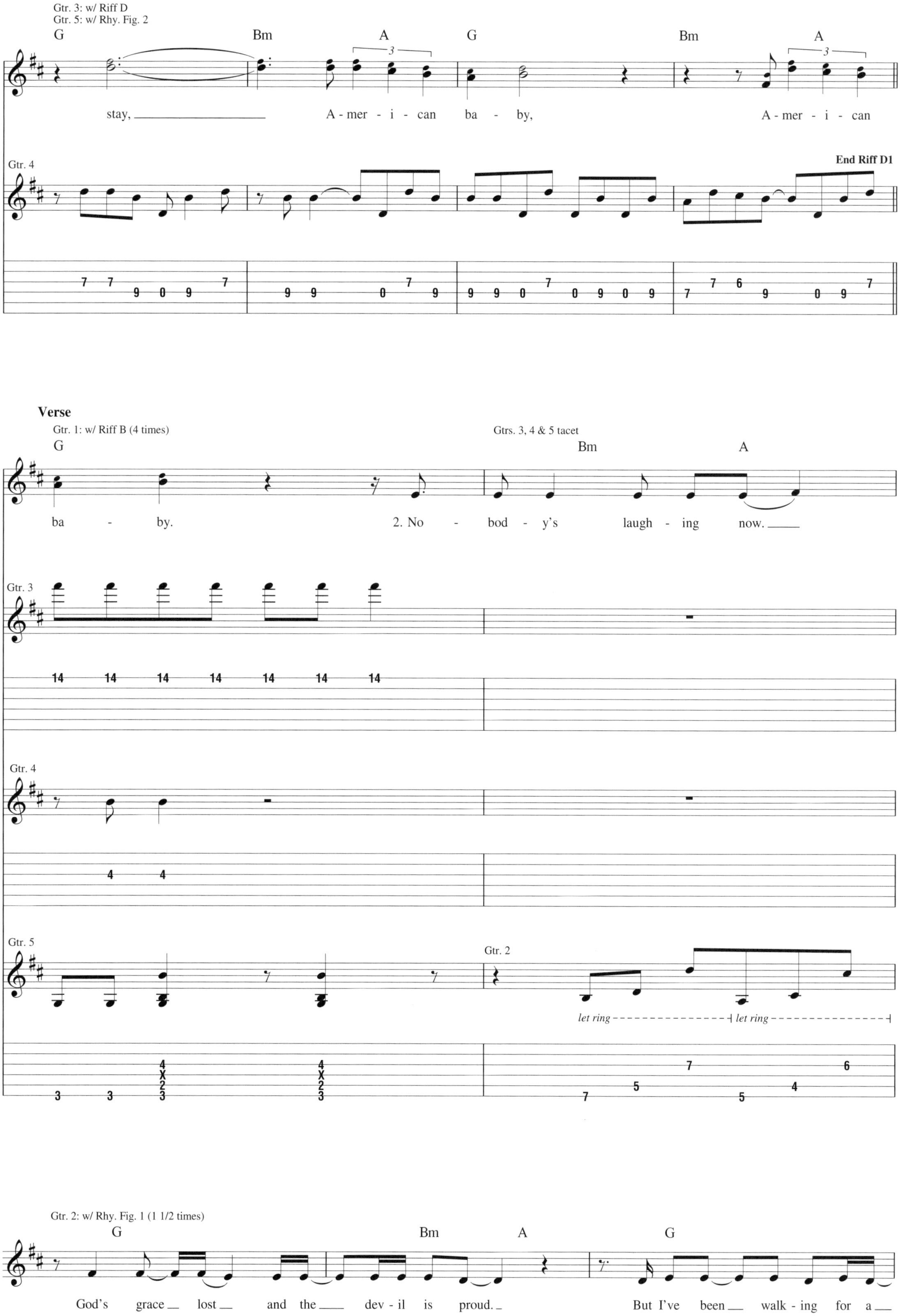

LOUISIANA BAYOU
From *Stand Up* (2005)

The last song in our exploration of the music of Dave Matthews Band is "Louisiana Bayou," a Cajun-flavored number from 2005's *Stand Up*. Awash in layered acoustic and electric guitars, the festive music barely conceals a menacing tale of backwoods corruption, moral squalor, and worse.

THEORY

Harmony

"Louisiana Bayou" is essentially a modal song. The verse and chorus sections are based on the A Mixolydian mode (A–B–C♯–D–E–F♯–G), with harmony generated by multiple single-note parts instead of chords. The overall tonality in these sections is A7. This harmony remains static until the bridge, where we encounter our first real chord progression, which moves from A5 to G5 and F5 power chords. It's another example of modal interchange, in which the A Mixolydian mode is temporarily transformed into the A Aeolian mode. The power chords represent i, VII, and VI, respectively, and are followed by a single note line that continues descending through the Aeolian mode back to its tonic, landing on E (v), D (iv), C (III), B (ii), and A (i) along the way. In the clavinet-driven interlude heard later in the song, this progression returns in a more sophisticated, fully realized guise. In this instance, the two modes are mixed together, rather than substituted for each other, so that we begin on an A triad (I), and descend to a Dm chord (iv) in 1st inversion (with its 3rd, F, in the bass), the two chords connected by a passing G in the keyboard's left hand part. Next, we return to the A chord, with a series of descending bass notes beginning on E and working themselves back down the (Mixolydian) mode, passing D, C♯, B, and A along the way. It's the same step-wise motion heard in the bridge, altered only by raising the C to a C♯ to accommodate the A major chord above. It should be noted that it's not at all unusual, particularly in classical composition, to "borrow" chords from a parallel minor mode to add tension to a major harmonic sequence. In "Louisiana Bayou," the borrowed Dm/F chord accomplishes this rather dramatically, especially after we've heard one basic tonality (A7) for so long; it resolves beautifully down to the A/E chord that follows, with the F descending to E while the D moves down to the C♯ on top.

Rhythm

There are a number of overdubbed guitar parts on "Louisiana Bayou," all of which feature varying degrees of rhythmic syncopation. If you've been diligent about working your way through this book, our earlier studies of broken 16th phrases should really help to ease the way here. Take your time learning the individual parts; many are auxiliary and are (obviously) omitted when the song is performed live, as Matthews is usually the only guitarist on stage. Two critical phrases are the opening instrumental motif played by Gtr. 1, and the chorus riff played by Gtr. 5, shown in the examples below. Let's look at the intro lick first.

What makes this lick particularly challenging is the close juxtaposition of both broken 16th note and eighth note triplet figures. Try the exercise below, which mixes 16th notes and triplets while gradually adding rests, to get a grip on this often difficult rhythm and its variations. As always, proceed slowly and carefully—this one gets a little tricky. When playing (or tapping) the broken triplet rhythms, try to imagine a note in the place of each eighth or 16th note rest.

That was a little awkward, wasn't it? Through struggle comes advancement, however, so your work here and on our earlier rhythm studies should leave you well equipped to deal with most of the demanding 16th note and triplet phrases you'll encounter in Matthews' music and beyond. The phrase below, taken from the chorus, should be a breeze after all that.

Be sure that your first A falls on the "and" of beat 2, not the "a" as for the note that immediately precedes it (a C bent up a quarter tone). As you work through the song, you'll encounter numerous similarly syncopated rhythms. Count them all out—don't just rely on your ear and the recording to do the work for you.

Scales

The single note lines and licks of "Louisiana Bayou" are all based on the A Mixolydian mode (A–B–C♯–D–E–F♯–G), except for the bridge and interlude material, which employs the A Aeolian mode (A–B–C–D–E–F–G) as well. Both modes are explored in detail in the examinations of "What Would You Say" and "So Much to Say" found earlier in this book. The music example below includes an upper octave, three-notes-per-string fingering of the A Mixolydian mode in the region of the opening lick of "Bayou." It's important to learn all of your scales and modes in multiple keys, fingerings, and registers, particularly if you'd like to have access to them at a moment's notice in any region of the neck.

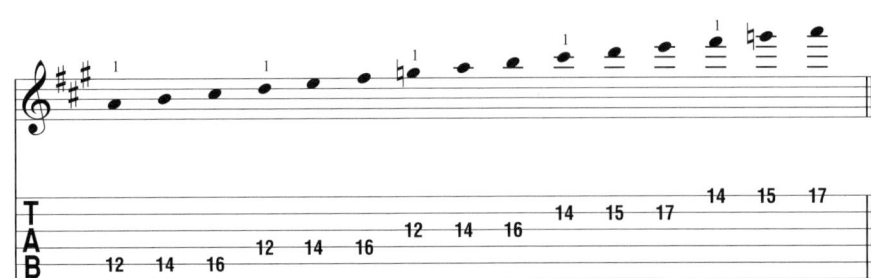

Composition

The pastiche of single-note lines in "Louisiana Bayou" makes it a fairly unique song in the band's repertoire. There's a lot that's unusual about this song, actually, from Dave's quasi-Cajun whooping in the chorus, to the use of clavinet (a classic 1970s keyboard sound most closely associated with Stevie Wonder's "Superstition"), and the incredibly dense, conversational feeling of all of those layered guitars. They're used almost like colors on an artist's palette to paint a lush backdrop upon which the song's story is told. Of course, this being Dave Matthews Band, there's a handful of favored devices at work here, particularly the modal interchange between the A Mixolydian and Aeolian modes. There's the use of repetition to build intensity. And there's the clear expression of the song's emotional essence—in this case, violence and menace—that has been a hallmark of Matthews' writing for some time now. The radical shifts of groove and numerous section changes of old have long since been abandoned for simpler structures that explore their limited materials more deeply than ever before. Case in point—the revisiting (and re-imagining) of the bridge's harmonic sequence and rhythmic pattern in the interlude, where fresh textures (the clavinet) expand upon previously heard material. "Louisiana Bayou" also marks a return to the funky jams so prevalent in the band's earlier repertoire, making for interesting comparisons with the songs on *Under the Table and Dreaming* and *Crash*. The music and the musicians have the same spirit and soul, but they've been rendered wiser, deeper, and even a little sadder. Matthews and his mates have seen more of the world and, inevitably, more of its injustices as well.

TECHNIQUE

The multitude of single-note guitar parts in "Louisiana Bayou" calls for a number of specialized techniques, including slides, hammer-ons, pull-offs, and the many unison bends (played by Gtr.4) heard off in the distance, buried at a fairly low volume in the mix. The example below is from the three measures immediately preceding the first verse; similar bends are played, with variation, throughout the tune.

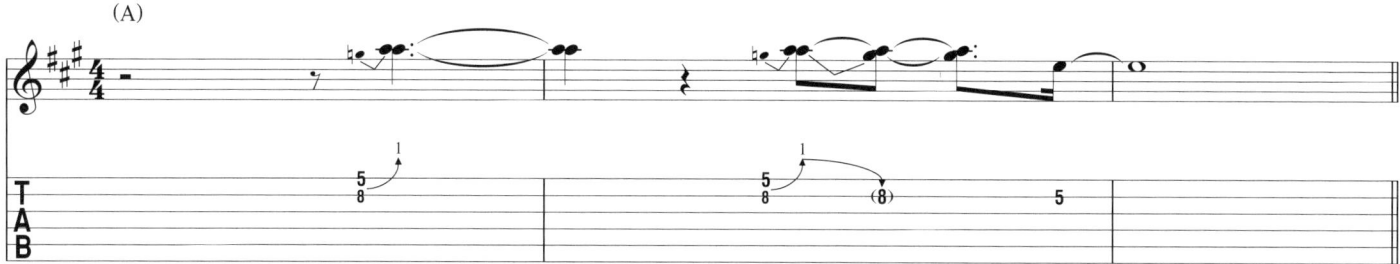

Play this lick with your index finger on the A (5th fret of the high E string) and your ring finger, assisted by the middle finger behind it, pushing the B string up a whole step. Because you're bending up to match an unbent tone on a higher string, intonation shouldn't be much of a problem. Simply match the bend to the A above—your ears will tell you if you went too far or fell short of the mark. In the second measure of the example, repeat the process and then release the B string down to its unbent position while leaving the A in its stationary position on the high E string. As you work your way through the song, you'll encounter a number of similar bends, some in different registers or moving up to different pitches. There are gradually released bends and G-string bends as well, but the same general technique applies: Match the sound of the upper, unbent pitch exactly, use your ring finger, and line the middle finger up behind it to assist in the push.

In the chorus, an additional clean-toned guitar (Gtr. 6) enters, adding a series of bell-like harmonics to this musical gumbo. The part continues throughout much of the song, combining natural harmonics with *harp harmonics*, which require you to touch the string lightly with your finger at the fret indicated (don't press down) while picking from behind, on the headstock side of the neck. The example on the top of the next page includes the first four measures of this part.

A

*Harp harmonics achieved by lightly touching string w/ index finger
at fret indicated in parenthesis and picking from behind.

Play the harp harmonics by touching the string at the fret indicated in the parenthesis while plucking with your pick hand at the lower fret shown just to their left. Switch to "regular," natural harmonics in the second half of the phrase, laying your finger lightly over the string where indicated and picking in the normal fashion. It's a bit awkward at first, but the relatively slow pace at which the harmonics go by makes things a bit easier. It's a very cool technique and one worth exploring for use in your own music.

Speaking of which, it's time for this author to say goodbye and leave you with the music at hand. We've dug deep into the songs of Dave Matthews Band, and you've hopefully gained a greater understanding of what they're all about. It's my sincere wish that you've used this book to gain a deeper understanding and greater command of your instrument as well. So go grab your ax, fix yourself a plate of jambalaya, and dive into that "Louisiana Bayou." Just watch your back—it's a dangerous place after dark!

LOUISIANA BAYOU

Written by
Dave Matthews Band and Mark Batson

*Chord symbols reflect basic harmony.

End Riff B

End Riff B1

Verse

Gtr. 1: w/ Riff B (2 times)
Gtr. 3 tacet

Gtr. 3: w/ Riff B1

A

Gtr. 4

1. No, no, Ma - ma cried dev - il; they do - si - do.

Two young boys ly - in' dead by the side of the road.

And the coins on their eyes rep - re - sent the mon - ey they owe.

No judge or ju - ry ev - er gon - na hear the sto - ry told. Down by the

Chorus

Gtr. 1: w/ Riff B (2 times)

Gtr. 3: w/ Riff B1

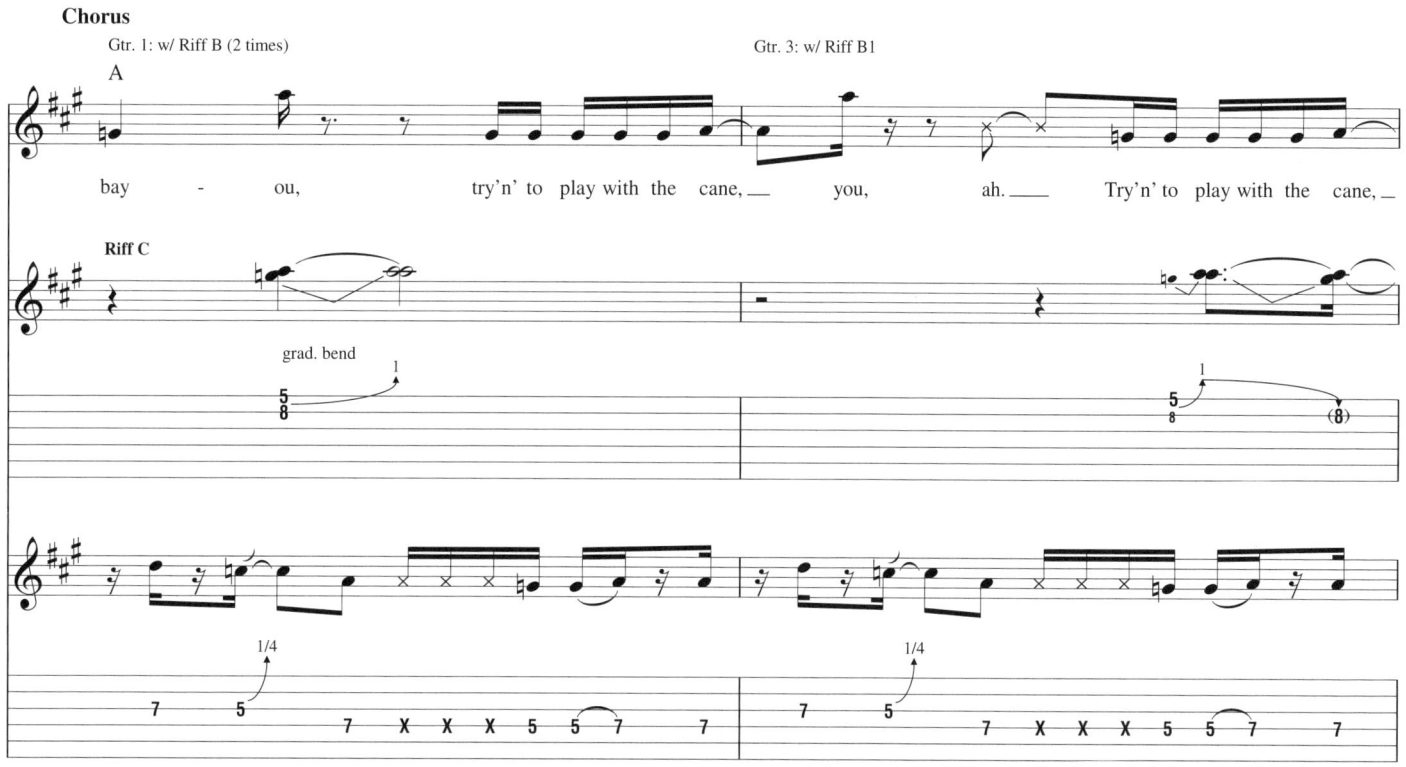

bay - ou, try'n' to play with the cane, you, ah. Try'n' to play with the cane,

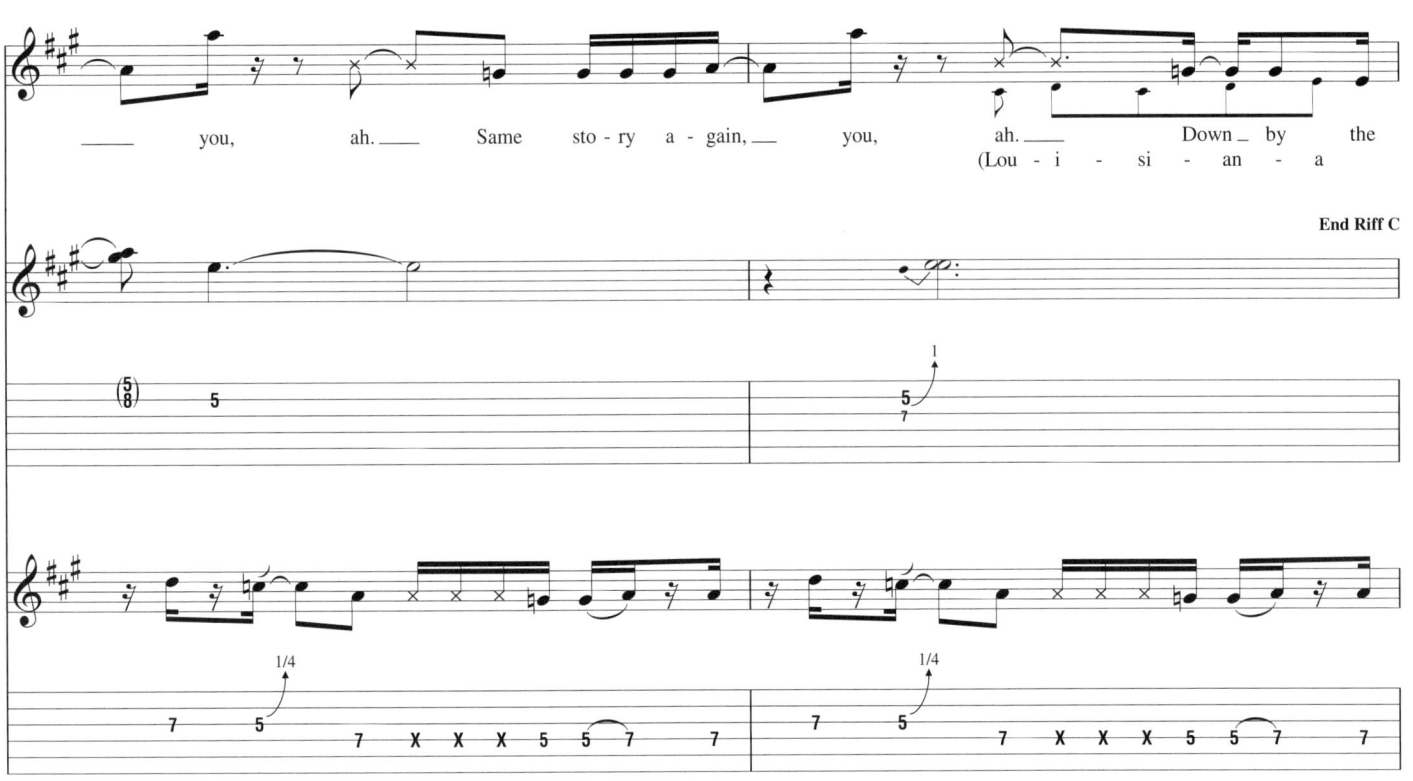

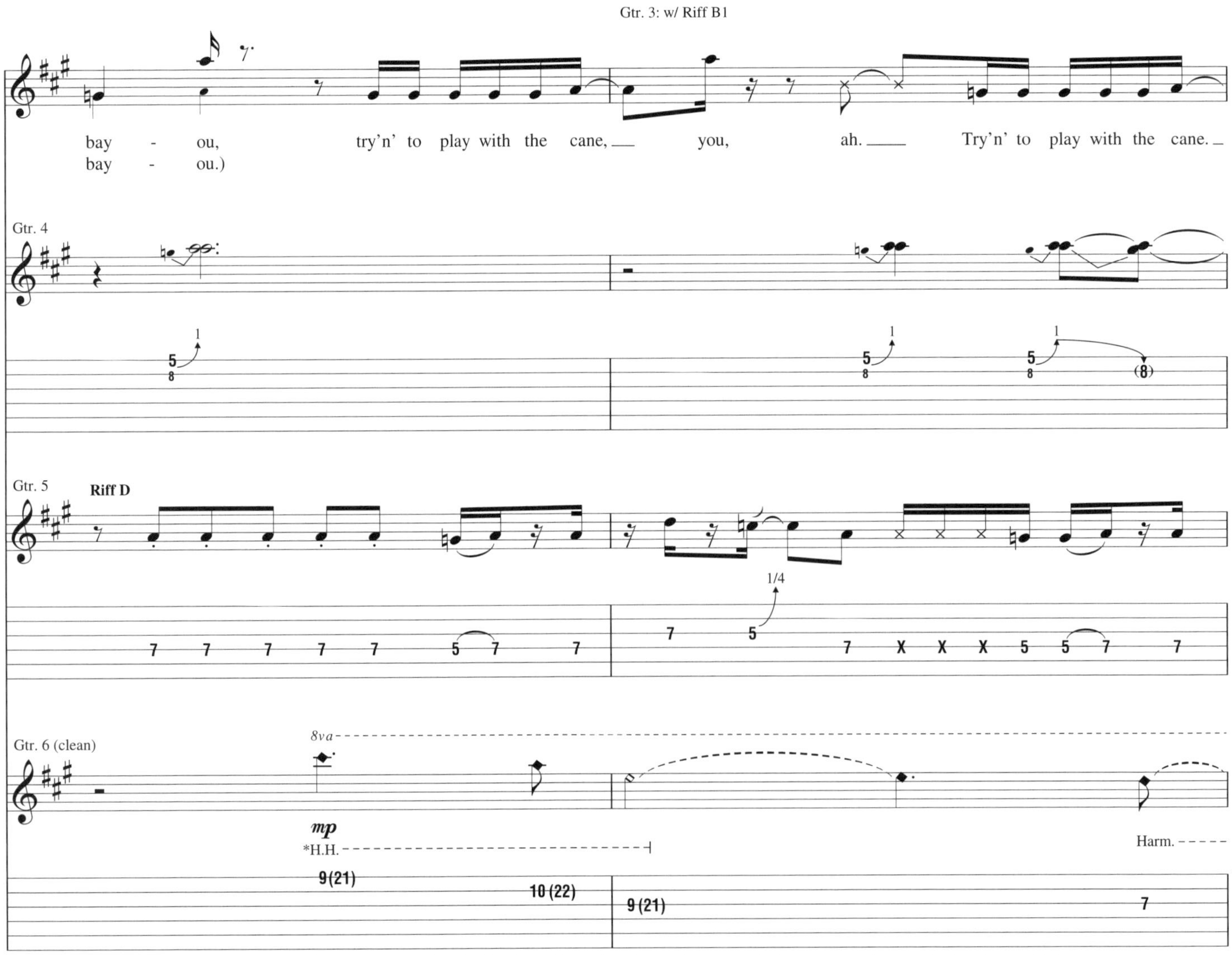

*Harp harmonics achieved by lightly touching string w/ index finger at fret indicated in parentheses and picking from behind.

you, ah. Same sto - ry a - gain, you, ah. (Lou - i - si - an - a

Bay - ou.
bay - ou.)

Gtr. 2: w/ Riff A (2 times) Gtr. 3: w/ Riff B1

N.C.

Gtr. 1

Gtr. 4

Gtr. 6

End Riff D

Pitch: D B G D

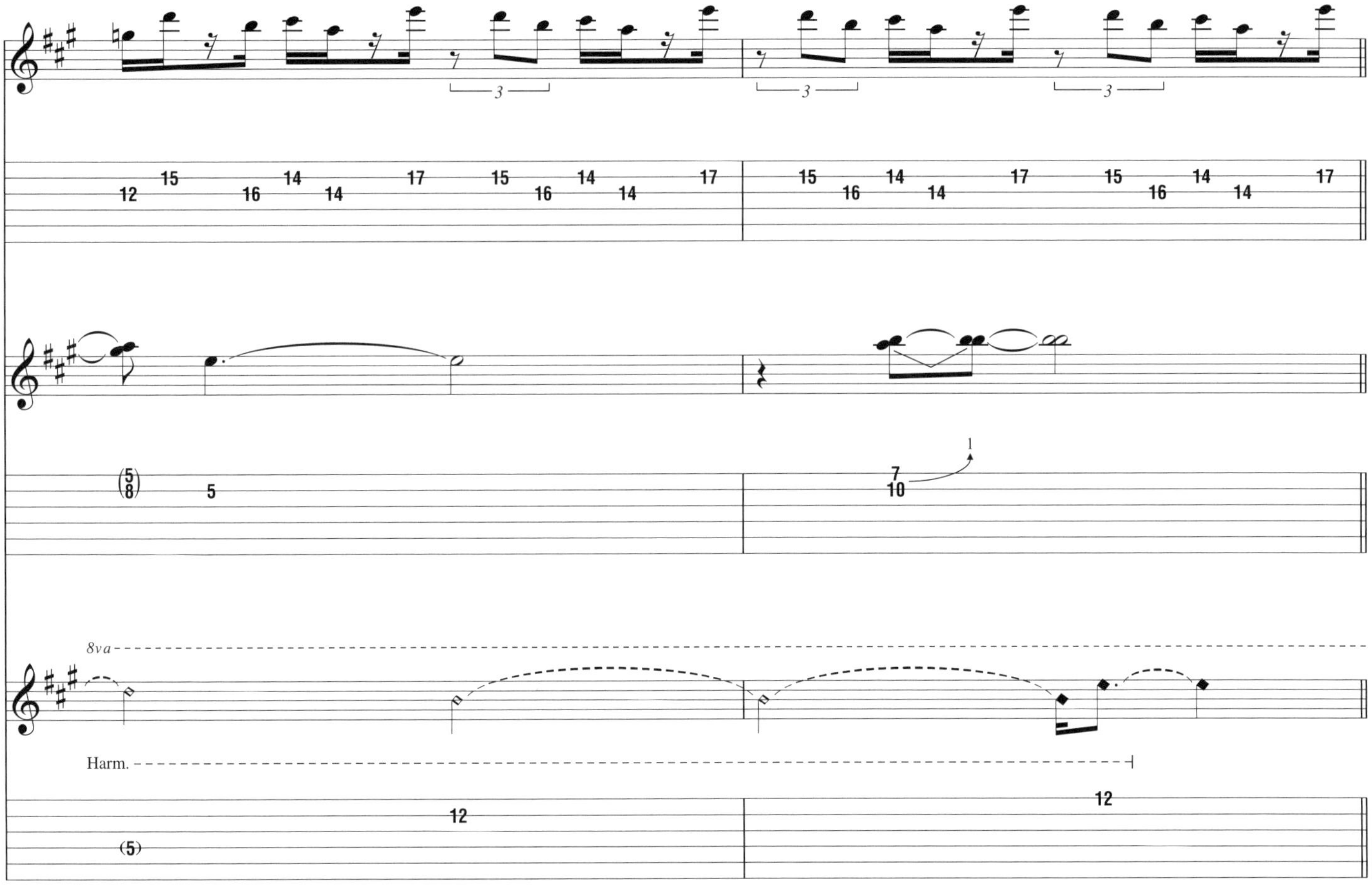
8va
Harm.
15 14 17 15 14 17
12 16 14 16 14
15 14 17 15 14 17
16 14 16 14
(5)
(8)
5
1
7
10
12
(5)
12

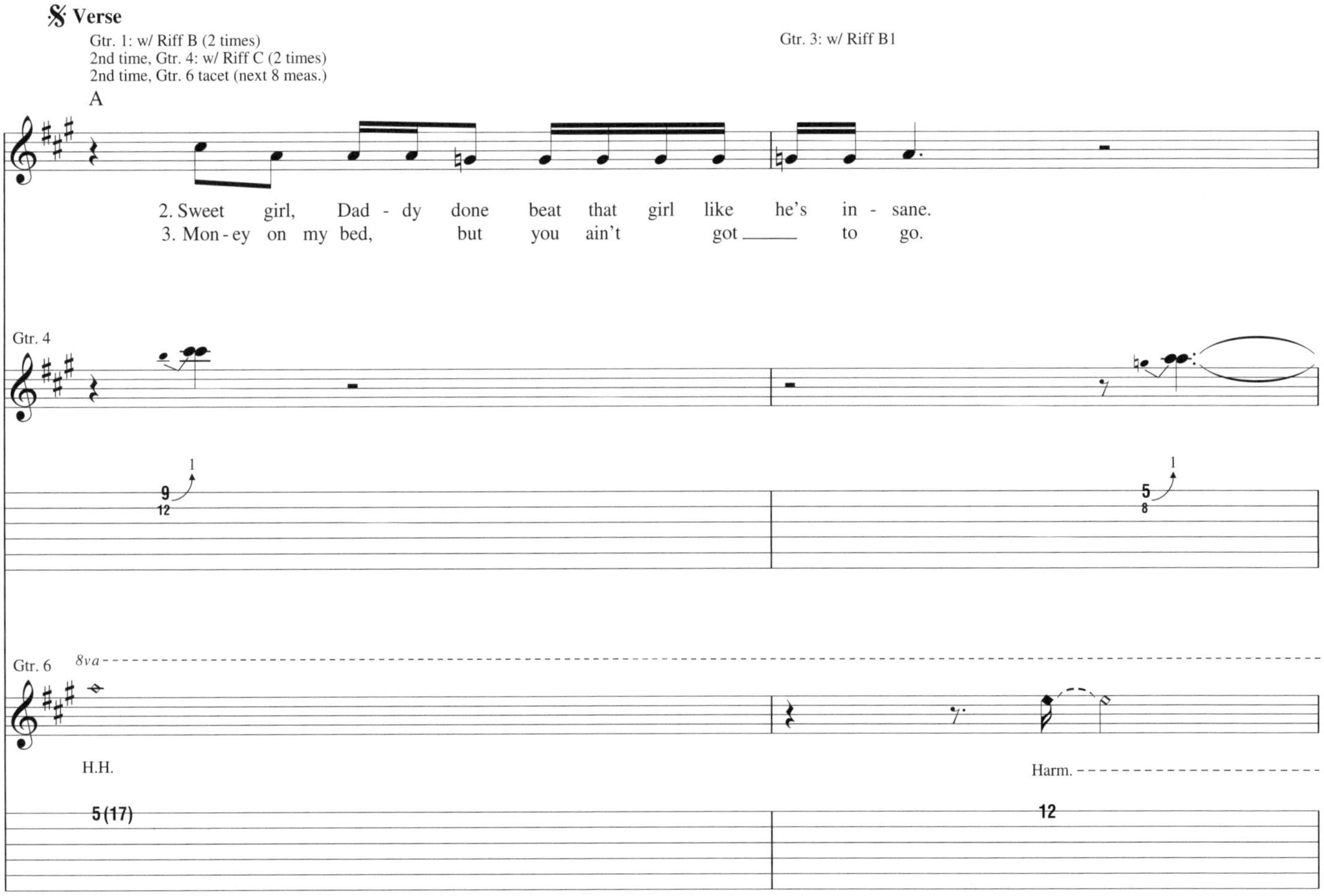
Verse
Gtr. 1: w/ Riff B (2 times)
2nd time, Gtr. 4: w/ Riff C (2 times)
2nd time, Gtr. 6 tacet (next 8 meas.)
Gtr. 3: w/ Riff B1
A
2. Sweet girl, Dad - dy done beat that girl like he's in - sane.
3. Mon - ey on my bed, but you ain't got to go.
Gtr. 4
1
9
12
1
5
8
Gtr. 6
8va
H.H.
Harm.
5 (17)
12

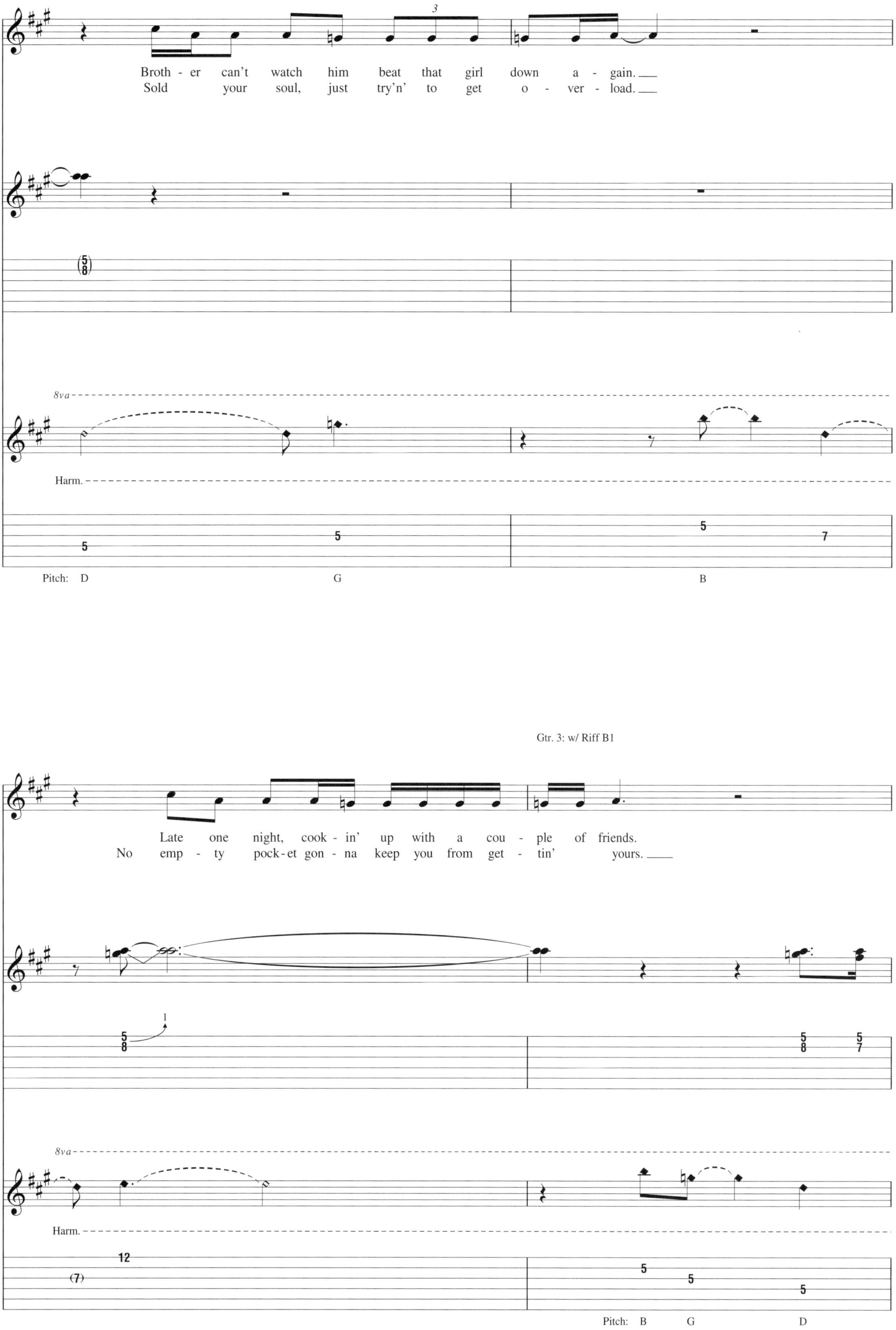
3
Broth - er can't watch him beat that girl down a - gain.
Sold your soul, just try'n' to get o - ver - load.
8va
Harm.
Pitch: D G B
Gtr. 3: w/ Riff B1
Late one night, cook - in' up with a cou - ple of friends.
No emp - ty pock-et gon - na keep you from get - tin' yours.
8va
Harm.
Pitch: B G D

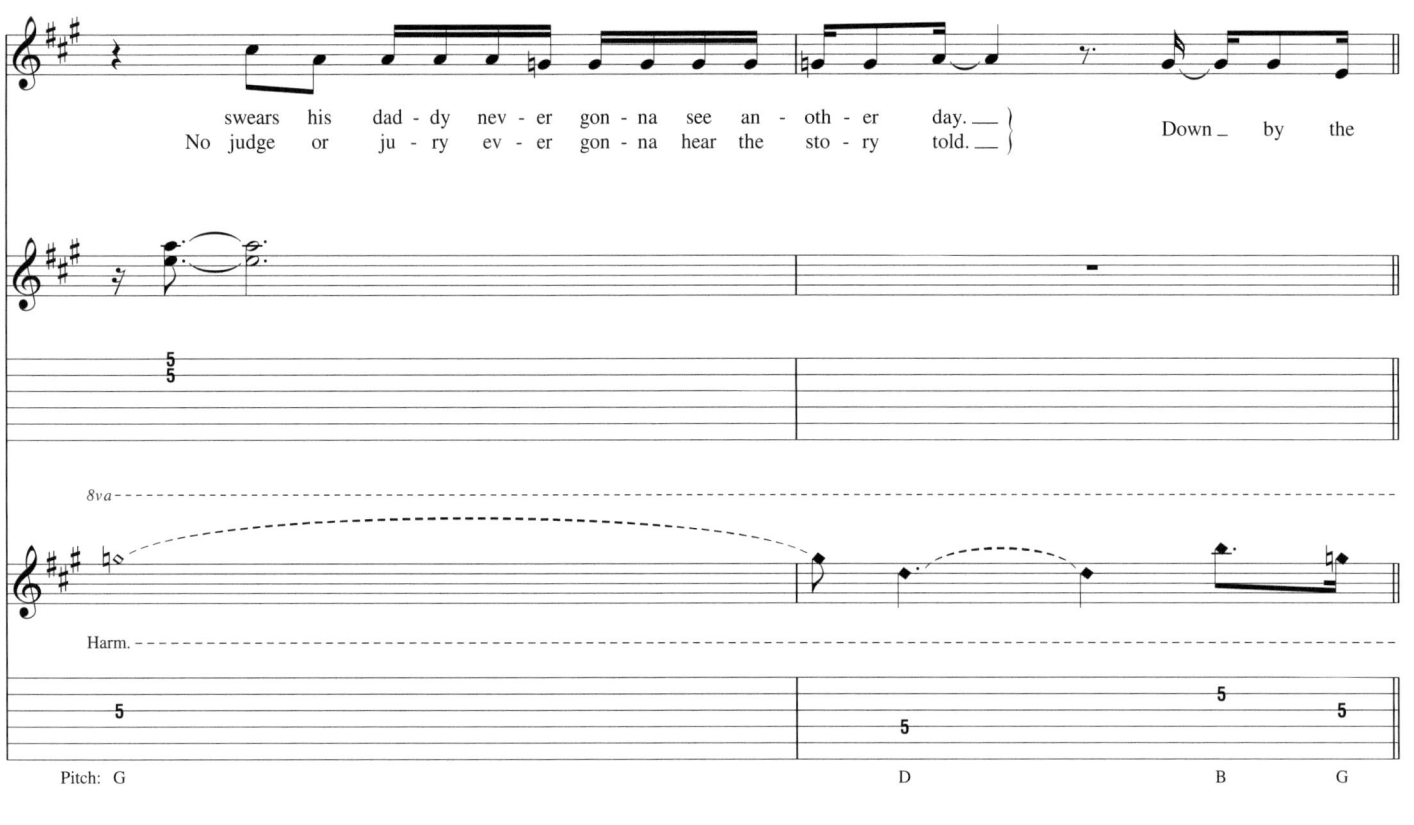

Pitch: G   D   B   G

Chorus

Gtr. 1: w/ Riff B (3 times)
Gtr. 4: w/ Riff C (2 3/4 times)
Gtr. 5: w/ Riff D (2 times)

Gtr. 3: w/ Riff B1

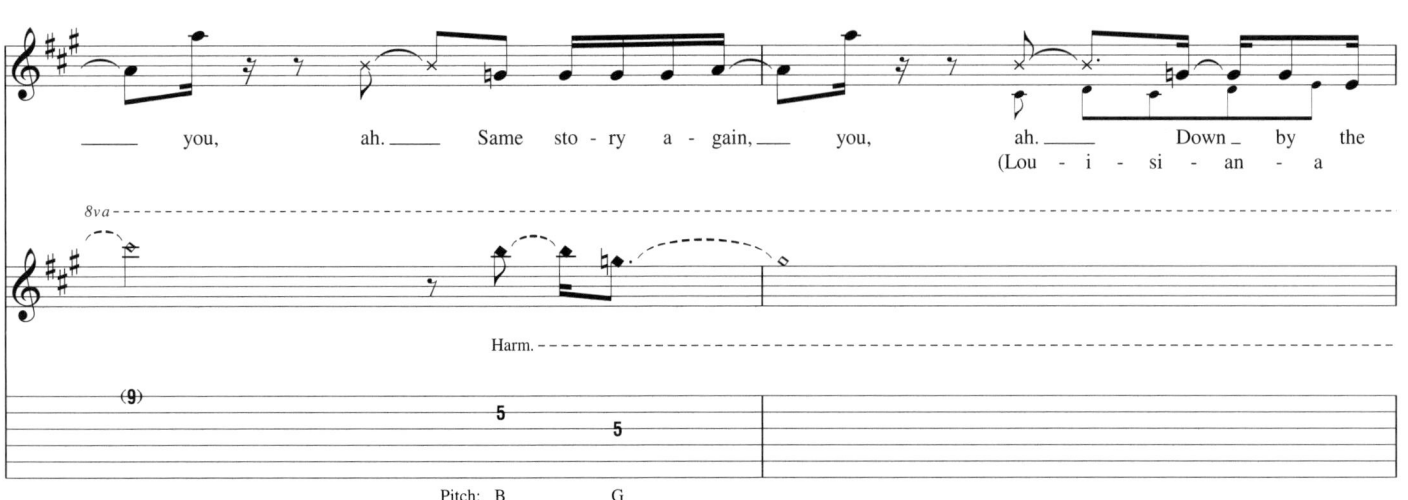

Pitch: B   G

Gtr. 3: w/ Riff B1

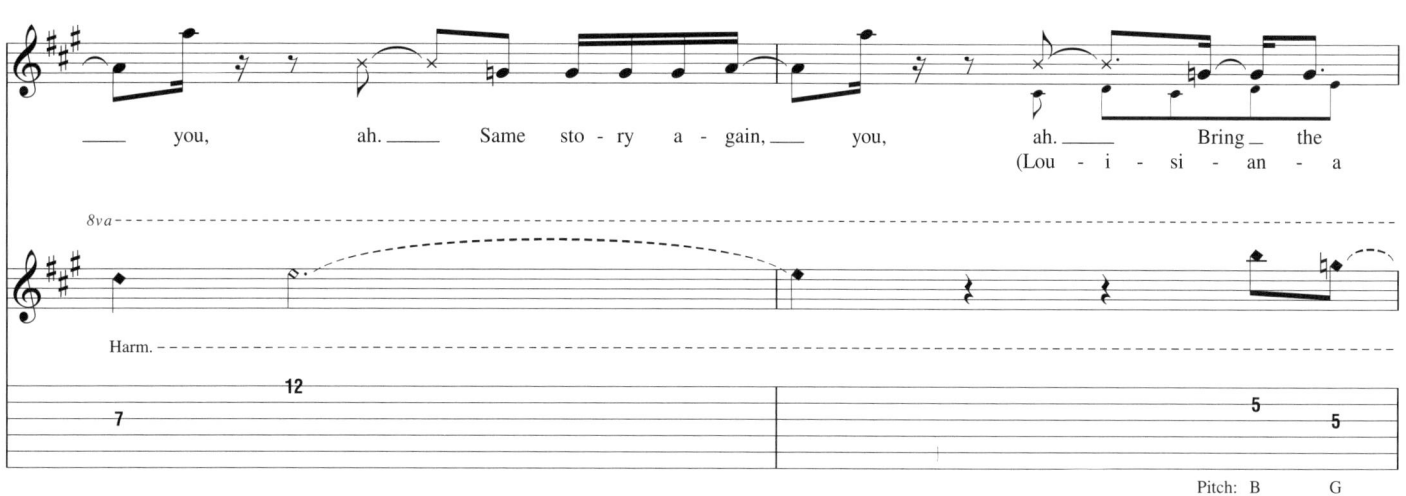

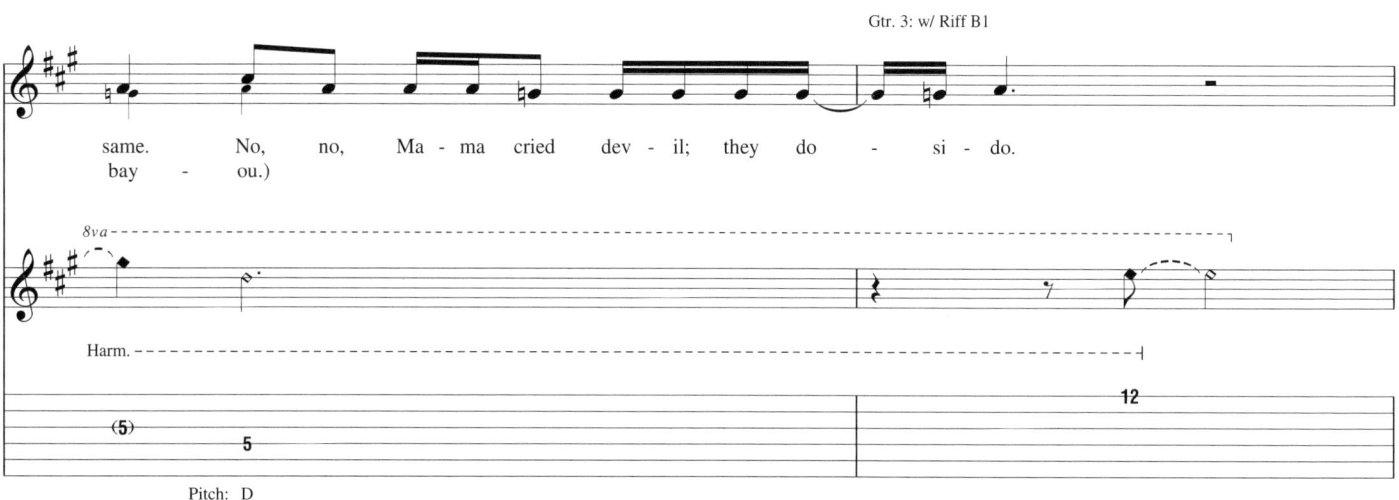

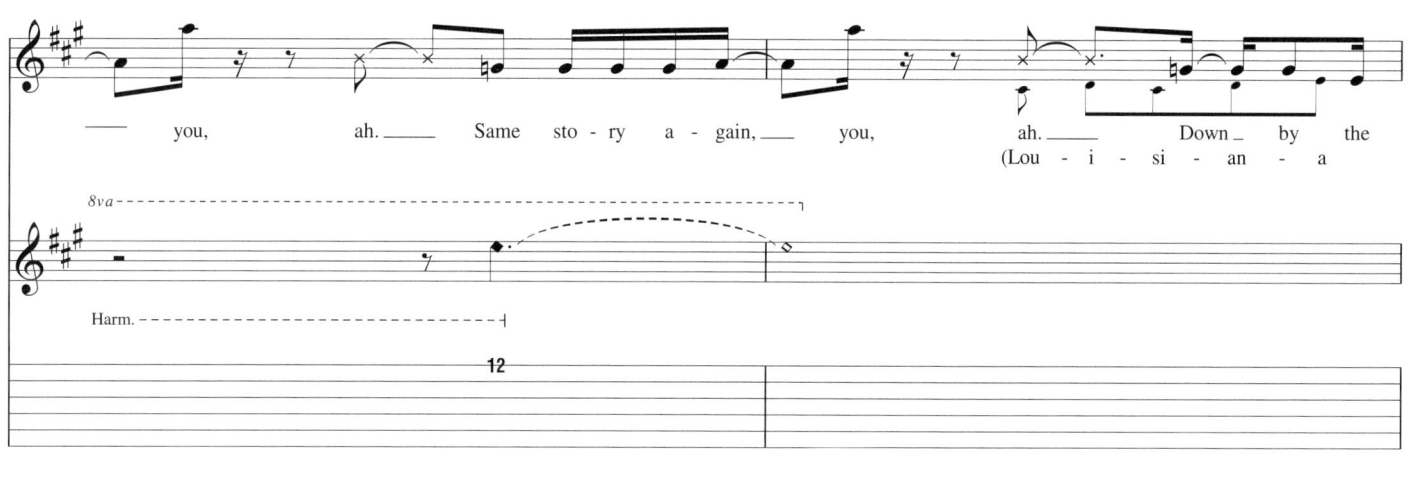

you, ah. Same sto-ry a-gain, you, ah. Down by the
(Lou - i - si - an - a

8va
Harm.
12

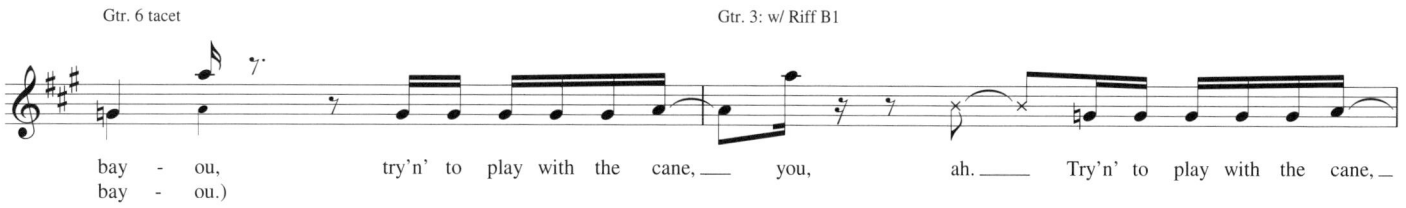

Gtr. 6 tacet
Gtr. 3: w/ Riff B1

bay - ou, try'n' to play with the cane, you, ah. Try'n' to play with the cane,
bay - ou.)

you, ah. Same sto-ry a-gain, you, ah.
(Lou - i - si - an - a

Gtr. 5: w/ Riff D (1st 2 meas., 2 times)
Gtr. 3: w/ Riff B1

No, no, Ma - ma cried dev - il; they do - si - do.
bay - ou.)

Gtr. 6

1/2

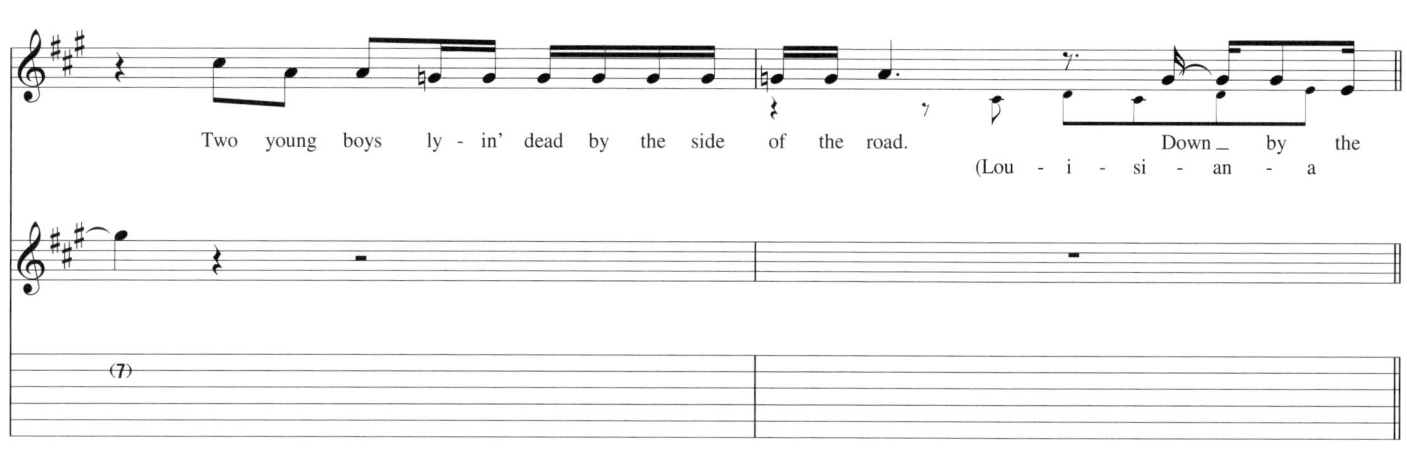

Two young boys ly-in' dead by the side of the road. Down by the
(Lou - i - si - an - a

(7)

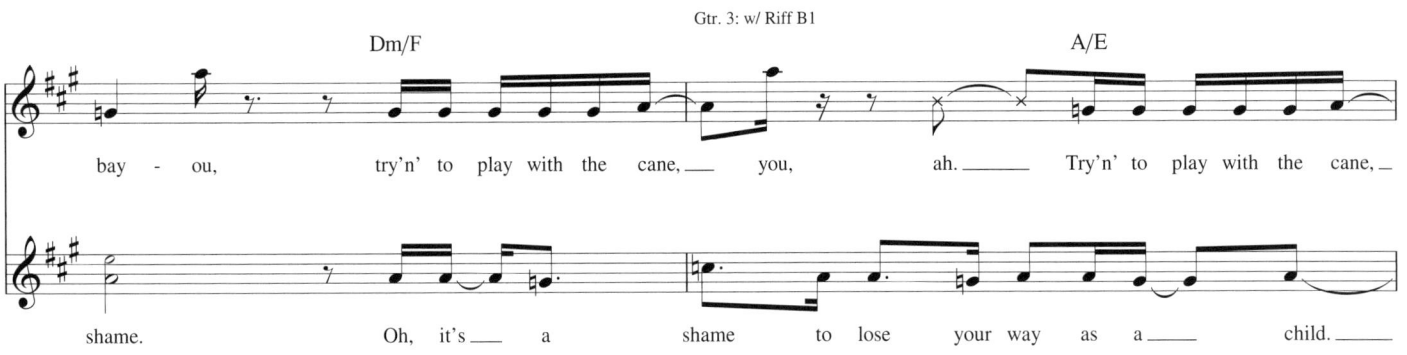

Outro

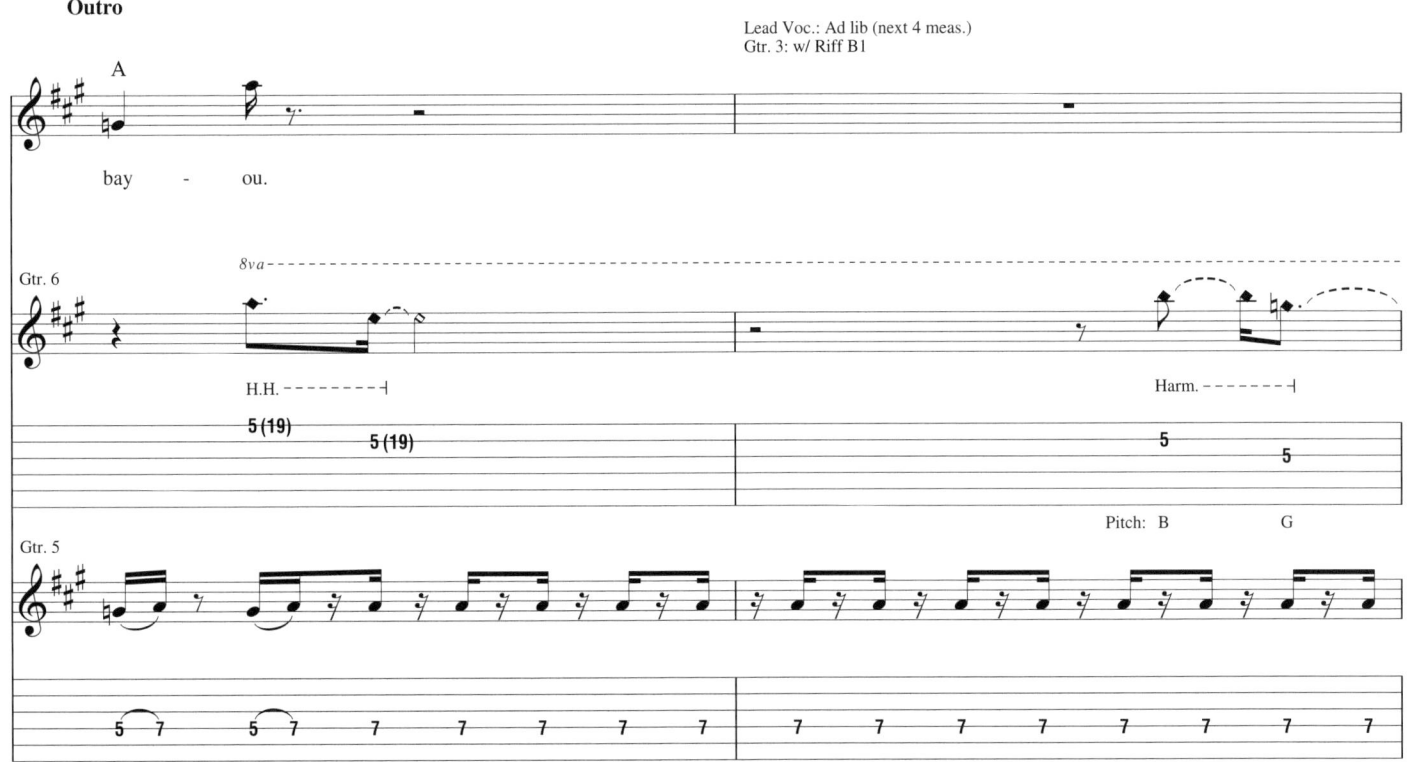

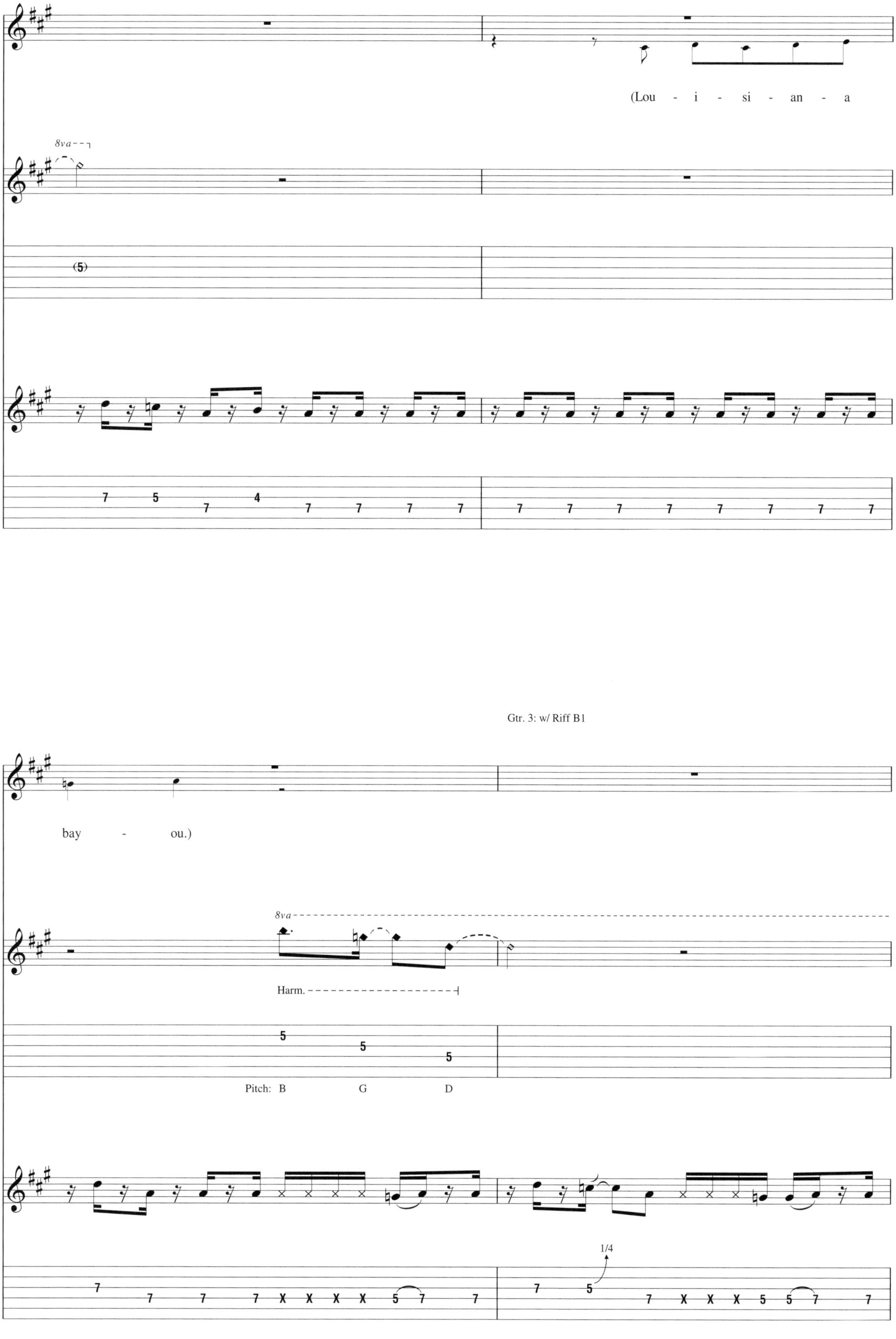
(Lou - i - si - an - a
8va
Gtr. 3: w/ Riff B1
bay - ou.)
8va
Harm.
Pitch: B G D
1/4

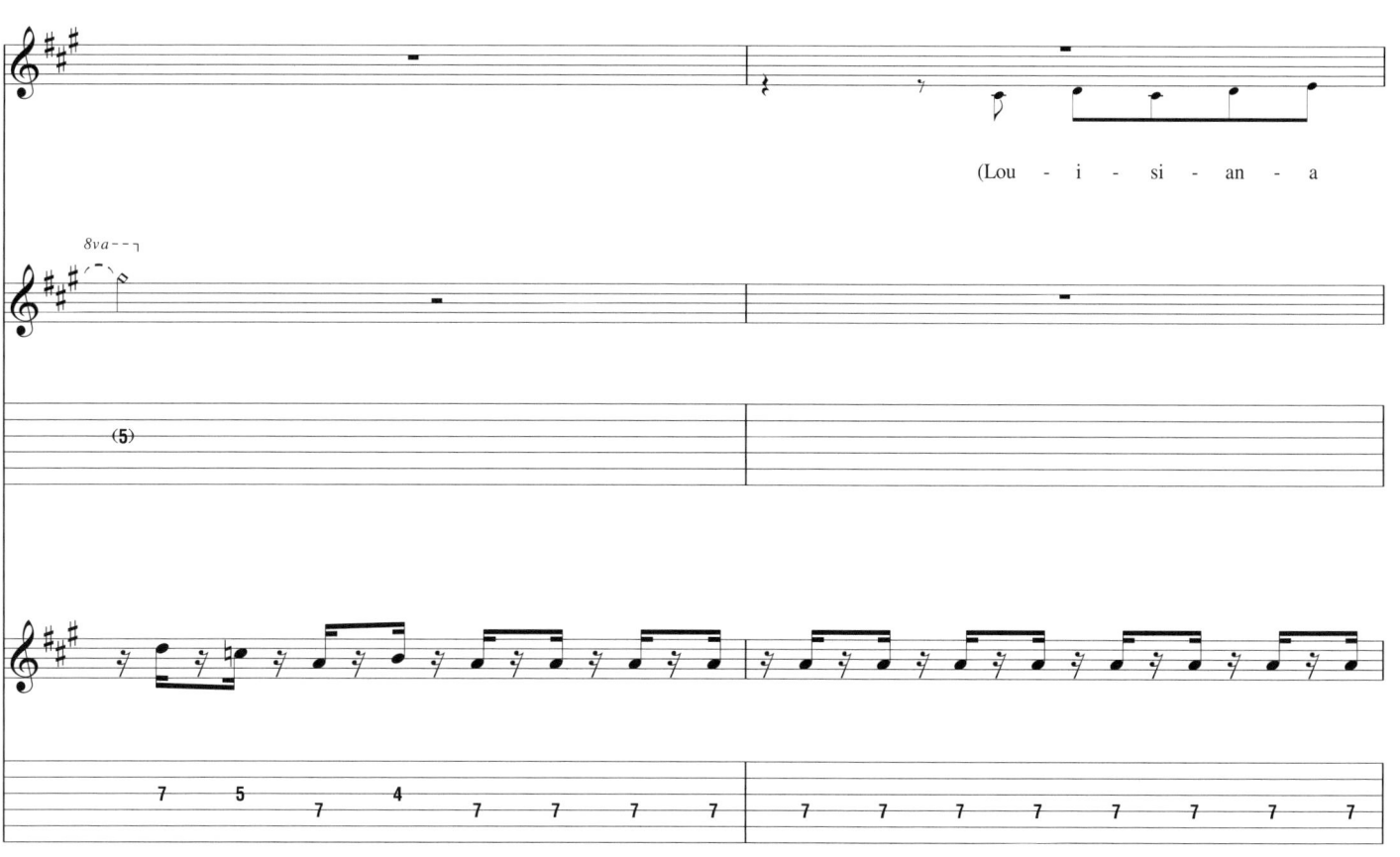